Sauternes
and other sweet wines
of Bordeaux

FABER BOOKS ON WINE

General Editor: Julian Jeffs

Bordeaux (new edition) by David Peppercorn
Burgundy (new edition) by Anthony Hanson
French Country Wines by Rosemary George
German Wines by Ian Jamieson
Haut-Brion by Asa Briggs
Italian Wines (new edition) by Philip Dallas
Sherry (new edition) by Julian Jeffs
The Wines of Alsace by Tom Stevenson
The Wines of Australia (new edition) by Oliver Mayo
The Wines of Greece by Miles Lambert-Gócs
The Wines of the Loire by Roger Voss
The Wines of the Rhône (new edition) by John Livingstone-Learmonth

SAUTERNES
and other sweet wines of Bordeaux

STEPHEN BROOK

faber and faber
LONDON BOSTON

First published in Great Britain in 1995
by Faber and Faber Limited
3 Queen Square London WC1N 3AU

Phototypeset by Intype, London
Printed in England by Clays Ltd, St Ives plc

A CIP record for this book
is available from the British Library

ISBN 0-571-17316-0

To Maria

Contents

Acknowledgements

This book could never have been researched without the co-operation of the growers and winemakers of the Sauternes region, who put up with my repeated visits and responded to my questions with good humour and generosity. Both the Ambassade de Sauternes and the Syndicat des Crus Classés de Sauternes et Barsac have enabled me to visit the region for lengthy periods to complete my research. My thanks go to Monique Achard and Christian Médeville of the former, and to Sita Garros and Comte Xavier de Pontac of the latter. Pierre Benaitier of the Maison du Vin at Cadillac organized my visits to Sainte-Croix-du-Mont, Loupiac and Cadillac. For many years, Jean and Suzanne Perromat have made me welcome at the Château de Cérons and introduced me to the growers who produce the wine from this neglected appellation. Catherine Manac'h of Sopexa in London has also been helpful over many years in organizing visits to the region.

In Sauternes and Barsac, I wish to thank for their hospitality Pierre Castéja, Pierre Dubourdieu, Jean Gérard David, Michel Garat, Jean Lalande, Comte Emmanuel de Lambert des Granges, Comte Alexandre de Lur-Saluces, Pierre Meslier, Comte Xavier de Pontac and Comte Henri de Vaucelles. Michel Garat, Denis Dubourdieu and Jean-Pierre Jausserand were of great help in discussing some of the more technical aspects of the vinification of Sauternes, though any errors should be attributed to me rather than to them. Mme Valérie Lailheugue responded thoroughly to my many questions about Yquem.

In the other sweet-wine appellations, I am indebted for their hospitality to Yves Armand, Michel Boyer, Patrick Dejean, Jean Médeville and his extended family, Arnaud de Sèze, and Bernard Solane.

ACKNOWLEDGEMENTS

I have always enjoyed the warmest of welcomes at Château Nairac, initially from Tom Heeter in the 1980s and in recent years from Nicole Heeter-Tari and her son Nicolas. They have accommodated me at the château on a number of occasions, and provided the comfort and hospitality writers crave when immersed in research.

I received much of my early education in Sauternes at the tastings organized by Liz and Mike Berry of La Vigneronne in London, and more recently Richard Brazier of Clapham Cellars has often invited me to tutor tastings of Sauternes, thus giving me the opportunity to encounter very rare vintages, which is always a fascinating experience.

Introduction

Like many others of my generation, my first acquaintance with 'Sauternes' took the form of a noisome yellow liquid routinely served at undergraduate orgies and labelled 'Spanish Sauternes'. So rather than encouraging the association of the name with the noblest of sweet wines, 'Sauternes' became indelibly linked with memories of screeching hangovers. Unlike some of my fellow revellers, I was at least slightly aware that Spanish Sauternes was a travesty of a great name. It was on election night in 1964 that my hosts opened a bottle of Château Climens to celebrate the Labour victory under Harold Wilson. I don't recall the year, but the bottle came from the cellars of one of Oxford's wealthiest colleges, and no doubt the vintage was a sound one. Since that first sip, I have always loved Sauternes.

With hindsight, it was not so extraordinary that the British shippers of the very worst white wine Spain had to offer from its capacious reserves should have availed themselves of one of Bordeaux's greatest names. The 1960s were a terrible time for the sweet wines of Bordeaux. Demand had collapsed and only a handful of estates could either be bothered or afford to maintain the exacting standards that the production of fine sweet wine requires. The slump continued right through the 1970s as many of the *Premiers Crus* released shamefully inadequate wines on to the market. By the mid-1980s the market had changed beyond recognition and Sauternes was once again a name to conjure with.

The reputation of Sauternes is relatively recent. Samuel Pepys was sufficiently impressed by his first taste of Château Haut-Brion – or Ho Bryan, as he cheerily referred to it – to note it in his diaries in 1663. But no accolades greeted the top growths of Sauternes until well over a century later. Its international acclaim dates from the

mid-nineteenth century, when a vintage of Yquem found special
favour with the Russian court, which had always had the sweetest
of teeth.

There were probably vines planted south of Bordeaux in Roman
times, but we can only speculate about their style and flavour.
Bordeaux's medieval prosperity derived from vines planted in the
Graves region to the south of the city and, again, it is likely that
the Sauternais provided some of those wines. It is also probable
that the wines were sweet. The Romans certainly loved sweet
wines; the British taste, on which the Bordeaux trade was initially
founded, was also for sweet wines, a propensity shared by the
Dutch, who succeeded the British as major players in the French
wine trade. The region also prospered as a source of sacramental
wine, which had to be sweet, but, according to Professor Ribéreau-
Gayon, the majority of the wine would have been *clairet*, a light red
or rosé.[1]

Sweet wines were favoured not just for their flavour, but for
entirely practical reasons. The major production problem from
earliest times lay in stabilizing the wine. Without temperature-controlled fermentation, levels of volatile acidity often must have been
perilously high, and for many wines it could only have been a
matter of months before the grapy drink in the amphora or cask
turned into vinegar. With the additional risks of bacterial infection
and premature oxidation, most wines would have had to have been
consumed within one year of the harvest. The problems of conser-
vation were compounded when wines had to be transported.

There were two ways to prop up a wine and keep it from rapidly
spoiling. One was to add alcohol or brandy, a method still used to
produce port or French *vin doux naturel*. The other was to leave
residual sugar in the wine, which would also act as a preservative.
The easiest natural way to do this was to pick the grapes late, when
the sugar content was at its peak. Fermentation would grind to a
halt before all the grape sugar had been consumed by the yeasts,
leaving a measure of natural sweetness in the wine. That, in essence,
is how Sauternes is made. However, it was no doubt more efficacious to add substances to the wine – such as sugar or fruit
juices – to provide the sweetness. Adulteration of wine was a major

1 Pascal Ribéreau-Gayon, *The Wines and Vineyards of France*, p. 102

industry in the nineteenth century and, as the occasional death in modern-day Italy reminds us, it is still with us.

Even a wine with natural residual sugar did not have guaranteed stability. There was always the risk of secondary fermentation, as dormant yeasts awoke and found the supply of sugar in the wine had not been exhausted. The warmer the weather, the more likely this was to occur. One modern method of suppressing the yeasts is to add sulphur dioxide, during both vinification and the bottling process.

This use of sulphur dioxide was well known to the Germans and Dutch in the seventeenth century. It enabled Dutch merchants in Bordeaux to increase the stability of the local wines, notably the sweet white wines that their customers prized above all others. Not only did such wines obtain the highest prices, but they were also shipped in the largest quantities. Dutch links with Protestant Bergerac, the source then as now of sweet Monbazillac, as well as with the region around Bordeaux, guaranteed a flourishing market for these wines not only in the Netherlands, but also in many parts of northern Europe. To this day, the Dutch remain deeply fond of Sauternes and Monbazillac. British merchants too, such as Henry Thompson, whose records survive from the 1640s, made large purchases of sweet wines from the Sauternais at high prices.

Sauternes owes its reputation to the fact that its best wines are made from grapes affected by noble rot. As will be explained in greater detail later, noble rot provokes a multitude of chemical reactions in the afflicted grape; these profoundly affect and improve the aroma, flavour and viscosity of the wine. A merely sweet wine from the Sémillon grape is not a drink of much distinction. To test this proposition, go into any French supermarket and buy the cheapest sweet white Premières Côtes de Bordeaux on the shelf. It may be sweet, but it won't be very agreeable.

The arrival of noble rot is a hit-and-miss affair. It is reasonable to expect that, at most, the Sauternes region will be blessed with it in one vintage out of two. It is hard to base an industry on chance. Inevitably there are vintages when noble rot is absent and even the most conscientious estates in Sauternes have difficulty producing a distinguished wine. In the seventeenth century, it is probable that the consumers were less exacting and were content with wines that were indeed no more than merely sweet.

We know for sure that grapes were harvested late in Sauternes – it is the obvious thing to do if your intention is to make sweet wine – but the extent to which noble rot was regarded as a beneficial infestation is less certain. The climate of the region has not altered radically, so noble rot must have occurred quite frequently. Modern grape growers can easily distinguish between noble rot and the more ignoble forms of infestation that signal the imminent destruction of the crop, so there is every reason to suppose that the farmers of a few centuries ago had the same skills. Moreover, the taste of a nobly rotten grape is luscious and sweet, and somebody must have produced wine from infested bunches and found it to their taste. By the early eighteenth century, the Hungarian wine from the Tokay region was one of the most celebrated in Europe and it was evidently made from nobly rotten grapes, so the connection between the condition of the fruit, and the flavour and longevity of the wine was no secret. Yet the scanty records that survive from the Sauternes region do not confirm that winemakers sought out nobly rotten grapes until the eighteenth century. There are references to mould in eighteenth-century wine notes, but no clear indication as to whether it was welcome in vineyards dedicated to sweet white wine.

In the early eighteenth century, Abbé Bellet kept vintage notes at Cadillac, a sweet-wine district across the river from the Sauternais, and he refers to rotten grapes. But, as Hugh Johnson has observed, 'he is silent on whether the mouldy ones were used or rejected. The general inference is the latter.'[2] It is, however, entirely possible that nobly rotten grapes were picked and that their qualities were recognized, but that such harvesting methods were not advertised. After all, it must have been more trouble than it was worth to explain to a merchant or consumer that the nectar before him owed its excellence to a fungal infection.

By the mid-eighteenth century, harvesting in Sauternes was done by the method known today as *tries successives*. It means that harvesting was an operation repeated at least three or four times, as pickers were dispatched into the vineyards in search of only those grapes that were in optimal condition. Although it is true that different grape varieties – and there were probably six or more widely planted in the Sauternes district – ripen at different times, it is at least plausible to suggest that one reason for adopting this

2 Hugh Johnson, *The Story of Wine*, p. 264

costly procedure was that pickers were indeed instructed to seek out nobly rotten grapes, since the infection in most vintages is random and irregular.

It had certainly been a tradition to harvest the grapes very late. Bernard Ginestet refers to a document dated 4 October 1666, in which the owner of Yquem, François Sauvage, specifies that 'in order not to harm the reputation of the said wine harvesting shall be done only when the grapes are fully ripe. It is the practice in Bommes and Sauternes to harvest every year about October 15.'[3] This was about a month later than the commencement of the harvest elsewhere. By mid-October, noble rot would usually have made its presence felt in the Sauternes. Fifty years after Sauvage gave his orders, a regional official, Lamoignon de Courson, was referring explicitly to the late harvesting of grapes that were at least touched by noble rot: 'At harvest time the grapes are selected and only those which are almost rotten are gathered, with the result that harvesting can sometimes last right through to the month of December.'[4] This applied not only to the Sauternais itself, but also to the areas on the other side of the Garonne where sweet wine was produced.

Similarly, the Yquem cellar-book chronicles the harvest in 1810, which began early in October and concluded on 11 November. It is reasonable to assume that the sole reason for protracting the harvest to such an extent was to search for nobly rotten fruit. Had the pickers been instructed to look only for grapes that were overripe and thus full of sugar, there would have been no need to wait until late in the autumn, with its attendant risks of rain and rot.

Patterns of land ownership became more stable in the eighteenth century. A few fortified châteaux and farms survived from medieval times – still visible at, among other properties, Yquem, Lafaurie-Peyraguey, Coutet and Ménota – but it was towards the end of the eighteenth century that the splendid country mansions of Filhot and Nairac were constructed. They were not built solely from the profits derived from winemaking. Just as many New World wineries are founded by prosperous businessmen in search of a more bucolic

3 Bernard Ginestet, *Sauternes*, pp. 18–19
4 Ibid., p. 19

life, so successful merchants and politicians built showplaces in the countryside around Bordeaux.

This newly acquired flamboyance was to prove short-lived for many of the proprietors. Quite a few aristocratic owners lost their heads during the Revolution and most noble estates were sold off, though in some cases the original owners were able to buy back their estates in the nineteenth century. The immediate aftermath of the Revolution was to leave the vineyard area in disarray and some time was to elapse before the region regained a measure of prosperity. The turn of the century also saw the consolidation of many of the top estates in the hands of the Lur-Saluces family, whose principal asset was Château d'Yquem. In 1846, Charles Cocks wrote that 'Coutet, the first *cru* [of Barsac], belongs to the family of Lur Saluces, who own almost all the best *crus* of this white wine country.'[5] Two centuries later, it sometimes seems as if nothing has changed. Although the Lur-Saluces family today owns a mere two estates – Yquem and Fargues – their distant cousins seem to own a sizeable proportion of the rest.

It was the 1847 vintage that put Yquem firmly on the map and gave a boost to the region as a whole. Michael Broadbent, who has enjoyed the privilege of tasting this wine on several occasions, is astonished by its power, richness and intensity, and concludes: 'One of the greatest wines ever tasted.' It must have made a comparable impression on the brother of the Russian tsar, Grand Duke Constantine, when he tasted the wine in 1859, for he promptly ordered a 900–litre *tonneau* for the amazing price of 20,000 gold francs. Yquem has never looked back.

By this time there was no doubt that the best Sauternes was made from nobly rotten grapes. The most learned surveyor of nineteenth-century viticulture, André Jullien, was quite explicit: 'Grapes are picked only when they are rotten and when their skin, having acquired a brown tinge, sticks to the fingers. This means the harvest can last two months, especially in the *crus* which make the finest wines.'[6] The English physician J. L. W. Thudichum, writing in the 1890s, recalled: 'We have been present at Château Suduiraut on an occasion when the vintagers passed through the vineyard for the

5 Charles Cocks, *Bordeaux*, p. 188
6 André Jullien, *Topographie de Tous les Vignobles Connus*, 1866, p. 20

tenth time, each time collecting single berries, and it was believed that they would have to pass once or twice more.'[7]

The Sauternais themselves propagated the idea that delaying the harvest until the onset of noble rot was an invention of the nineteenth century. In Germany, where the same phenomenon gives birth to the rare *Beerenauslesen* and *Trockenbeerenauslesen*, the invention of the style is attributed to the delay in securing permission for the harvest at Schloss Johannisberg in the Rheingau in 1775. By the time authorization for the harvest had been secured from the local bishop, goes the story, noble rot had set in. The pickers rapidly harvested the shrivelling, discolouring fruit and made rapturously wonderful sweet wine. So entrenched is this legend that Schloss Johannisberg has erected a statue of the courier whose tardiness accidentally caused the happy discovery. It's a myth, of course, and so is the story of M. Focke, the owner of Château La Tour-Blanche, who travelled to Germany in the 1830s and supposedly brought back with him the secret of noble rot. The fact is that the revelation of the phenomenon would have come as no surprise to Sauternais farmers, who must have known about it for decades, if not centuries.

However, not all Sauternes was sweet. Dr Thudichum remarks at the very end of the nineteenth century: 'The dry fine wines of Sauternes were once amongst the great favourites of the oenophilists' cellars, but they have now almost entirely disappeared.'[8] In the 1930s, Maurice Healy also refers to dry Sauternes, though he adds that they are 'very rarely found now'.[9] The closest approximation to their taste is probably Ygrec, the strong dry wine produced in certain years by Château d'Yquem.

Nowadays we think of Sauternes as a dessert wine, customarily served at the conclusion of a meal as a special treat. In the nineteenth century, it was more usual to find the wine poured as an accompaniment to a course on a typically lavish menu – with the turbot, perhaps. Our palates balk at coping with a sweet wine before meat and red wines, but Victorian and Edwardian gastronomes were made of sterner stuff.

Yet despite the growing popularity of the wines, the region was

7 J. L. W. Thudichum, *A Treatise on Wines*, p. 118
8 Ibid., p. 119
9 Maurice Healy, *Claret*, p. 133

plunged into fresh crises in the latter half of the century. Oidium plagued the vineyards in the 1850s, mildew was a constant problem and Sauternes was not able to avoid the eventual onslaught of the destructive louse known as phylloxera, which devastated most of the vineyards of Europe in the late nineteenth century. There is a high sand content in the soils of Sauternes, which lies close to the dunes of the Landes, and this retarded the affliction. As late as 1899 and 1900, Château d'Yquem was harvesting all its fruit from ungrafted vines, but before long the region had to follow the example of the rest of Europe by grafting vines on to phylloxera-resistant American rootstocks.

The fortunes of the region remained mixed during the twentieth century. The Russian taste for Yquem, sweet Roederer Champagne and Imperial Tokay came to a rapid end in 1917. Two world wars hampered trade and Prohibition put the dampers on exports to the United States. The *appellation contrôlée* for Barsac and Sauternes was issued in 1936, laying down the rules and regulations by which the wine was to be harvested and structured. There was a spurt of interest in sweet white wine during the world wars and again after the Second World War, but only at the cheapest end of the market. As had no doubt been the case in medieval times, sweet wine was sought less for its flavour than for its nutritional content. Sugar, rationed and in short supply, could be sampled instead in liquid form. Vast quantities of insipid sweet wines were produced on both sides of the Garonne. Instead of assisting the ailing châteaux which were trying to maintain high standards in the face of a sales slump that must have seemed never-ending, the glut of cheap and mostly nasty sweet wine had the opposite effect, wrecking the reputation of Sauternes. (Decades later the German wine industry made the same mistake in Britain by assiduously promoting its worst wines, with the result that sugary, watery Müller-Thurgaus produced in industrial quantities began to be seen as representative of the best of German wine, while top estate wines became almost impossible to sell.)

During the 1960s and 1970s, even among classified growths, standards plummeted. Yquem itself released a wine from the 1963 vintage that was rightly derided as a disgrace and the 1968 vintage was not a great improvement on the 1963. In 1976, Comte Maximilien de Pontac, the owner of the *Deuxième Cru* Château de Myrat, uprooted his vines, since he found it no longer worth his while financially to cultivate grapes. (Myrat has been replanted, but it came very close to extinction.) Other estates, such as the *Premier Cru* Château Guiraud, produced substantial quantities of dry white and red wines to make up for slack sales of Sauternes. Château Coutet marketed dry white wine under its prestigious label, even though the grapes were not from the Sauternes region. Yquem too mopped up some surplus production by releasing it in the form of a strong dry white called Ygrec, although this is a wine of real distinction and not merely a way of using up grapes. In the sweet white wine regions on the other side of the Garonne – in Loupiac, Sainte-Croix-du-Mont and the Premières Côtes – the same trend was discernible.

The slump led to instability. Many fine properties changed hands. In some cases, such as Châteaux d'Arche and Raymond-Lafon, the new owners were closely linked with the region; in other cases, such as Châteaux Guiraud and Nairac, the new proprietors were outsiders. There was surprisingly little resentment against the influx, as the long-settled estate owners recognized that new investment and new blood were essential for the survival of the region and its wines. If Guiraud had come into the hands of a rich Canadian businessman and his ambitious sons, so much the better for this neglected property.

The turning point in the fortunes of the Sauternais was 1983. Just as the interest in claret was intensified by the splendour of the 1982 vintage, so the superb 1983 vintage in Sauternes kindled a new curiosity in the sweet wines of Bordeaux. The American market in particular rose like Lazarus and an appreciation of fine wine became a social asset among a generation that had probably been raised on Budweiser and Dr Pepper. When the 1983 Sauternes came on to the market, they were still relatively inexpensive – top wines were selling *en primeur* for about £100 a case in 1984 – and their quality persuaded many cautious wine lovers that there was something special about Sauternes after all. Meanwhile in the Sauternais, the proprietors, instead of simply pocketing the proceeds of the 1983 vintage, wisely ploughed the profits back into their estates, making viticultural and technological improvements that were long overdue. *Premiers Crus* such as Suduiraut, La Tour-Blanche and Rabaud-Promis abandoned the short cuts they had taken in the 1970s and reinvested in *barriques* and other essential equipment.

By the time of the next great vintage in 1986, the region was ready for it. Many estates made better 1986s than 1983s, and felt justified in raising their prices. The consumer may have gasped at first, but the fact is that until the early 1980s the wines had been so underpriced that only the most philanthropic of proprietors could afford to take the pains necessary to produce top sweet wine. *Tries successives*, low yields (the average crop is almost one-third of that in the Médoc) and long ageing in *barriques* do not come cheap, and the frequency of washed-out vintages only adds to the overheads.

1988 was another glorious vintage, which was followed by the opulent 1989s. By then, prices had risen to such an extent that, as far as this ardent wine lover was concerned, Sauternes had almost priced itself out of the market. It was possible to buy two cases of 1983 Château Climens for the same price as one case of the 1988, and the 1989s were even more expensive. True, the quality was unimpeachable, but estates such as Suduiraut and La Tour-Blanche increased their opening prices so steeply that they encountered a quite justified resistance both among merchants and wine lovers, whose incomes had been reduced by world-wide recession.[10]

The 1990 vintage was, if anything, even greater than the two preceding ones, but it was no longer feasible for the Sauternais to raise their prices again and the 1990s proved slightly cheaper than the 1989s. But by this time, the reputation of the region and its wines had been restored and the estates were equipped to maximize the potential of future vintages. Just as the Sauternais felt justified in resting on their laurels, just as they were reflecting on how they had snatched survival from the jaws of commercial disaster, a new crisis loomed.

The vintages of 1988, 1989 and 1990 were unprecedented in that they offered three great vintages in a row. Two in a row, such as 1928 and 1929, or 1975 and 1976, had not been that unusual, but no one had experienced three successive triumphs. To punish the Sauternais and dissipate any complacency that may have set in, the weather gods inflicted three appalling vintages on them: 1991 was the year of the frost, the crop was of good quality, but tiny; 1992 and 1993 were dreadful. The large estates were not too concerned: Château Suduiraut rather grandly took the step of not bot-

10 Opening prices from some châteaux were as follows: Doisy-Daëne, 80 francs; de Malle, 85 francs; Doisy-Védrines and Rabaud-Promis, 95 francs; La Tour-Blanche, 120 francs; Sigalas-Rabaud, 135 francs; Guiraud, 155 francs; Suduiraut, 175 francs.

tling any wine from those three vintages. But Suduiraut is financed by a giant French insurance company. For the small growers, or for the de Pontac brothers at Château de Myrat, who had bravely replanted the vineyard but had yet to harvest a saleable crop from its vines, the situation was disastrous.

In the late 1970s, the average price per *tonneau* (900 litres) of generic Sauternes was about 7,000 francs, which, as an earlier study of Sauternes has pointed out, was about the same price as generic Saint-Émilion, which is far less expensive to produce.[11] By 1985, with the watershed vintage of 1983 just entering the market-place, there was a greater differential between the two wines, with Sauternes fetching 21,003 francs against 14,606 francs for Saint-Émilion. As we have already seen, prices continued to rise steadily through the 1980s, but in 1989 there was a considerable leap upwards, with many prices rising by 40 per cent. Since then prices have declined, as the market would no longer tolerate very high prices even for undeniably great wines. Some châteaux discreetly lowered their prices in an attempt to dispose of unsold stock piling up in their cellars. With the rash of bad vintages in the early 1990s, the need to raise cash became ever more urgent. For the proprietors of Sauternes, the great irony is that the splendid vintages, for which the highest prices can be obtained, are the cheapest to produce. In 1990 everyone had good grapes and, if they didn't mess up the fermentation, the wine was of outstanding quality. In 1991, the Barsac proprietor Mireille Daret told me, the quantity was minute and, because of harvesting conditions and other factors, the wine cost twice as much per bottle to produce as the 1990. With virtually no good wine made in 1992 and 1993, most estates holding large amounts of stock were able to dispose of their surplus.

By 1990, the price per *tonneau* for Sauternes had climbed to 45,000–50,000 francs, but it plummeted to 16,000–20,000 francs for the worst wines in 1992. By 1994, the price had risen to just above 30,000 francs. According to Xavier de Pontac of Château de Myrat, the president of the region's Syndicat des Grands Crus Classés, prices had to reach 30,000 francs for small estates to be certain of survival. Of course, statistics such as these are misleading, since they do not reflect the difference in demand for good wines as opposed to bad. Pierre Meslier of Château Raymond-

11 Jeffrey Benson and Alastair Mackenzie, *Sauternes*, p. 37

Lafon has encountered Bordeaux merchants who are seeking 'Sauternes' that can be on the shelves six months after the harvest. Such wines undoubtedly exist, even though they must taste frightful, and they have nothing in common with classic Sauternes produced by the good estates, despite sharing the same appellation and being entitled to the same label. None the less, many students of the economic life of the region believe that the profits made during the late 1980s by every producer and the gradual increase in wholesale prices in the mid-1990s means that most growers will somehow struggle through.

Despite the indisputable fact that the quality of Sauternes is probably finer than it has been for many decades, the wine remains difficult to sell. In June 1994, a leading London wine merchant with a core of rich customers discounted one of the top 1989 Barsacs from £290 per case to £199. In his list he commented: 'Cost price. Lovely wine, but can't sell it.' At about the same time Laytons, another London merchant, was offering similar discounts on dozens of cases of Coutet, Climens, Suduiraut and Rieussec from 1988, 1989 and 1990, as well as 1986 Yquem; Sauternes doesn't get much better than those wines. There are many explanations for the failure of such wines to sell – a severe recession, excessive price increases when the wines were released, and so forth – but it has to be bad news for the region when truly great wines have to be reduced to the price of a modest Burgundy or a smart *Cru Bourgeois* claret in order to find a market.

The region's difficulties would doubtless be eased were growers permitted to make dry wines in mediocre vintages. David Peppercorn has argued:

What is needed is a smaller production of top-quality wines. But in order to achieve this, producers must be able to make other, more commercial everyday wines from the same vineyards. Let us hope that the authorities respond to what is a crisis situation with some common-sense solutions. Sauternes and the other great sweet wines of Bordeaux cannot survive much longer on philanthropy.[12]

12 David Peppercorn, *Bordeaux*, p. 634

Peter Vinding-Diers, a winemaker of great experience now based at Château Landiras in the Graves, agrees:

> From the start the authorities should have allowed dry white wine to be made in Sauternes under the Graves appellation. Then the committed winemakers could have concentrated their efforts on making Sauternes, and the lazy growers who happen to own a few hectares in the region could have played safe and made dry wines. But the old Marquis de Lur-Saluces was against it at the time, and that was that. The consequence, though, is that many growers with no interest in making good sweet wine churn out mediocre Sauternes that damages the region's reputation.

The suggestion sounds reasonable, but the experience of other appellations where this approach has been followed is not encouraging. Cérons is a sweet-wine appellation just north of Barsac, but its growers are also entitled to make dry wines under the Graves appellation. The advantages of opting for the latter are obvious: you don't have to wait for a moment beyond the day when your grapes attain ripeness, you can enjoy yields about twice those required to make good-quality sweet wine and the wines can be sold months, rather than years, after the harvest. The consequence? Cérons has been in steady decline for decades and, until the great 1989 vintage, seemed on the brink of extinction. Many properties had abandoned the production of sweet wine altogether, others produced a small quantity in certain years just to satisfy eccentric clients with a fondness for such wines, while only a handful of estates made a conscientious effort to make sweet wine of high quality. There were times when Sauternes estates, such as Guiraud, made abundant quantities of dry red and white wines. But that proved no guarantee that the smaller quantities of Sauternes that they did produce were of high quality. One can only have sympathy for the owner of a small *Cru Bourgeois* in Sauternes who has to contemplate a near-empty cellar for the third year in succession. But if the production of sweet wine were to become just one option out of many, then Sauternes might become an ultra-expensive wine made in minute quantities for the ultra-rich.

This recent history and the issues raised by Peppercorn are a useful reminder that making sweet white wine in Bordeaux is a lottery. None of the certainties that apply to winemaking in most other regions apply here. In Germany, an absence of noble rot doesn't prevent Riesling growers from making abundant fine wine, but a failure of the climate in Sauternes can leave the proprietors with no wine to sell and no income to invest. I don't doubt that there will always be dedicated, even maniacal, estate owners who will battle against the odds of nature for the satisfaction, even if only twice or thrice in a decade, of astonishing us with the unrivalled beauty of their wines. But connoisseurship is no substitute for a sound commercial basis. In future years we are likely to see the absorption of estates by large and diversified companies. If Rieussec or Suduiraut makes a loss in a few vintages, their owners, Lafite-Rothschild and AXA, can balance that against their profits from the Médoc. That is not possible for proprietors whose sole asset is an estate in the Sauternes and their long-term future is surely in doubt.

Xavier de Pontac sagely remarked to me: '*On fait jamais sa fortune à Sauternes. Heureusement il y a toujours ceux qui pense* . . . ' ('Nobody will ever make a fortune from producing Sauternes. Fortunately for the region, there are always people who believe the opposite . . .').

Maps

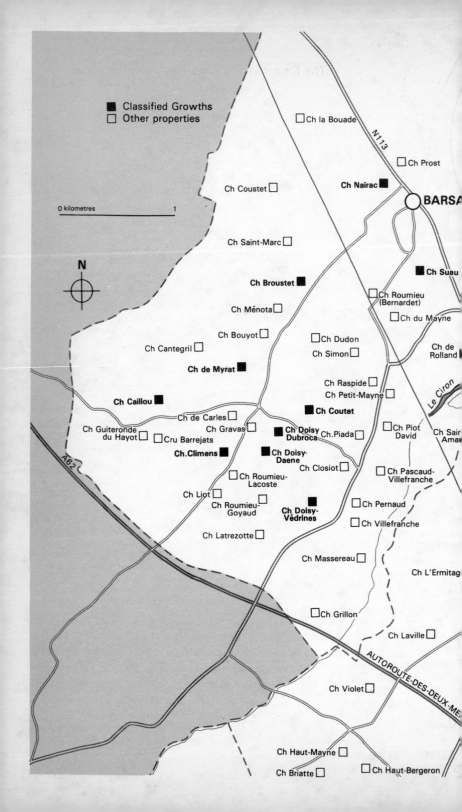

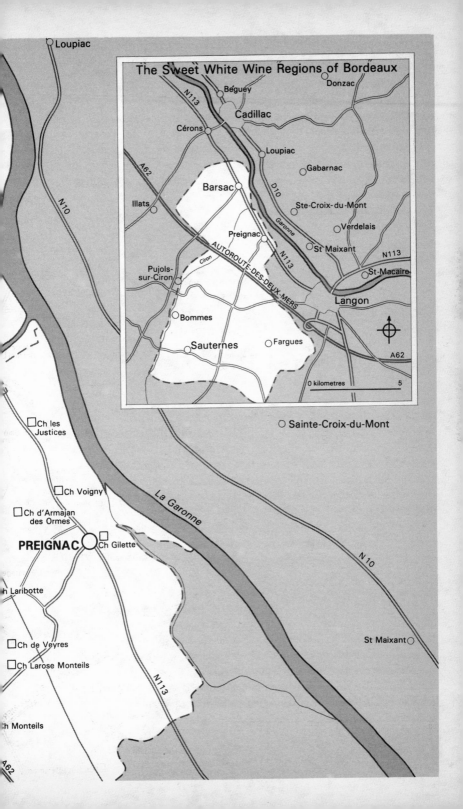

Loupiac

The Sweet White Wine Regions of Bordeaux

Donzac

Béguey

Cadillac

Cérons

Loupiac

Gabarnac

Barsac

Illats

Ste-Croix-du-Mont

Verdelais

Preignac

St Maixant

St-Macaire

Pujols-sur-Ciron

Ciron

AUTOROUTE-DES-DEUX-MERS

Garonne

N113

Langon

Bommes

Sauternes

Fargues

A62

0 kilometres   5

N113

N10

A62

D10

Garonne

Sainte-Croix-du-Mont

Ch les Justices

Ch Voigny

Ch d'Armajan des Ormes

PREIGNAC

Ch Gilette

La Garonne

N 10

h Laribotte

Ch de Veyres

Ch Larose Monteils

St Maixant

N113

h Monteils

A62

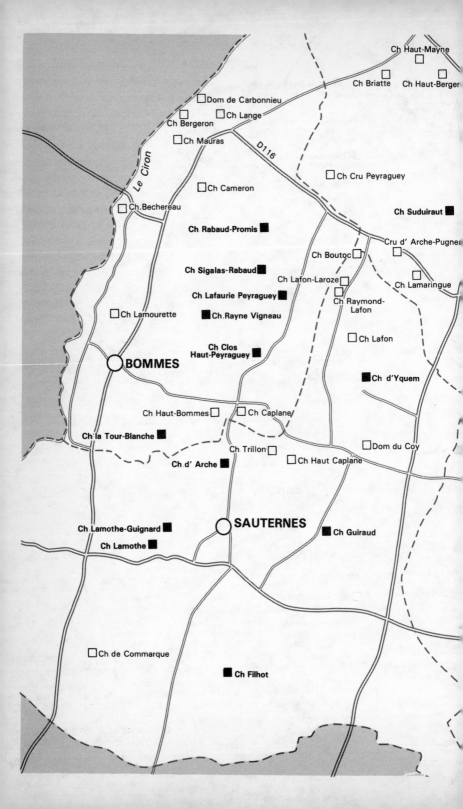

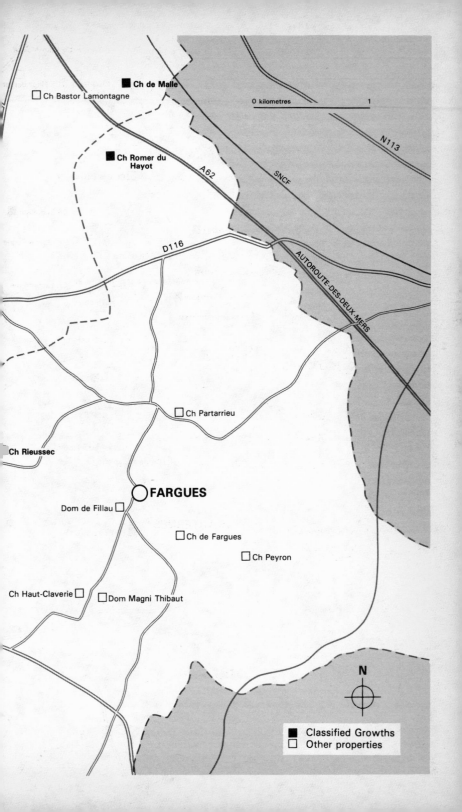

SAUTERNES

I

The Classification of Sauternes

━━━━━━

The classification of 1855 established the hierachy of the Sauternes region that is still used today, but this was by no means the first attempt to rank the wines. In 1846, Charles Cocks was writing confidently of the characteristics of the five communes of which the region is composed – Sauternes, Preignac, Bommes, Fargues and Barsac – and devising a classification of his own. He proposed three tiers rather than the two adopted by the 1855 classification.

His *Premiers Crus* were, retaining Cocks's spelling: Yquem, Guiraud, Vigneau (now Rayne-Vigneau), La Tour-Blanche, Peyraguey (now Lafaurie-Peyraguey and Clos Haut-Peyraguey), Rabaut (now Rabaud-Promis and Sigalas-Rabaud), Soudiraut, Mareillac, Coutet, Climenz, Myrat and Daune (now Doisy-Daëne?). All these properties still exist with the exception of Mareillac, but since Mareilhac was the name of the owner of what is today Rieussec, these two properties are probably one and the same.

The *Deuxièmes Crus* were: Filhiol (now Filhot), Baptiste, Lasalle, Pechotte, Lamontagne (now Bastor-Lamontagne), Montalier (which appears not to be the same as the present-day estate of that name), de Malle, Les Ormes (now Château d'Armajan-des-Ormes), Amé, Charon, Vedrine (now Doisy-Védrines), Chemizard, Pernaud and Suhaute.

The *Troisièmes Crus* were: d'Arche, Rabat, Lafon (now Lafon and Raymond-Lafon), Nérac (now Nairac) and Guitte-Ronde (now Guiteronde).[13]

The 1855 classification was compiled by the wine merchants of Bordeaux. Hence it was based on commercial considerations as much as on the supposed but ill-defined superiority of one *terroir*

13 Charles Cocks, *Bordeaux*, pp. 199–200

over another. Still, it is safe to assume that after a few centuries of buying and trading the wines of Sauternes, the Bordeaux merchants had a shrewd idea about where the best and most consistent wines were to be found. The resulting classification was as follows:

Premier Grand Cru

Château d'Yquem	Sauternes

Premiers Crus

Château La Tour-Blanche	Bommes
Château Peyraguey	Bommes
Château Vigneau	Bommes
Château Suduiraut	Preignac
Château Coutet	Barsac
Château Climens	Barsac
Château Bayle	Sauternes
Château Rieussec	Sauternes
Château Rabeaud	Bommes

Deuxièmes Crus

Château Mirat	Barsac
Château Doisy	Barsac
Château Pexoto	Bommes
Château d'Arche	Sauternes
Château Filhot	Sauternes
Château Broustet-Nérac	Barsac
Château Caillou	Barsac
Château Suau	Barsac
Château de Malle	Preignac
Château Romer	Preignac
Château Lamothe	Sauternes

Inevitably changes of ownership have forced a revision of the list. Bayle is now Guiraud. Rabeaud was later divided into two properties, as was Lamothe. Pexoto was absorbed by what is now Rabaud-Promis. Châteaux Broustet and Nérac have been split into two separate properties, whereas Doisy has been divided in three. Rieussec and Romer were placed within Preignac, whereas subsequent boundaries would place them within the commune of Fargues.

In 1867, a M. Daney attempted a revised classification in which he changed the ranking. Yquem remained top dog, but the *Premiers Crus* were listed in the following order: Vigneau, Peyraguey, Guiraud, Tour Blanche, Rieussec, Suduiraut, Coutet, Climens, Rabaut. The *Deuxièmes Crus* consisted of Peyxotto, Doisy-Védrines-Boireau, Myrat, Doisy-Daëne, Filhot, Arche, Caillou, Dudon, Daney (Preignac), Lamothe, Raymond-Lafon and many others.[14]

Today the classification preserves the choices made in 1855, but makes no attempt to rank the wines within each category:

Premier Grand Cru

Château d'Yquem	Sauternes

Premiers Crus

Château Climens	Barsac
Château Clos Haut-Peyraguey	Bommes
Château Coutet	Barsac
Château Guiraud	Sauternes
Château Lafaurie-Peyraguey	Bommes
Château La Tour-Blanche	Bommes
Château Rabaud-Promis	Bommes
Château Rayne-Vigneau	Bommes
Château Rieussec	Fargues
Château Sigalas-Rabaud	Bommes
Château Suduiraut	Preignac

Deuxièmes Crus

Château d'Arche	Sauternes
Château Broustet	Barsac
Château Caillou	Barsac
Château Doisy-Daëne	Barsac
Château Doisy-Dubroca	Barsac
Château Doisy-Védrines	Barsac
Château Filhot	Sauternes
Château Lamothe	Sauternes

14 Edouard Féret, *Statistique Générale . . . du Département du Gironde* (1874)

5

Château Lamothe-Guignard	Sauternes
Château de Malle	Preignac
Château de Myrat	Barsac
Château Nairac	Barsac
Château Romer-du-Hayot	Fargues
Château Suau	Barsac

In the 1960s, the accuracy of the classification looked doubtful. At least half the *Premiers Crus* were producing wines scarcely worthy of any classification, let alone the top tier. The principal explanation was human weakness, not the inadequacies of soil or microclimate. The great trio of vintages at the end of the 1980s has vindicated the original classification. Most of the modifications one would wish to make would be the promotion of unclassified properties; only a few classified growths definitely deserve demotion. At present the classified growths own 43 per cent of the appellation's vineyards.

The American wine writer Robert Parker has bravely attempted his own classification, though he has somewhat unfairly included special *cuvées* in the top rank rather than rating the overall quality of a particular estate. It's not difficult in a fine vintage to make a special selection of the very best lots, then bottle and market it separately and to great acclaim. Here is the Parker classification of 1993 from his *Wine Buyer's Guide*:

Outstanding Producers

Château Climens	Barsac
Château Coutet (Cuvée Madame)	Barsac
Château de Fargues	Fargues
Château Raymond-Lafon	Sauternes
Château Rieussec	Fargues
Château Suduiraut (Cuvée Madame)	Preignac
Château d'Yquem	Sauternes

Excellent Producers

Château Coutet	Barsac
Château Doisy-Dubroca	Barsac

Château Gilette	Preignac
Château Guiraud	Sauternes
Château Lafaurie-Peyraguey	Bommes
Château Rabaud-Promis	Bommes
Château Suduiraut	Preignac
Château La Tour-Blanche	Bommes

Good Producers

Château Bastor-Lamontagne	Preignac
Château Doisy-Daëne	Barsac
Château Doisy-Védrines	Barsac
Château Lamothe-Guignard	Sauternes
Château de Malle	Preignac
Château Rayne-Vigneau	Bommes
Château Sigalas-Rabaud	Bommes

My own personal classification would be as follows:

Summa Cum Laude

Château d'Yquem	Sauternes

Outstanding Producers

Château Climens	Barsac
Château de Fargues	Fargues
Château Lafaurie-Peyraguey	Bommes
Château Rabaud-Promis	Bommes
Château Raymond-Lafon	Sauternes
Château Rieussec	Fargues
Château Suduiraut	Preignac

Excellent Producers

Château d'Arche	Sauternes
Château Coutet	Barsac
Château Doisy-Daëne	Barsac
Château Doisy-Dubroca	Barsac
Château Doisy-Védrines	Barsac
Château Gilette	Preignac
Château Guiraud	Sauternes

Château Haut-Bergeron	Preignac
Château Lamothe-Guignard	Sauternes
Château Nairac	Barsac
Château Rayne-Vigneau	Bommes
Château Sigalas-Rabaud	Bommes
Château La Tour-Blanche	Bommes

Good Producers

Château Bastor-Lamontagne	Preignac
Château Broustet	Barsac
Château Clos Haut-Peyraguey	Bommes
Château Les Justices	Preignac
Château de Malle	Preignac
Château Saint Amand	Preignac

However, readers are urged to take all such personal classifications with a large pinch of salt. There are some properties with a lowly classification or no classification at all that have made excellent wines in recent vintages; but consistency is also an important factor, as is the ability to make a good wine in a modest vintage.

2

Communes, Soils and Grapes

The Sauternais lies some twenty-five miles south of the city of Bordeaux, where it forms an enclave within the larger region known as the Graves. It is bordered by two rivers: the tidal Garonne and the smaller Ciron which rises from cold springs in the Landes. The conjunction of these two rivers between the villages of Barsac and Preignac spawns the autumnal mists which form such a congenial environment for the spores that carry noble rot on to the ripening grapes.

The Graves is named after the shallow gravel outcrops that are the region's distinctive feature. They were formed during the Tertiary period, when the Gironde was inundated and the receding waters left sedimentary deposits of gravel and sand layered in alluvial terraces. Gravel outcrops are present in the Sauternais too, but here the soil is more complex, with ample clay, and with hills and slopes more conspicuous than those encountered in the northern Graves. The layers of gravel offer excellent drainage and aeration, and the pebbly soil retains the warmth of the atmosphere for some time after sunset, a warmth which is reflected back on to the lowest-lying bunches, helping them to ripen. Where there is a heavy clay content in the soil, as at Château d'Yquem, good drainage is essential.

The Sauternais is composed of five communes. Barsac and Preignac lie close to N113 between Bordeaux and Langon and thus close to the Garonne. Sauternes, Bommes and Fargues lie further inland. The total area planted with vineyards is about 2,100 ha. (hectares), one-third of which is located in Barsac. The landscape is very gently undulating, but towards the south-west of the region, notably around Sauternes and Bommes, there are hilly outcrops where most of the best estates are located. The soil is poorer towards the top of the slopes and thus better adapted to the cultivation of the vine.

SAUTERNES

In this commune, 369 ha. are planted on soils composed of gravel, clay and sand; the subsoil consists of clay, as well as gravel and iron. The presence of the clay in the soil means that vineyards with good drainage are nearly always superior to those on flatter sandier sites, where there is a risk of the vines becoming waterlogged. At its southern border, vineyards merge into a typical Landes topography of pine woods. The gently hilly nature of the terrain means that there is a great variety of exposures, with slopes orientated towards the north as well as the east and south. It is often maintained that in wet years Sauternes has a more successful vintage than Barsac, while the reverse is true in dry years.

The population of the village is about 600. Here you can find two restaurants, the rustic and inexpensive Auberge les Vignes, opposite the church, which specializes in steaks cooked over vine branches (*sarments*); and the more elegant Le Saprien, which has an excellent range of Sauternes by the glass. In the main square is the Maison de Sauternes and the Caveau du Sauternais; both sell wines directly to the consumer. Opposite the church is the Caves des Lauréats, which offers a smaller selection of wines, as it is owned by Château Lamothe. It is often cheaper to buy directly from the estates, but in the case of the many properties that do not sell directly to the public, it is easier to track down their wines here.

Accommodation is available at Château de Commarque about 2 kilometres from the village. This secluded and peaceful mansion, owned by Dr Nigel Reay-Jones and his wife, has eight rooms, from 180 to 375 francs. It is closed in February. The reasonably priced restaurant offers many dishes prepared with Sauternes.

BOMMES

A total of 349 ha. are under vine here, the best sites being on the slopes above the Ciron valley. Here gravel is again an important component of the soil structure, as well as clay. Lower-lying land has a high sand content. The subsoil is stony, blending clay and limestone. In 1846, Charles Cocks claimed that the wines from Bommes have a fresher and lighter character than those from Sauternes itself.

With 518 inhabitants, Bommes is little more than a hamlet. Its one restaurant is the Auberge du Dix Cors.

FARGUES

The village is dominated by the ruined castle of Fargues, which remains the property of the Lur-Saluces family. The village itself is tiny, but there has been some suburban development between the hamlet and the outskirts of Langon, bringing the population of the commune to over 1,200. Only 218 ha. are planted. The soil around the village and the slopes just south of it is composed of clay and limestone, while on low-lying land there is sand and gravel. Almost all the vineyards are on the higher land. The subsoil is gravelly, with considerable clay content. The wines are a touch lighter than those from Sauternes.

PREIGNAC

This is a substantial little town with just over 2,000 inhabitants and is bisected by the *route nationale*. The recently restored eighteenth-century church of St Vincent contains, along the south wall, the Renaissance stone tomb of Pierre Sauvage, whose family owned Château d'Yquem in the mid-sixteenth century. It was erected in his memory by his widow Jeanne, and has fine carvings and inscriptions.

The 543 ha. of vineyards, apart from Château Les Justices and a few other small parcels, lie to the west of the town, and stretch beyond the *autoroute* to the boundaries with Sauternes and Bommes. The soil is very varied, with alluvial deposits to the north and east, but with much heavier clay and gravel to the south. The western parts of Preignac have a lighter sand and gravel soil, and the whole commune rests on a clay and gravel subsoil. In 1846, Charles Cocks asserted that the wines were, in general, less fine and less perfumed than those of Sauternes.

Wine can be bought from the Maison du Vigneron along the main road in the centre of town.

Preignac has a few restaurants, of which the most congenial is the inexpensive Restaurant du Cap, located on the riverbank. Along the main road is Braises et Gourmandises, which has a garden, and just south of the village is the slightly cheaper Les Érables. In the hamlet of Boutoc, not far from Château d'Yquem, is the inexpensive Restaurant La Table du Sauternais (closed Mondays), which is owned by the Château d'Arche-Pugneau opposite.

BARSAC

Barsac is far more distinctive than the other four communes. It lies to the north-west of the Ciron and is characterized by its subsoil of permeable limestone bedrock. Indeed, many of the vineyards are surrounded by limestone walls probably constructed when the fields were originally cleared for planting. The other feature of Barsac soil is the presence of red sand, the colour denoting its high iron content. The 520 ha. of vineyards surround the village of Barsac, which lies along the *route nationale* and is about the same size as Preignac. A few estates, such as Nairac, Prost, Suau and Rolland, have vineyards along the main road. Not surprisingly, given the proximity of the Garonne, the soil is more alluvial.

Most of the best sites are located between the railway line and the *autoroute*, which forms the boundary of the commune. Towards the *autoroute*, the essentially flat land of Barsac rises slightly to form what is known as Haut-Barsac, a plateau all of 20 metres above sea level. Production figures throughout the 1980s were 13,000–15,000 hl. (hectolitres), giving an average yield of about 20 hl./ha. (hectolitres per hectare). In terms of area under vine, Barsac is easily the largest of the five communes. It enjoyed an economic bonus until the end of the nineteenth century, as the Ciron was used to transport timber from the Landes to Bordeaux via the port of Barsac.

In 1846, Charles Cocks reported that the wines of Barsac, once regarded as highly as those from Sauternes itself, 'have now fallen in estimation'. That is no longer the case and the wines are greatly admired. They do have a character of their own, derived primarily from the limestone subsoil. They tend to be lighter and fresher than the wines from the other communes, with more citric characteristics in the aromas and a greater raciness on the palate. This lightness can be deceptive. Traditionally, Barsac was vinified to give higher alcohol and less residual sugar than Sauternes itself, and a few growers tell me they still aim to balance their wines in this way. (In 1829, Paguierre declared that Barsac wines had more body than either Sauternes or Bommes, a statement which surprises us today, when the prevailing view is the exact opposite. He added that the wine becomes drier after ten years, acquiring a flavour of almonds.[15]) Nor should 'lightness' be interpreted as short-lived. Perhaps because of their acidic backbone, top Barsacs age beautifully. I have often tasted *Premiers Crus* from the 1920s that were in impeccable condition.

The commune maintains the Maison de Barsac, its own tasting and sales room, in the middle of town along the *route nationale*.

There are two hotels in Barsac. Hostellerie du Château de Rolland is just south of the town in the midst of the vineyards. It has nine rooms and enjoys a mixed reputation, especially as far as the cooking is concerned. In 1993, an attractive mansion in the village, the Château de Valmont, opened as a comfortable hotel. Meals are available only for residents and room prices in 1994 ranged from 295 to 595 francs.

The church, with its fine vaulted interior, is worth a visit. Just inside the entrance you can see the lines drawn to record the water levels during the spring floods of 1770 and 1930.

It is sometimes remarked that each commune has its own character. With the exception of Barsac, I find this hard to substantiate in practice. Sauternes is said to be the most luscious and honeyed of the wines, with Bommes and Preignac having a more floral and slightly leaner character. In the early nineteenth century, André Jullien felt that the style of Preignac blended those of Barsac and Sauternes. Sometimes, yes, but not invariably. There are too many other factors at play: variations in microclimate, the maturity of the grapes when picked and the degree of noble rot, the use of new oak in the *élevage* of the wine, the balance between alcohol and residual sugar, and so on. Rieussec is from Fargues (just), but in certain vintages, if tasting it blind, I would swear that it was from Sauternes. Lafaurie-Peyraguey and Sigalas-Rabaud are both Bommes, but made in very different styles, which affects our perception of their overall character.

Of equal significance in establishing the character and balance of

15 M. Paguierre, *Classification et Description des Vins de Bordeaux*

a particular estate's wine is the blend of the grapes planted. Only three grapes are planted in the Sauternais: Sémillon, Sauvignon Blanc and Muscadelle. Muscadelle is becoming quite rare and many estates eschew it altogether. Sémillon is easily the dominant variety, and a few estates such as Climens and Doisy-Daëne use nothing else. Château d'Yquem, however, is more typical of the region in favouring a balance of 80 per cent Sémillon and 20 per cent Sauvignon.

The Sémillon grape is quite large, turns a golden colour in autumn and the formation of the bunches is relatively tight. A naturally high-yielding variety with thin skins, it attracts noble rot quite easily. The substantial leaves are five-lobed with a downy underside; the stems can have a deep reddish colour.

The thicker-skinned Sauvignon is less susceptible to noble rot than Sémillon, but is prized for the freshness and acidity it brings to the finished wine, in contrast to Sémillon, which has a low natural acidity. The leaves are three-lobed and, like Sémillon, downy on the underside; the grapes are smaller than those of Sémillon and more oblong in shape. Although it ripens relatively late, many growers pick it quite early during the harvest, again in order to preserve its acidity and vigour. Growers try to avoid planting Sauvignon on soils that are excessively humid as the tight bunches can be susceptible to *pourriture grise* or grey rot.

It is not always clear whether Muscadelle has fallen from favour because growers do not like its aromatic character or because they simply find it too troublesome to farm. As an early ripener, it is susceptible to grey rot, which renders its fruit useless. Like Sémillon, its leaves are quite large and five-lobed. The grander estates have little fondness for Muscadelle and aim to keep it out of their vineyards, but there are other properties, such as Château Broustet, where the owner not only preserved the existing old vines of Muscadelle, but also replanted the variety to maintain the traditional varietal mix in the field. Christian Médeville, the owner of Châteaux Gilette and Justices, retains a small proportion of Muscadelle in his vineyards because it offers *support aromatique*: 'It's like salt in cooking.' A grower in Sainte-Croix-du-Mont claims that when there is frost damage in the spring, Muscadelle is more likely to give a second crop than the other two varieties.

Two centuries ago there were other varieties planted in the Sauternais. There were dark rumours that Riesling had been planted at Château Rabaud in imitation of Schloss Johannisberg in the Rheingau, and I know of a Barsac estate where Riesling vines frolic in the fields, though I have no evidence to suggest any of it has ever ended up in a bottle labelled Sauternes. Another grower in Barsac assures me that Marsanne, a variety commonly encountered in the Rhône valley, used to be planted in the region; however, it proved more resistant to noble rot than the other varieties and the last vines were grubbed up in the 1950s. Cocks, in listing the varieties found in 1846, mentions Sémillon and Sauvignon, of course, but also refers to Rochalin, a late-ripening variety akin to Sauvignon; Verdot Blanc, another late-ripening variety, with large dark leaves, middling-sized bunches, small grapes and a fine flavour; Blanc-doux, which I have seen referred to in some modern sources as a synonym for Sauvignon[16] and in others as a synonym for Sémillon;[17] and Prueras, high-yielding with 'large savoury grapes'.[18] In 1829, Paguierre also referred to Prunilla, Muscadet Doux and Chalosse, though he intimated that the dominant varieties in Barsac and Preignac were Sémillon, Sauvignon and Malvoisie.[19] Maurice Healy, writing in 1934, mentions another grape found in the region, the Metternich, which was almost certainly Riesling planted in the previous century.[20] It was banned in the 1930s under the new *appellation contrôlée* regulations.

Verdot is a synonym for Petit Verdot, and although Cocks may have been referring to a white grape that bore this name, it is entirely possible that red grapes were encountered here in the first half of the nineteenth century. Thomas Jefferson's *Travel Notes* of 1787 describes Sauternes as a wine 'made from grapes with red skins' but 'pale rose in colour, for, being made without being pressed, the colouring matter of the skin does not mix with the juice'. What is probable is that a small proportion of red grapes was vinified together with the dominant white varieties, and that the treading of those grapes lent a light coloration to the finished wine.

There is considerable controversy about the merits and faults of the two leading varieties and this applies to their contribution to dry white wine as well as sweet wines. The great oenologist Émile

16 Cocks and Féret, *Bordeaux et Ses Vins*, 1949
17 Jancis Robinson, *Vines, Grapes and Wines*, p. 119
18 Charles Cocks, *Bordeaux*, 1846, pp. 142–3
19 M. Paguierre, *Classification et Description des Vins de Bordeaux*
20 Maurice Healy, *Claret*, p. 128

Peynaud, who acts as a consultant to many estates in the region, doesn't think much of Sémillon, though he concedes that it is the best grape for sweet wines. There is a problem with Sémillon: its essential neutrality. Its character is derived either from the soil in which it is planted or from the changes wrought by noble rot. In Australia's Hunter Valley, for instance, even when vinified entirely in steel, it acquires a nutty, toasty character easily mistaken for the aromas and flavours acquired after oak-ageing. But Sémillon planted on indifferent and over-fertile soils can be exceedingly dull, as anyone with wide experience of Californian Sémillon can confirm. Sémillon's natural character is often described as waxy and reminiscent of lanolin or linseed oil. This is apt, but not very inviting. Of course, noble rot alters that character dramatically. Where it scores over Sauvignon is in its capacity to age. This is particularly noticeable in dry white Graves, where wines dominated by Sémillon tend to age more interestingly than those made principally from Sauvignon. It also attains high alcoholic levels with relative ease, which is important for a style of wine such as Sauternes.

Sémillon is not a uniform variety, but one that exhibits subtle differences acquired after clonal or massal selection. The young vines planted nowadays, claim most growers, are selected so as to offer a more regular rather than an excessive production. The vines tend to be long-lived and can easily live for up to fifty years before deracination and replanting become unavoidable. Modern-day selections not only offer regular yields, but also ensure that the vine is resistant to many diseases. The issue of selections is a contentious one in many French wine regions, notably Burgundy where inappropriate clones had been planted, but it is of less importance in Sauternes. One of the purposes of clonal selection is to diminish susceptibility to rot, but that frailty is precisely the one that Sauternes growers most seek.

Sauvignon Blanc is admired not only for the freshness it contributes, but also for its stronger aromatic personality. Sémillon is far more neutral in this respect. The tightness of the Sauvignon bunches and the grapes' thick skins mean that noble rot finds it harder to anchor itself in Sauvignon than Sémillon. Although acidity is a crucial component in wines that are long-lived, Sauvignon Blanc is not a variety known for the longevity of its wines, although I have encountered dry wines from the Loire and the Graves that have not tired after decades in bottle. But they are surely exceptional, and it is prudent to keep the proportion of Sauvignon in a wine intended to be aged, such as Sauternes, to a modest level. Other drawbacks of Sauvignon include its susceptibility to eutypiose, a fungal infection driven by wind and rain from vine to vine and to which there is no effective solution. It is also more prone than Sémillon to suffer from *coulure*: if the flowering, which usually occurs in June, is irregular, clusters of young berries can drop off the vine, reducing its production.

Given such drawbacks, it is strange to record that Sauvignon was undoubtedly the more prized variety of the two in the early nineteenth century. In 1846, Charles Cocks wrote in *Bordeaux*:

> It is now generally understood today that the Sauvignon is the basis of the best white wines, and that Yquem owes its superiority chiefly to this plant. This has, in some measure, been proved by the success of the proprietor of La Tour-Blanche, who, for the last 30 years, has been replanting the whole of his estate with this species of grape, where he has brought it almost on a par with Yquem.

Cocks's speculation was confirmed when in 1855 the classification of Sauternes placed La Tour-Blanche at the head of the *Premiers Crus*, thus hailing it as the best wine of the region after Yquem. But at about this time it was discovered that Sémillon was more resistant to oidium, so it began to replace Sauvignon when replantings occurred. Moreover, after the devastation caused by phylloxera from 1879 onwards, even more Sauvignon was replaced by the more productive Sémillon. By the time Dr Thudichum was writing his book in 1894, Sémillon, he estimated, accounted for two-thirds of the plantations in the Sauternais.

Although Sauvignon vines are reputed to be less long-lived than Sémillon vines, the oenologist Denis Dubourdieu claims that this is not the case and that Sauvignon vines can live for just as long, provided they are properly cared for. In Sainte-Croix-du-Mont, some growers were telling me that Sauvignon needed to be replanted after twenty-five years, but this suggests poor viticultural practices rather than any inherent feebleness of the Sauvignon vine.

In this regard, it is instructive to read in Cocks's *Bordeaux* that red vines were capable, *on average*, of surviving for 100 to 150 years. He refers to some vines in Pauillac that are two centuries old and to others in Pessac, in the northern Graves, which were planted in the fourteenth century. Naturally such undocumented claims must be treated with utmost scepticism. The longevity of the vines, he writes, varies according to the structure of the soil in which they are planted, but it is sandy or gravelly soils (such as Sauternes possesses in abundance) that permit the longest duration. Nowadays it is very rare to encounter white vines that are more than a century old, and it would be routine practice in the Graves and the Sauternais to replant vines that are between thirty and fifty years old. The reasons for replanting them may have as much to do with diminishing productivity as with diminishing quality, since it is widely recognized that old vines give the best and most concentrated wine. After replanting, a vine can only be cropped for Sauternes from its fourth year onwards.

The vines are usually planted to a density of 6,600 plants per ha. Sémillon and Sauvignon are pruned differently. Sémillon and Muscadelle are pruned by the *taille à cot* method of spur-pruning: the wood from the previous year's growth is cut off, leaving two, or at the most three, stumps, each with two or three eyes, from which the new shoots will spring. As the shoots grow, they are trained on to wires. Sauvignon, on the other hand, is pruned by the widespread *Guyot simple* method: a single stem (or *aste*) with up to eight eyes is left as the fruit-bearing arm, while a short stem is retained to provide the shoots for the following year's crop. It is not always the case that different methods are used on the same estate; some growers simplify their pruning tasks by adopting a single technique for all varieties, especially where the varieties were intermingled in the vineyard, as used to be the case. The object of severe pruning (*taille courte*) is to limit the yields. It is important that the vine be vigorous and fruitful, but equally important that it is hindered from bearing too much fruit. The risk involved in *taille courte*, which is generally undertaken in February, is that it increases the risk of frost damage in the spring, but that is a hazard which Sauternes growers are used to.

3
Viticulture and Noble Rot

There are few substantial viticultural differences between the cultivation of vines intended for the production of sweet wine and that
of vines destined for dry wine. The crucial difference is the limi-
tation of yields. Depending on the grape variety, yields of about 30
to 50 hl./ha. (2 to 3.3 tons per acre) will still allow a winemaker to
produce wine of a high standard and with reasonable concentration
of flavour. In Germany and the New World, many growers obtain
considerably higher yields without, they insist, any serious decline
in quality.

None of this applies to Sauternes. The regulations stipulate that
the maximum yield shall be 25 hl./ha., though in certain vintages
authorization may be given for a crop of up to 30 hl./ha. Yet very
few top estates achieve even these relatively low yields, though
there have been a few vintages when the crop has been of high
quality as well as generous in quantity. But that is very much the
exception. Since the aim of the serious winemaker in Sauternes is to
pick only grapes affected by noble rot, it is evident that in most
vintages a certain percentage of the fruit will be lost. Some bunches
will fail to ripen sufficiently, others will be ripe but not nobly rotten,
and others may succumb to attacks by insects, pests or hail. Set-
backs such as *coulure* (a failure of pollination that causes the young
unfertilized fruit to drop from the vine) or *millerandage* (a consequence of imperfect fertilization, which leaves stunted grapes that
will ripen unevenly) can occur during the flowering, especially if the
season is wet, and reduce the size and quality of the crop.

From the outset, yields must be restricted by severe pruning,
otherwise the grapes will not attain the high must weights essential
before great sweet wine can be made. Yquem estimates that its
average yield is 9 hl./ha., which is equivalent to one glass of wine

per vine. Sometimes a low yield in the vineyard will be further diminished after unsatisfactory lots have been rejected during the *assemblage*. Yquem is an extreme case and its astronomical prices require it to be more exacting than any other estate if it is to maintain its exalted status, but there are many other classified growths routinely attaining yields of 12 or 15 hl./ha., yields that enable them to make first-rate Sauternes.

Grapes destined for dry white wine will be picked at a potential alcohol level of about 13° in a good vintage. Some of that potential alcohol will be lost during the vinification process, but the result will still be a wine of between 12 and 12.5°. In years when the grapes fail to attain optimal ripeness, the must can be chaptalized, which simply means that, in the absence of sufficient natural grape sugar, sugar is added to the must to give the yeasts additional material to convert into alcohol. A good Sauternes will have a balance of about 14° of alcohol and 4° of residual grape sugar. This means that grapes must be picked with a must weight or potential alcohol of at least 18°. In cool or damp years this is not always possible, but this is what the conscientious grower must aim for. If the vine is bearing too much fruit, it will be that much more difficult for a sufficient concentration of sugar in the grape to be achieved. As Edward Steinberg has put it, 'Doing what comes naturally, vines are like parents who conceive more children than they have the means to bring up properly.'[21]

When describing vinification and specific wines in the chapters that follow, there will be many references to must weight or potential alcohol, since this measures the sugar content of the grapes at harvesting. Unfortunately, different scales of measurement are used. The measurement the grape grower makes is of the relative density of the juice. This is established by using a hydrometer or refractometer. The sweeter the juice, the greater its density and the greater the refraction of the light, which is calibrated by the refractometer, then read off by its user. To use this device, a little juice is smeared on to a glass plate, a plastic lid is flipped down which presses against it, then the calibrated reading is given by looking through an eyeglass. In France, the figure for relative density is converted into degrees Baumé or potential alcohol, which are not quite the same. Thus grapes picked at 18.7° Baumé will probably produce a

21 Edward Steinberg, *The Vines of San Lorenzo*, p. 37

finished wine with a total of alcohol and residual sugar of 18.1°, perhaps 14° of alcohol and 4.1° unfermented, and thus expressed in terms of residual sugar. But this is only a rule of thumb. There are various factors that can produce slight variations in the outcome, such as the activity of the yeasts and the temperature of fermentation. When figures are given in the chapters that follow for must weight, it must be borne in mind that such figures, often provided by winemakers, are usually but not necessarily given in terms of Baumé. In any event, what the wine tastes like is far more important than its statistical analysis.

Pruning is the simplest and most efficacious way to limit yields. It is not always effective, however. The vine is a living plant and can sometimes respond to the growing season with a burst of unwonted vigour. Even the most conscientious grower may find that by the summer the vine is bearing more fruit than is compatible with a low yield. At this stage in the growing cycle, it is becoming increasingly common for green-harvesting to take place: bunches are snipped off and allowed to go to waste. The consequence is that sugars and other nutrients are distributed among a smaller number of bunches and grapes, thus increasing the concentration of flavour. This practice horrified old-timers, for whom grapes are a foodstuff; such wastage seemed scandalous. But a younger generation of growers sees the need to increase quality if Sauternes is to maintain its reputation. There are others who criticize green-harvesting on the grounds that it is a consequence of cultivating over-productive vines in the first place and that it is better to control yields by curbing the vigour of the vine through improved viticultural practices.

Yves Armand of Château La Rame in Sainte-Croix-du-Mont says: 'The problem with green-harvesting is that the vines adapt themselves and begin to over-produce. Furthermore, the more you cut back the grapes, the more bunching occurs, which increases the risk of rot. It's far better to cultivate the vine so that it regulates itself.' That may well be so, but it is still preferable to remove bunches than to allow them to dilute the crop.

Other practices that are becoming commonplace in French vineyards have made little impact in the Sauternais. Vine growers are increasingly turning to organic or non-interventionist methods of farming. Excessive chemical treatments have impoverished the soil and there is a growing movement away from pesticides and other interventions. Where a decade ago the rows between the vines would have been free of vegetation, now, in many vineyards, grass and herbs grow freely, creating competition for nutrients with the vine roots (and thus limiting naturally the vigour of the vines) and forming the basis for a mulch that will later be dug into the soil.

There is little evidence of such enlightened viticultural practices in Sauternes. This is not solely because of obscurantist conservatism among growers. Much of the soil in Sauternes, especially in the south-western half of the region, is rich in clay and by working the soil in order to dispose of vegetation growing between the rows, there is a risk of turning clay slopes into muddy troughs impassable to tractors. Michel Garat of Château Bastor-Lamontagne acknowledges that treatments can damage the soil and also harm the microclimate. On the other hand, he and other growers do not want to impose harsh limits on the vines. Eventual yields may be 20 hl./ha. or less, but to attain those yields the vines must be capable of generating double. Consequently, growers are loath to engage in practices that could further diminish that natural productivity, nor do they want to encourage predators that could inflict damage on the already limited crop. Growers must protect their vines against problems such as *vers de la grappe*, a grub that hangs from the buds and is capable of penetrating the grapes when they ripen, thus exposing the fruit to grey rot.

In addition to copper-sulphate spraying and other treatments to guard against fungal infections or rapacious insects, some green-harvesting will take place in over-fertile years, and in the early autumn some leaves will be removed to allow the free circulation of air around the bunches. By this stage in the growing cycle, the grapes are deriving less and less nourishment from the leaves. Green leaves are left on the vine, but those that are yellowing are usually removed. The purpose of this ventilation procedure is to keep the grapes healthy and free from mould. It also allows the autumn sun more direct access to the ripening fruit. There is nothing novel about this. William J. Flagg noted in 1869 that 'leaf pruning is practised to excess, beginning early in September'.[22]

About one hundred days after flowering, which is normally in mid-June, the grapes should be ripe. Sauvignon Blanc has a slightly shorter growing season than Sémillon, so although it tends to flower later, the two varieties usually ripen at about the same time.

22 William J. Flagg, *Three Seasons in European Vineyards*, p. 68

It is from this point onwards that growers cross their fingers and wait for noble rot.

Whether or not it arrives is a function of the local climate. The climate of the Sauternais is not particularly benign. Winters can be cool and wet, with average temperatures in January of 5.2°C (41°F). Spring temperatures are variable, but there is often a mild spell in March or April that accelerates the development of the vines and buds. But a warm spring is often followed by a cold snap, which, if it takes the form of frost, can do great damage. The spring of 1991 was a case in point. On 21 April a particularly harsh frost gripped the region, as it did much of France. When the growers surveyed their vines the next day, many of them were shocked by the extent of their losses, especially in low-lying vineyards that are always more susceptible to frost. This kind of exceptionally severe frost, *gel noir*, is relatively rare.

More frequent is the kind that occurred on 16 April 1994. The thermometer sank to only a couple of degrees below zero, so the trauma to the vines was relatively light. The real problems began at sunrise. The sky was cloudless, the weather remained cold, and by mid-morning the sun was shining brightly. The overnight frost had encased the buds in ice and when the sun rose it shone on the vines and burnt the tender buds. During the afternoon I toured Barsac with Pierre Dubourdieu of Château Doisy-Daëne. Around Châteaux de Myrat, Caillou and Cantegril, the vines had turned black. The damage had been done and the proprietors could only hope that a second budding would produce a small secondary crop by the autumn.

There is little the growers can do to protect themselves against frost. On the morning of 16 April 1994, I could see black smoke besmirching the blue sky as tyres were being burnt in the vineyards. This environmentally unfriendly act was designed to impede the harmful action of the sun's rays by interposing the thick black smoke generated by the burning tyres. But that morning, the wind was blowing in the wrong direction and the smoke was carried away from the vines it was intended to protect.

No sooner has the danger of spring frosts passed than the risk of summer hail grows. Hail can be tremendously destructive, bruising and gashing the grapes, and tearing off the green leaves from which they take their nourishment. Once the fruit has been damaged in this way, it becomes susceptible to grey rot and mould. Fortunately, hail tends to be extremely localized. There was a heavy hailstorm on 6 July 1989, but it only affected parts of Sauternes and Bommes. First reports suggested that at some estates up to half the crop had been lost, but at the end of the day the damage was considerably less than had initially been feared. (Cynics assert that hail and frost damage are always exaggerated, especially if an insurance claim is being contemplated.)

In a normal year, a successful flowering in June would be followed by a warm summer, probably enlivened by some very hot days in August and relieved by intermittent rainfall. The forests of the Landes protect Sauternes from Atlantic breezes and summers can be distinctly hot. Without rain, the maturation process can grind to a halt, especially with young vines that have not yet sunk their roots down to the moisture and nutrients below the topsoil. By mid to late September, the grapes should have ripened. Autumns tend to be mild in the region, as the forests of the Landes shelter the Graves from the winds screeching off the Atlantic. The proprietors of the Sauternes may cast an envious glance at their neighbours in the Graves, who will be busily picking their grapes for dry wines at this time. Noble rot thrives in humid conditions and, as has already been mentioned, the confluence of the cold Ciron and the warmer Garonne generates morning mists that the spores find congenial. In an ideal season, noble rot will begin its work by mid-September or early October, when the grapes should be fully ripe. The morning mists will burn off after a few hours and the warm autumn afternoons will encourage the further development and desiccation of the grapes and discourage attacks from undesirable fungi or mould. An hour or two after dawn, the mist will rise again and the process will repeat itself until the infection of noble rot is widespread, sugar contents are soaring and the harvest begins. Picking rarely begins before ten in the morning, as it is wise to wait for the morning moisture to dry off before wielding the secateurs. Moisture on the surface of the skin will only dilute the must.

Should there be any signs of unwelcome grey rot, or a significant presence of underripe bunches, the owners may instigate a *trie de nettoyage*, a cleaning-up operation to remove the offending fruit, which will have been taking nourishment better offered to the ripe and healthy bunches. Grey rot is also produced by botrytis when the spores attack grapes that are either unripe or damaged by hail, insects or birds. The damaged or torn berries can admit bacteria which will rapidly instigate the terminal decay of the juice.

The subsoil can also have an effect on the microclimate and encourage the onset of noble rot. Xavier Planty, the manager of Château Guiraud, points out that in Sauternes itself, which is some distance away from the Ciron, condensation is generated by the difference in temperature of the subsoil; this forms a heavy dew that also spurs on the action of noble rot.

The botanical name for noble rot is *Botrytis cinerea*, occasionally referred to as *Botrytis acinorum*. It is a tiny parasitic fungus that belongs to the *Ascomycetes* family and its spores are carried by the wind on to the grapes. It is important for the production of good Sauternes that the grapes should be fully ripe before botrytis attacks. Its attack takes the form of producing minute filaments called *hyphae* that penetrate the skin of the grape. The fungus then spreads within the skin, not just on its surface. It takes a few days for the benign rot to spread widely. One of its effects is to make the skin permeable. The skin discolours, becoming an ever more repellent purple-brown, and the desiccation process shrivels the grape. Thus the term 'noble rot' is somewhat deceptive. Despite its unwholesome appearance, a botrytized grape is not being destroyed, as the term 'rot' would suggest, but instead it is being chemically transformed and ameliorated. As the grape loses water, its sugar content increases and become more concentrated. Botrytis also increases the level of glycerol, which will give the must greater viscosity, and releases tannins from the skins into the juice.

The whole process is a delicate balancing act. The steady alternation of morning humidity and afternoon sunshine provides an ideal environment for noble rot to work its magic while preserving the grapes from other infection. Should the process be interrupted by prolonged spells of rain, the delicate and increasingly porous skins, already invaded by botrytis spores and susceptible to other forms of rot, can be attacked by mould that can spread rapidly and render the crop unusable. In such circumstances the grower must begin to harvest as rapidly as possible, in the hope of saving at least part of the crop before malignant moulds do too much damage. This is invariably a race against time. Sometimes the undesirable forms of rot are detectable only by skilled harvesters. Take *moisissure*, a kind of white fungus provoked by excessive humidity which attacks the inside of the bunch. If harvested by inattentive or inexperienced pickers, it will give the wine disagreeable aromas and flavours that cannot be rectified. *Moisissure* is spotted by checking the interior of the bunch before applying the secateurs. If the white crumbly mould is present, the bunch must be eradicated. In 1993 there was widespread *moisissure* and some lots were so badly tainted by it that they had to be poured down the plug hole.

Alternatively, there can be a lack of moisture. If the weather is too dry, the action of botrytis will be erratic and incomplete. This does not spell disaster, but it does mean that the grapes will be dry and raisiny rather than properly botrytized. Perfectly good wine can be made from such fruit, but it will lack the extra dimensions that botrytization will bring to the grapes. Ideally there should be some light rain during this final period in the evolution of the grapes. By late autumn, the normal growing processes of the vine have shut up shop and any rainwater that seeps down to the roots will not be absorbed any longer. As long as any rainfall is followed by dry weather, or better still sunshine, no serious damage will ensue.

Heavy rain can also enter botrytized grapes through their dehydrating skins; this will give swollen grapes with diluted juice and a much lower sugar content. At such periods, picking will stop until the fruit has dried off, though the process known as cryo-extraction (see Chapter 4) does allow for wet botrytized fruit to be salvaged and used.

It is not only wine lovers who seek ultra-ripe grapes; birds and wasps love them too. Both these creatures break the skins and oxidize the interior, allowing access to bacteria; these turn the juice to vinegar, as you can tell by bringing such a grape close to your nose. This unfortunate condition is known as *pourriture aigre* and can also be provoked by hail.

During the early stages of botrytis, before the spores have spread the infection too far, the grapes will become purple-green rather than chocolate-purple. At this stage they are still full of juice and are referred to as *pourri plein*. Inexperienced pickers may be tempted to harvest such grapes, but this is far from desirable. *Pourri plein* grapes are only in the first stages of botrytis infection, in which the botrytis is consuming sugar without effecting any concentration; consequently such grapes are usually slightly *less* sweet than very ripe golden grapes that have not yet been infected. Sometimes, though, *pourri plein* grapes are picked if the alternative is to pick nothing at all. Once the desiccating action of the botrytis is complete, the grapes are said to be *confit* or *rôti* and in perfect condition for harvesting. By now the grape is a shadow of its former healthy self. The botrytis will have consumed much of its contents, notably the various acids present in its juice; its weight loss will be considerable. Grape sugar too will have been guzzled by the botrytis, but what remains, whether in the form of sugar or acids, will be far more concentrated than when the grape was merely *pourri plein*. In addition, botrytis will have generated glycerol, dextrin and other compounds which will contribute to the texture and complexity of the little juice that is left. At this point, the botrytized grape will be in optimal condition. This is the kind of fruit of which every Sauternes producer dreams.

But it doesn't occur by itself. Estates such as Yquem and other top properties want grapes with a must weight of 20° by the time they pick. This is not solely because it will result in wines of pleasing richness. At 20°, as François Amirault of Château de Fargues points out, the level of acidity will also be high and this is essential to maintain the freshness in an unctuous wine destined for long ageing. Moreover, grapes picked at this level will not require chaptalization and will give musts that are well balanced and will ferment easily.

For the noble rot to boost the sugar content to 20°, the grapes need to have a potential alcohol of 15° before the botrytis gets to work. This is another reason why severe pruning and low yields are so essential; without them, it is exceedingly difficult to achieve such ripeness. These days, the sugar content is easily established with the help of a refractometer. With experience, you can pop a botrytized grape in the mouth and that will tell you all you need to know. It takes some courage to eat something that looks like a fuzzy wart, but nobly rotten fruit is delicious. Occasionally the refractometer will register 25° and highly selective picking can sometimes produce entire lots with incredibly high must weights. But what you gain in sugar content you lose in volume. Since harvesting is often a race against time, you must be content with anything that will give you an average must weight of 18.5° or more.

There are vintages, such as 1989 and 1990, in which uniformly botrytized fruit is abundant. All you have to do is rush out and pick it before something goes wrong. More commonly, however, the infection is erratic, which is why *triage* is essential. There have been some vintages, such as 1985, when a few conscientious estates continued picking well into December. There was plenty of desiccated fruit on the vine much earlier in the autumn, but the dry weather had kept botrytis at bay. Only in the very late autumn did botrytis finally arrive and the patient were rewarded with a small but fine crop.

This is why the harvesting process is so crucial in Sauternes. In most years, patience is required if you are hoping to pick botrytized grapes. But patience entails risk. At any moment the weather can turn and your grapes will be turned to unsightly grey mush by rot and mould. There are vintages, such as 1982, when it paid to pick sooner rather than later, before rain stopped play. Ironically such vintages favoured the less conscientious estates, who routinely pick early as an insurance policy. The following year, 1983, many growers picked too soon, making respectable wines, but not the sublime wines achieved by those who were patient. Thus it is misleading to place too much importance on vintage alone. It may have been a great year in 1983, but not every estate by any means made great wine; 1991 was a minor vintage, but I can name two estates – Climens and Lafaurie-Peyraguey – that picked at exactly the right moment, had a small crop of nicely botrytized fruit and made beautiful wine.

Propagandists for the region, and for the other sweet-wine regions of Bordeaux on the other side of the Garonne, would have you believe that harvesters pick grape by grape. It can and does happen, but it is not usual. If the spread of botrytis is sparse and irregular, it may be necessary to search out individual grapes. It is far more common, however, whatever the books may say, for entire bunches or parts of bunches to be picked. At many estates there is a further selection process that takes place when the grapes arrive at the presshouse. Although this safety net may encourage some pickers to be less fastidious in their harvesting than they should be, it does ensure that insufficiently ripe or otherwise defective grapes don't enter the press.

Picking grapes destined for Sauternes is highly skilled work. The *chef de culture* or sometimes the cellarmaster will give precise directions to the team of harvesters, specifying not only which parcels are to be picked, but also whether clusters or individual berries should be selected, whether to concentrate on *pourri plein* grapes or to select only grapes that are fully *rôti*. Among each team of pickers there will be one or two overseers who constantly monitor that these instructions are being followed. Any failure to do so can lead to the vinification of poor-quality grapes that can tarnish the flavour and health of the crop. The pickers are trained to distinguish between grapes that are nobly rotten and grapes that are suffering from other kinds of malaise, such as grey rot or larvae. What makes the task so tricky is that healthy and unhealthy grapes can flourish on the same bunch. The fruit is placed in plastic baskets known as *bastes* and taken to the presshouse by tractor.

Botrytis, it must be remembered, makes it *easier* to produce fine Sauternes, because the action of noble rot sends the must weight soaring. Estates such as Yquem will pick fruit only with a potential alcohol of between 19 and 21°, which is usually impossible to attain without botrytis. *Surmaturité*, or overripeness alone, will push the potential alcohol up to 15 or 16° at the most. To make Sauternes from such grapes you must resort to chaptalization, which is far from ideal, as will be explained in the next chapter. *Triage* also gives you more cards to play with. Many top estates keep each day's harvest separate after the grapes have been pressed. Months later they will assess the outcome, perhaps blending an excessively botrytized barrel with a fresher batch of lightly botrytized Sauvignon, while discarding altogether some indifferent and merely overripe Sémillon.

There are few stars among the *Crus Bourgeois* of Sauternes because very few owners of such estates can afford to delay the harvest beyond October. If the grapes are ultra-ripe, the temptation to pick can be overwhelming. Such growers will reason that it is better to have a good quantity of rich sweet wine, even without honeyed botrytis character, than a tiny crop of luscious botrytized wine. If you are a small grower who derives almost his entire income from the production of a wine that is by its very nature irregular, the temptation is fierce. *Triage* is also very costly, since you must keep your team of well-trained pickers available for up to two months. This is not an expense that smaller estates can easily bear.

Those who are prepared to take the risks are, with few exceptions, the classified growths, who have the financial security or the pride to gamble on the fickle botrytis spores doing their work at the right time. As wine lovers, we can only bow with respect towards those who, year after year, play this lottery with the climate. When they win, we win. When they lose, we make do without a vintage while they contemplate an empty cellar and dwindling financial reserves. No wonder there have been moments when Sauternes as a style of wine has seemed on the verge of extinction.

4

Making Sauternes

This chapter is about vinification, but the fact is that Sauternes, more than any other wine, is made in the vineyard. Denis Dubourdieu, Professor of Oenology at Bordeaux and a fine winemaker in his own right, expresses the point perfectly:

> As far as sweet wines are concerned, vinification doesn't really exist. The wine is determined by the time the grape is picked. The vinification process consists of the controlled digestion of sugar. In the case of sweet wines such as Sauternes, fermentation begins after the digestion has taken place. The whole process of *élevage* is one of protecting and refining the wine you have made. But you don't need to protect Sauternes. A grape that has been attacked by botrytis has seen everything.

None the less, the grapes have to be processed and the first process they must undergo is extraction of juice from the pulpy, raisiny fruit brought to the presshouse in *bastes*. The grapes are either lightly crushed or tipped into the press, stalks and all. A cloud of spores rises into the air as the grapes tumble from the baskets. In former times they would have been trodden briefly before being pressed. One advantage of crushing is that it allows the winemaker to get far more grapes into the press, especially when a hydraulic press is used. This speeds up the pressing process, which is useful when the crop is abundant. On the other hand, the resulting must is murkier and less clean. Some winemakers like a clear, clean juice; others believe the murkier juice is richer in nutrients.

Three types of press are used. The most venerable is the basket, hydraulic or vertical press. The grapes are emptied into a slatted wooden basket which is placed in a trough into which the juice will run. Straw mats (*paillons*) are placed between layers of grapes to ensure the pressure is evenly spread and a wooden cover is placed on top of the grapes. The press operates by bringing a metal plate down with increasingly powerful pressure on the top of the basket; the juice extracted runs from the basket into the trough and thence into an underground vat or other container. After this first extraction, the cakey pulp or *marc* remaining in the basket is broken up with forks or in a machine known as an *émietteur*, then pitchforked into another hydraulic press and given its second pressing; the must from this pressing is usually kept separate from that from the first pressing. Sometimes a third pressing follows. The total pressing time is about six hours.

The first pressing, which extracts about 60–75 per cent of the juice, is usually regarded as the best in terms of its balance and flavour. But it is the subsequent pressings that are richer in sugar. The problem is that the third pressing in particular also extracts less desirable flavours, and there is a greater chance that the must will be slightly oxidized. Some estates discard the third pressing, despite its high sugar content. On the other hand, highly desiccated grapes will yield virtually no juice on the first pressing, so subsequent pressings are essential. If the grapes are not perfectly healthy, it may be that only the first pressing is used, as at Château Nairac in 1994, for fear that subsequent pressings would extract unwelcome flavours.

The hydraulic press is slow – each pressing takes about two hours – old-fashioned and cumbersome. It is also hard work to operate. Nevertheless, many estates – including Yquem, Nairac and Coutet – swear by it. They applaud its gentleness and the clarity of the juice it extracts, which means that a lengthy *débourbage*, or decantation to clarify the must, is rarely necessary. The second kind of press is the horizontal press, of which the Vaslin is the most commonly encountered. It employs a revolving cage to press the grapes and is considered somewhat rough in its handling of the fruit. It has been replaced in many estates by the far gentler, and far more expensive, pneumatic press, of which the Bucher is the most common brand. With this machine an inflatable bag exerts pressure on the grapes and, as in the horizontal press, the juice seeps through slats into the tray below. Some estates, such as Caillou, argue that the juice from a pneumatic press is too clean and they prefer the horizontal press because they find the must richer in nutrients.

The must is usually allowed to rest so that any gross lees can sink to the bottom of the vat and be eliminated, although, as already mentioned, the clear juice derived from hydraulic pressing often eliminates the need for a lengthy *débourbage*. There is less emphasis than there used to be on squeaky-clean musts before fermentation, except in years when moulds could be present that might impart off-flavours to the wine. Fermentation takes place either in a vat made from stainless steel, cement or some other impermeable material, or in oak *barriques*. The advantage of the former is that the temperature can be controlled easily. In precocious vintages such as 1989 and 1990, the grapes had to be picked in very warm weather and it was difficult to control the temperature of fermentation. In such circumstances, stainless-steel tanks that can be cooled offer an ideal vehicle for fermentation. One of the drawbacks of barrel-fermentation is that volatile acidity, always present when botrytized musts are fermented, can rise to worrying levels and this is less likely to occur when the temperature is controlled. It is heat that encourages the yeasts to produce acetic acid and if this is not kept under control, the winemaker can end up with vinegar. Many old vintages of Sauternes produced before temperature control was possible – other than by throwing blocks of ice into the vats – suffer from excessive volatile acidity, to which many tasters (though fortunately I am not among them) are exceedingly sensitive.

Fermentation in barrel, however, is gaining more and more converts. They point out that temperature control, even when the outside temperature is unusually warm, is rarely problematic with barrel-fermentation because the volumes are small. It is larger containers, such as cement vats without the benefit of temperature control, which can allow temperatures to rise to dangerous levels that can damage the wine. In casks of 225 litres, the standard *barrique bordelaise*, the fermentation temperature is usually about 20°C, which is fine. Fermentation is a prolonged process, usually taking four to six weeks. If the winter is particularly cold, or some lots are particularly rich in sugar, the process can continue for months.

There are usually enough indigenous yeasts in the vineyards to allow fermentation to begin without adding cultivated yeasts to give the process a kick-start. The issue of cultivated yeasts is less contentious in sweet-wine vinification, as the residual sugar will partially mask any aromas or flavours imparted by the yeasts. With dry white wines, the use of cultivated yeasts can alter aromas and flavours significantly.

During fermentation, the winemaker may add sugar to the must. This is known as chaptalization, after Jean-André Chaptal, the nineteenth-century legislator and reformer. It is simply a way of boosting the must weight. If you have picked fruit with a potential alcohol of 16°, the eventual balance of the wine is likely to be 13° of alcohol and 3° of residual sugar. This is just about acceptable. It is legal to add enough sugar to raise the potential alcohol by 2°. With a must weight of 18°, a more satisfactory balance of 14° of alcohol and 4° of residual sugar can be achieved.

Some of the top estates declare that they never chaptalize. If nature won't provide sufficiently rich juice, then they will have to forgo a vintage declaration and sell the inadequate wines off to the wholesale trade for eventual sale as generic Sauternes. Other top estates admit that, on occasion, they do chaptalize and see little harm in the process if it will improve the balance of some of the lots. A rigorous estate such as Yquem regards the need to chaptalize as an indictment of one's viticulture. If you have ripe grapes on low-yielding vines and wait for botrytis to attack, there should be little difficulty in achieving high must weights of 19° or more.

The question one needs to ask is: does a chaptalized wine taste different, and inferior, to wine made without recourse to the process? If they are indistinguishable, then there can be no reasonable objection to the procedure. It is not an easy question to answer. The gustatory argument against chaptalization is that some of the added sugar will not be converted into alcohol by the yeasts but will remain in the wine, as will some of the natural grape sugar, in the form of residual sweetness; when this occurs, the wine will lack the complexity of an unchaptalized wine and will convey an impression of mere sugariness. I am inclined to accept this view, though I cannot back it with irrefutable empirical evidence. However, I have often tasted wines, especially from modest vintages, that have excessive sweetness in relation to their body and alcoholic strength, and this can only derive from the sack of sugar added during fermentation. The result may be a sweet wine, but not a very agreeable sweet wine.

An alternative consequence of chaptalization is that the yeasts seize greedily on the extra 2° and consume them, giving a wine that is over-alcoholic in relation to the residual sugar. It is rightly pointed out that a high degree of alcohol can mask faults in the wine and swamp the fruit. It is a common fault in Barsac, where many growers insist that the local tradition of vinification requires more alcohol and less *liqueur* (residual sugar) than in the other communes. The result is heavy, clumsy wines. In addition to excessive chaptalization, the use of vigorous cultivated yeasts can also produce over-alcoholic wines.

I am not one of those totally opposed to chaptalization. If used discreetly to boost some lots by a degree or so, and if those lots are then blended with 'natural' wines, I can see no great objection if the winemaker is convinced that it will improve the balance and structure of the final blend. If in a coolish year the owner of a *Cru Bourgeois*, financially barred from practising Yquem-like perfectionism, indulges in some chaptalization to give his wine a tad more richness, it would be churlish to complain too loudly. What I am opposed to is the routine chaptalization of the entire harvest as an alternative to lowering yields and to waiting for noble rot to reach the vines.

If the winemaker chooses not to chaptalize, how then does he balance the wine? He may seek a $14°$ plus $4°$ formula, but fermentation is not always that obliging. The balance will depend upon the year. In a wet vintage such as 1992, when it was necessary to pick before the entire crop succumbed to destructive rot, the musts may well have been undernourished. The desirable balance in such a vintage may be $13.5°$ plus $3.5°$, but the yeasts' hunger may not be appeased when the alcohol reaches $13.5°$. They may munch on, leaving a wine of $15°$ plus $2°$, which is likely to taste unbalanced. In a fine vintage, when the must has a potential alcohol of $19°$ and the ideal balance would be $14°$ plus $5°$, or $14.5°$ plus $4.5°$, the fermentation may well grind to a halt of its own accord. If some lots were slightly unbalanced in one direction, they could be blended with others unbalanced in the opposite direction. At the end of the day, all would be well.

That's the theory. When I first visited Château d'Yquem in the 1980s, I asked the *régisseur*, Pierre Meslier, how they stopped the fermentation. The answer he gave me was that botrytis generated an antibiotic called botryticine that joined with the alcohol in inhibiting the appetite of the yeasts; the eventual consequence was that fermentation halted of its own accord at about $14.5°$. It sounded too good to be true, especially since other winemakers are full of stories about awkward vintages when they have major problems with the fermentation and had to struggle to end up with a well-balanced wine.

I have made further investigations and the consensus view seems to be that there is indeed a natural antibiotic called botryticine which acts as a brake on the fermentation process, just as alcohol itself does, but there is no guarantee that the alcohol and botryticine will halt the fermentation at the desired moment. If they do, all well and good. If they do not, then the winemaker must intervene. It is possible that at a very large estate such as Yquem, all fermentations are allowed to pace themselves and any imbalances in the finished lots can be rectified by blending or, in some stubborn cases, by eventual rejection. I specifically asked Guy Latrille, Yquem's cellarmaster for many decades, whether they ever add sulphur to stop the fermentation and he replied: 'Never.' I certainly would not want to doubt his word, but others are sceptical. Michel Laporte, the winemaker at Lafaurie-Peyraguey, estimates that about three-quarters of his *barriques* stop fermenting by themselves and many of the remaining lots can be dealt with by blending. But the truth is that most winemakers will intervene, especially if there is a risk of excessive alcohol in the wine.

In a vintage such as 1990, when must weights were exceptionally high, it was safe to allow some fermentations to continue until the alcohol level rose to 15.5°, as there was so much residual sugar left that the alcohol did not unbalance the wine. But that was an atypical vintage. It is rare that a winemaker will want to see an alcohol level much higher than 14.5°. If the fermentation does not stop by itself, then the yeasts must be suppressed.

However, it is worth pointing out that both Guy Latrille and Nicolas Heeter-Tari of Château Nairac stress that the difficulty they encounter during fermentation is in persuading the yeasts to bring the alcohol level up to 13.5°. High alcohol tends to be the last thing they need to worry about. They both suggest that wines in average vintages with alcohol levels of 15° are almost certainly chaptalized.

There are two ways to stop the fermentation. One is by chilling the wine to about 4°C, which will isolate the yeasts; the other is to add sulphur dioxide, which will kill them off. The objection to these procedures is that they could adversely affect the aroma or flavour of the wine. Certainly an excessive use of sulphur dioxide will have a deleterious effect, but if either technique or both is used judiciously, there should be no lasting damage to the wine. Chilling is probably the better procedure, if the winemaker has the facilities, or if the weather is cold enough in the *chai* to bring the temperature right down. Its effect is to block the yeasts, which will then fall to the bottom of the tank, from which they can be racked off. Then to be certain that any remaining yeasts are no longer active, some sulphur dioxide will be added, though in a smaller quantity than if the wine has not been subjected to chilling.

For many years, the excessive use of sulphur dioxide has been the bane of white Bordeaux, dry and sweet. Certain white Graves, such as Château Laville-Haut-Brion, are renowned for their longevity and it is true that some vintages that are thirty or forty years old are still excellent. My own theory about this is that, from the outset, the wines were probably so heavily dosed with sulphur dioxide that they must have been undrinkable for a decade or more. What they are displaying is not so much astonishing longevity, but retarded development. It is hard to describe the taste of excessive combined sulphur dioxide, though its physical effects make it easy to spot. On the nose there may be a whiff akin to burnt matches and on the palate there will be a stale, cardboardy taste, which may induce a swift coughing fit. With time, the unpleasant aspects of combined sulphur will diminish ('free' sulphur dioxide which has not got itself into a permanent clinch with the wine is less noxious). The winemaker will keep in mind that about one-third of any dose of sulphur dioxide will combine with the wine.

The problem for the Sauternes winemaker is that it is impossible to avoid the use of sulphur dioxide. It is added at various stages. Sometimes it is used during the harvest to prevent premature oxidation of the grapes or must. It is almost always used to help bring the fermentation process to a close, as already explained. Once the wine has been fermented, the process known as *élevage*, the rearing of the wine, begins. The wine is aged either in tanks or in *barriques*. *Barrique*-ageing is ideal in terms of the gradual evolution of the wine, but it is customary to rack the wine every three months to remove any dead yeasts or other solids that have gradually sunk to the bottom of the barrel. Before the racked wine is returned to its barrel, it is necessary to burn some sulphur inside the barrel. This must be repeated at each racking.

The aim is simple: to prevent bacterial infections and secondary fermentation. Where there is sugar in a wine, there is always a risk of secondary fermentation. But since at this stage the wine is finished and, one hopes, well balanced, any additional fermentation, which would increase the alcoholic content at the expense of the residual sugar, could render the wine almost undrinkable. To ensure that this does not happen, sulphur dioxide must be used after racking. A dose is also unavoidable during the bottling process, when as a security measure the winemaker will add sulphur dioxide before the wine begins its long slumber in bottle. If the wine in question is a light, fresh dry white, intended to be consumed within months of bottling, then the risk is slight. But sweet wine is intended to be aged in bottle. In 1983, Château Raymond-Lafon scrupulously reduced the amount of sulphur dioxide at the bottling stage, but eight years later it was apparent that some bottles of this very expensive wine were undergoing secondary fermentation. This is the kind of story that makes Sauternes winemakers shudder and reach for the sulphur dioxide.

Conscientious winemakers will do what they can to keep the use of sulphur dioxide to a minimum. Wines that used to suffer from an overdose, such as Climens, have now fallen into line and, except in very young wines, it is rare to find excessive sulphur in top-flight Sauternes. Many cheaper Sauternes and other sweet white wines of Bordeaux still do, I regret to say, exhibit far too much sulphur dioxide, which lightens the colour of the wine, flattens its flavour and can induce headaches. There are a number of ways in which the use of sulphur dioxide can be minimized without compromising the stability of the wine. The most ferocious is to use sterile filtrations which will strip the wine of its yeasts. But they can also have the effect of stripping the wine of its flavour. Château Doisy-Daëne employs sterile filtrations as a way of keeping down the sulphur-dioxide levels, and it certainly doesn't seem to harm the wine, but then Pierre Dubourdieu is one of the most skilled winemakers in France.

Other winemakers will add a good dollop of sulphur dioxide – about 25 milligrams per litre – immediately after fermentation, which will allow them to lower the doses thereafter. Cellar hygiene also plays its part in allowing levels of sulphur dioxide to be reduced: the cleaner the cellars, the less chance there is of bacterial infection. As has already been mentioned, the use of chilling will also allow the winemaker to reduce the amount of sulphur dioxide used. The authorities and the regulations imposed by export mar-

kets such as Japan have forced winemakers to lower the total sulphur-dioxide level to 350 milligrams from 400. This is to be
welcomed, but the consequence could be greater use of filtration
and chilling to stabilize the wine. None the less, most winemakers
in Sauternes report sulphur levels in their wines of just above or
below 300 milligrams.

The *élevage* will take place in tank or barrel, or in a combination
of the two. The usual period of *élevage* is between eighteen and
twenty-four months, but wines that are particularly rich and high in
extract – again, Yquem is the classic example – may be aged
in *barriques* for up to three and a half years. The current trend is to
bottle sooner rather than later, to avoid premature oxidation or a
too rapid evolution of the wine. In addition to regular rackings
(usually every three months, but at some estates, such as Caillou,
every six months), the wine may be subjected to other treatments. It
may be fined with bentonite (a colloidal clay), gelatine, or albumen
to clarify the wine by removing any impurities, or filtered for the
same reason. The fining agent is left in suspension for two weeks.
Some estates may chill the wine for a lengthy period to precipitate
tartrate crystals which, should they form after bottling, can
resemble slivers of glass. American importers in particular have a
horror of tartrate crystals, even though they are harmless. Light
fining and light filtration should not be too damaging to the wine,
but there are suspicions that excessive chilling is harmful.

The longer the *élevage*, the more likely it is that the wine will
have clarified itself by natural means. A few estates, including
Château d'Yquem, bottle without filtration, but the great majority
will employ a light filtration just before the wine is bottled.

During the bad years of the 1960s and 1970s, when demand was
exceptionally low and even top estates resorted to crude short cuts
to reduce their expenses, the *élevage* often took place in tanks.
Neutral containers of cement or steel may contribute little or
nothing to the flavour or quality of the wine, but they have the
advantage of being relatively inexpensive and easy to maintain.
Oak, in contrast, is a living material and must be monitored and
maintained. It is costly too, especially if a quantity of new *barriques*
is bought each year. An additional hidden cost is the evaporation
that takes place in barrels, though much of this loss is water, thus
increasing the concentration of flavour. A tank can be used year
after year, but *barriques* have an optimal life span of three years,

though they can be kept longer. However, after three or four years their influence becomes increasingly neutral. The advantages of oak barrels are that they allow the wine to breathe and permit a slow, controlled oxidation; the tannin present in the oak will give structure to the wine; and the oak itself will impart flavours to the wine that many consumers find attractive. Depending on how the wood has been conditioned by the cooper, those flavours will have a lesser or greater degree of toastiness. Many classified growths ferment and age the wine in oak; others ferment in temperature-controlled tanks and then age the wine in *barriques*.

I suspect that estates which practise the latter method do so for security reasons rather than out of conviction that the method is superior to barrel-fermentation. Certainly it is easier, cheaper and less risky to ferment in tanks, and then gain the benefits of wood maturation by using barrels for the *élevage*. New barrels will impart a much stronger flavour than those that are one or two years old. It is a matter of personal judgement. It is safe to say that the richer and more extracted the wine, the better able it is to cope with lashings of new oak. Yquem survives its three-and-a-half-year course with no difficulty, though for the first eight years of its life the wine is dominated by oak flavours; only subsequently does the full complexity of the wine become apparent. La Tour-Blanche and Raymond-Lafon are also aged in a substantial proportion of new oak, and this used to be the case at Château Nairac, though in recent years the proportion has varied. American wine writers and consumers do have a passion for new-oak flavours, but most Sauternes estates quite properly judge the proportion in relation to the richness and structure of their wine.

Once the new wine is about six months old, its quality and character become more evident, and it is time to think about blending. In the nineteenth century, as the harvesters were clearly instructed to search out only the most botrytized grapes, the first *tries* were often the richest. These lots, which comprised about 10 per cent of the harvest, were vinified separately and known as *crèmes de tête*. They were usually blended in with other lots from subsequent *tries*, but occasionally they were bottled separately and sold at a higher price. The second picking, which yielded about 40 per cent of the wine from the vintage, was called the *vin de tête*. The third and final picking, the *vin de queue*, collected whatever was left on the vine and was the largest but least rich of the three *tries*.

The practice of bottling *crème de tête* wines separately continues to this day. A few estates, notably Suduiraut, Coutet and Caillou, do still produce luxury *cuvées* from exceptional *tries*. Other estates frown on the practice as they feel it can dilute the *grand vin* if the finest lots are bottled separately. This may well be true of a small estate, but Coutet and Suduiraut are large enough for the loss of a few *barriques* from the final blend not to be too detrimental.

In the spring or summer following the vintage, all estates will begin their *assemblage*, eliminating the lots that they consider not up to standard and blending some of their remaining lots progressively or all at once. The blending is concerned with style as well as quality. For example, an estate may have light, fresh Sauvignon lots that either could be essential to balance the wine, or could inject floral aromatic tones that do not fit the stylistic continuity of the wine. Some estates like to make up the final blend as late as possible; others prefer to make up the blend of the *grand vin* relatively early in the *élevage*, so that the wine can age evenly. It is a matter of temperament and personal preference on the part of the proprietor and winemaker. At Yquem and other estates, each day's pickings are vinified separately, so there can be twenty or more lots that must be tasted, judged and blended – or rejected.

Not much has changed in the cellars of the Sauternais over recent decades. The classic winemaking at an estate such as Yquem or Climens has scarcely altered since the last century. But one major innovation has provoked considerable controversy: cryo-extraction.

In simple terms, cryo-extraction is a technique used to dry grapes which would otherwise be considered too wet, and thus too dilute, to be of use in producing Sauternes. Late-autumn rain often disrupts a promising harvest, but it is argued that cryo-extraction enables growers to save a portion of their crop that in normal circumstances would have to be sacrificed to the birds or sold off as generic Sauternes.

The technique was invented by two professors, S. Chauvet and P. Sudraud, at the Laboratoire de la Répression des Fraudes de Bordeaux at the University of Bordeaux. It requires a cold chamber: a large portable cabin in which the grapes can be chilled. The wet grapes are frozen by dropping the temperature within the chamber to about -5°C for twenty-four hours. The excess moisture on the surface of the skin and within the skin turns to ice. The grapes are then pressed. A pneumatic press is essential for this stage. Hydraulic presses are not suitable, as the uniform pressure turns the grapes into a solid frozen block. Only the botrytized juice flows into the tank below, since juice from nobly rotten grapes has a lower freezing-point than water. At the same time, the ice crystals remain in the press and are then discarded. Unripe or non-botrytized grapes freeze solid and emit no juice. The compacted nature of the grapes means that even though one might suppose that pressing them would melt the grapes and dilute the must, this does not happen.

The procedure was tested at Château Rayne-Vigneau with the co-operation of one of the estate's shareholders, Jean Merlaut. The experiments demonstrated to Merlaut's satisfaction that there was a significant improvement in concentration when wet botrytized grapes were used and no alteration at all when grapes harvested under good conditions were tested. Rayne-Vigneau was one of the first estates to invest in a cryo-extraction chamber. Critics of the procedure derided it as a short cut, but properties using cold chambers point out that it is pointless to cut corners in terms of the quality of the grapes used. If the fruit is not botrytized, then almost the entire moisture content of the grape would freeze and the amount of juice extracted would be negligible. So only botrytized fruit with a high moisture content added by wet weather is suitable for cryo-extraction. Possession of the equipment does not absolve the estate from *triage* and low yields, and all the other practices carried out to ensure high must weights and plentiful botrytis.

By 1987, a number of leading estates had invested in a cold chamber. In addition to Rayne-Vigneau, they included Yquem, La Tour-Blanche and Guiraud. The timing was perfect, as 1987 was a vintage ideally suited to cryo-extraction. There was botrytis, but rain left the fruit sodden and the grapes swollen. Rayne-Vigneau estimated that it doubled the quantity of usable must by employing this method; La Tour-Blanche used it on 30 per cent of their crop.

By the end of the decade, many other properties had followed the example of these *Premiers Crus*: Rieussec, de Fargues, Rabaud-Promis, Doisy-Daëne, Doisy-Védrines and Les Justices. In addition, three estates in Sainte-Croix-du-Mont acquired the chamber. Shortly before the harvest, some estates that could not justify the expense of acquiring a chamber of their own leased cold chambers in the nearby town of Langon, though whether the cost of so doing was justified is questionable.

Once word got around that prestigious estates in Sauternes were using this new technique, there was a startled and often critical reaction. Comte Alexandre de Lur-Saluces took the criticism particularly hard, even though it was clearly based on a misunderstanding of the process involved. There was also resistance within the region from some of the more conservative proprietors, who believed that cryo-extraction altered the style of the resulting wine for the worse.

Cryo-extraction is no longer acclaimed in the way it was in 1987. This is largely because the vintages that followed left the cold chambers idle. The sensational trio from 1988 to 1990 were made in almost perfect harvesting conditions. In 1991, thanks to the April frost, the crop was tiny. In 1992, the grapes were certainly sodden, but they were also mostly unripe and cryo-extraction would have been of no benefit. At Rayne-Vigneau, where some of the pioneering experiments with the technique were made, Patrick Eymery, the *régisseur*, now believes that it can help to produce a passable second wine, but that it can make no contribution to the *grand vin*. When in 1994 I asked Alexandre de Lur-Saluces what he now thought of the technique he had spoken of so admiringly (and defensively) in the 1980s, he admitted that his cold chamber had been rusting in the cellars ever since the 1987 vintage. It is useful only when the grapes are healthy and ripe, which is not often the case when the clouds open and the rains fall. Since the cold chamber costs about 500,000 francs, those who acquired one in the 1980s have not enjoyed a good return on their investment. Pierre Castéja of Château Doisy-Védrines, however, consoles himself by using his cold chamber to chill his wine to precipitate the tartrates before bottling. Another proprietor says it comes in handy for chilling beer when he gives summer parties.

There are those who use the cold chamber in fine vintages. One estate in Sainte-Croix-du-Mont used cryo-extraction in 1988 and the three succeeding vintages as an alternative to chaptalization. By freezing the grapes, the must became more concentrated. The oenologist Denis Dubourdieu also claims to have had good results from using cryo-extraction in good years, when he has increased the must weight from 19 to 21°.

The difficulty with assessing the utility of cryo-extraction is that reported experiences differ so widely and, without tasting the results side by side, it is impossible to judge whether claims made for or against the process are justified. Emmanuel de Lambert des Granges of Château Sigalas-Rabaud told me he used cryo-extraction in 1987 and 1993, although he doesn't have a cold chamber of his own. He insists that those who claim that it can increase the must weight give a false impression. If you pick wet grapes with 14° of potential alcohol, he says, you can't increase their must weight by freezing them, but you can save them from the effects of dilution that would otherwise reduce the must weight to a useless 12°. In other words, you can retain the original potential of your fruit, but you can't improve upon it.

Exactly the opposite is argued by Yves Armand of Château La Rame, a fine estate in Sainte-Croix-du-Mont. In 1993 he picked wet but healthy grapes with a must weight of 15.5–16°; after cryo-extraction it had risen to 18.5–19°. The colder the temperature at which you freeze the fruit, the more impressive the gain in concentration; however, at very cold temperatures the quantity of botry-tized juice declines. Freeze the grapes too hard and the loss of volume becomes economically unacceptable. However, Armand points out that if you pick grape by grape you also lose volume because of the concentration of the botrytized juice; what you lose in volume by cryo-extraction derives from less-ripe grapes that freeze and give no juice.

Armand believes it is possible to increase potential alcohol by up to 4°, which, if true, is considerable. Christian Médeville of Château Gilette also reports good results from cryo-extraction in 1993, but the consensus view in Sauternes is that the grapes were not healthy enough for cryo-extraction to be effective. Any faults or off-flavours present in the grapes when picked will be exaggerated by cryo-extraction, which is why it is essential that only healthy grapes are used.

Experimental lots made by cryo-extraction at Château Guiraud in 1985 were compared with conventionally made Sauternes. Cryo-extraction, it was then claimed, gave better extraction, fatter texture, more developed aromas and deeper colour; but the conventionally made wines were more elegant. I didn't taste those experimental lots, but those are not the results I would have expected. Cryo-extraction is a technological expression of the German *Eiswein* technique. In Germany, the grapes are left on the vine in the hope that a winter frost will seize them. When this occurs, the grapes are picked at night and pressed before the temperature rises. The water content is frozen and only the rich but rarely botrytized must emerges from the press.

One salient characteristic of *Eiswein* is its searing acidity, making such wines easy to spot in a blind tasting. As I understand it, the essence of the criticisms levelled at the Sauternais who used the technique in the late 1980s is that cryo-extraction changes the character of the wine, just as severe frosts in Germany alter the typicity of Riesling. The director of Château La Tour-Blanche, Jean-Pierre Jausserand, assured me that tests indicate that cryo-extraction actually lowers the level of tartaric acidity and leaves the level of total acidity unaltered. Even if one were to argue that cryo-extraction produces wines that, like *Eiswein*, are essentially one-dimensional, one must bear in mind, says Jausserand, that whereas *Eiswein* consists exclusively of wine made from frozen grapes, this is not the case with cryo-extracted wine, which forms one constituent in the blend. In his view, no Sauternes should contain more than 30 per cent of wine made by cryo-extraction.

Alexandre de Lur-Saluces disagrees. The conditions that make *Eiswein* possible provoke a concentration of sugar and acidity content in the must, but, he claims, cryo-extraction on botrytized grapes doesn't set off any comparable chemical changes. It only removes moisture and prevents dilution. Yves Armand also insists there is no difference in flavour between cryo-extracted fruit and grapes vinified in the usual way. The high acidity that could be derived from the fruit doesn't occur, because the non-botrytized fruit freezes completely and gives no juice, leaving only the more concentrated juice from botrytized grapes after pressing. This is a crucial point, explaining why *Eiswein*, made from non-botrytized fruit, is so high in acidity, while cryo-extracted Sauternes is not.

It is very difficult to resolve these conflicting claims. What seems clear is that the sceptics are on the increase, and that fewer and fewer experienced winemakers believe that cryo-extraction can be used to produce great wine. Nor is it possible to say what the long-term effect of cryo-extraction will be. The oldest commercialized wines made by this method date from 1987, and Jausserand estimates that we must let ten or twelve years go by before we can assess the claims for or against wines made partially by cryo-extraction. Although he has no qualms about using the technique when he considers it appropriate, he also has no doubt that in good vintages, nature does a better job of ensuring good-quality must than the cold chamber.

5
Château d'Yquem

———

Château d'Yquem dominates the landscape of the Sauternais, just as for two centuries the wine it produces has lorded it over the other sweet wines of the region. Lesser estates mention with pride that their vines adjoin those of Yquem. The castellated walls and pepperpot turrets of the fortified château are visible for miles around, forming a harmonious whole from very disparate elements. For hundreds of years, Yquem has been the centre of this particular universe. In certain vintages, other wines can claim to challenge the supremacy of Yquem, but no other estate, however ambitious, however conscientious, would seek to dispute that Yquem is indeed the sole *Premier Grand Cru* of the region.

As is evident from the exterior, the origins of the château are medieval, although the chapel wing dates from the sixteenth century and the north-facing wing containing the principal reception rooms was built a century later. The site was fortified in the sixteenth century, protected by the castellated wall on the south side. Sharing the hilltop site, 75 metres above sea level, with the mansion, its courtyard and its lawns, are the estate cellars, workshops and offices. From the west side there are superb views on to a string of *Premiers Crus*: Châteaux Clos Haut-Peyraguey, Rayne-Vigneau, Lafaurie-Peyraguey and Rabaud-Promis. The whole property is beautifully maintained, although now that the Lur-Saluces family no longer live at the château, its atmosphere is somewhat cold and manicured.

It was in 1593 that the château, then a royal estate, was acquired by the Sauvage d'Eyquem family. About two hundred years later, their descendants teamed up with the Lur-Saluces family of Château de Fargues, when the heiress of Yquem, Françoise Josephine de Sauvage, styled 'dame d'Yquem', married Comte Louis

Amédée de Lur-Saluces in 1785. The count was well connected and was the godson of King Louis XV. The Lur-Saluces family had been soldiers for many generations and were based at Château de Fargues until it burnt to the ground in 1687.

When Thomas Jefferson visited the Sauternes region two years after their marriage, he was most impressed by Yquem and Filhot. He placed a substantial order of 1784 Yquem for himself and subsequently ordered the 1787 for George Washington. This was to be the first of a series of dazzling impressions made by Yquem on distinguished visitors, all of which would combine to establish its lasting reputation as the greatest white wine of Bordeaux. Napoleon ordered the 1802. Even Joseph Stalin admired Yquem and asked for cuttings so that a Russian version could be produced.

Louis-Amédée died the year before the Revolution. During those turbulent years the Lur-Saluces family lost control of Yquem, but Françoise-Josephine eventually wrested control of the estate back from the state and lived at the château until her death in 1851.

The heir to the estate was Marquis Antoine-Marie de Lur-Saluces, who had been born at Yquem in 1786. While waiting for his inheritance, the heir had married Marie-Geneviève, the daughter of Gabriel-Barthélémy-Romain de Filhot. She was the owner of Châteaux Filhot, Coutet and Piada. After their marriage in 1807, these became part of the Lur-Saluces domaines, which already included Château de Fargues as well as Yquem itself. After Antoine-Marie's death, Yquem was run by his son Romain Bertrand, who was born in 1810. He devised the system of terracotta drainage channels which still plays a vital role in maintaining the quality of the estate's vineyards. Romain Bertrand died in 1867 and was succeeded by his son Amédée (1839–94), who implemented his father's plans in the mid-1880s. As Amédée had no children, he was succeeded by his nephew, Bertrand de Lur-Saluces.

Marquis Bertrand directed the affairs of Yquem through the first half of the twentieth century with great aplomb. He pioneered château-bottling shortly after the First World War and was president of the Union des Crus Classés de la Gironde for almost forty years. Two years before his death in 1970 at the age of eighty, he handed control of the estates to his younger brother's son Alexandre, who remains in charge. Comte Alexandre, who was born in 1934, is a slightly aloof figure, resulting from shyness, I suspect, rather than snobbery. Discreet and fastidious, always impeccably dressed and formal in his manners, yet looking younger than his sixty years, he sometimes gives the impression of being over-burdened by the great heritage that lies behind him. He may understandably experience a slight weariness at constantly having to play an ambassadorial role in spreading the gospel of Sauternes. There can be no doubt that he is a conscientious steward of the two estates he directs: no one can fault the quality of his wines since he took over.

Soon after he did so, the market for Bordeaux wines collapsed – coincidentally, of course. In 1974, Comte Alexandre sold a mere six cases of wine, and that year's vintage, like that of 1972, produced no saleable wine at all. Fortunately, matters soon improved and the two superb vintages of 1975 and 1976 boosted morale. Comte Alexandre was fortunate in having an excellent team under his command. Guy Latrille has been the *maître de chai* or cellarmaster for about forty years and the tenure of Yves Laporte, the vineyard manager, is about the same. Pierre Meslier was the *régisseur* from 1962 until 1989. Meslier left under clouded circumstances. Their falling-out is said to have had its origins in the municipal politics of Sauternes (of which Comte Alexandre was mayor from 1971 to 1989), but clearly there was more than that at stake. Meslier was, and still is, the owner of a small estate called Château Raymond-Lafon, where he produces wine to the same exacting standards employed at Yquem. It is not unusual for the *régisseur* of a great estate to have his own property in the region. Pierre Pascaud of Château Suduiraut owns Château Pascaud-Villefranche in Barsac; indeed, it has been in his family for four generations. Yet there must have been at least a suspicion in Meslier's case of a conflict of interest. Certainly the breach between Meslier and Lur-Saluces, publicly presented as a case of early retirement, seems final. After Meslier's departure Francis Mayeur, who was in his early thirties, was appointed in his place as production manager.

Yquem is a very large estate, with 111 ha. entitled to the Sauternes appellation. Some land is always left fallow before replanting, or is planted with vines too young to be cropped for Sauternes, so the actual area in production is 106 ha. The soil is very varied, which is one of the strengths of Yquem. Pierre Meslier used to say that it would be possible to make four different wines at Yquem, so varied are the soils on its slopes. Above the clay which dominates Yquem's soil is a stony, gravelly topsoil, only about 30 centimetres deep, which assists the drainage. Moreover, the quartz pebbles absorb the heat of the sun during the day and gently warm the vines after dusk. A band of clay mixed with limestone lies beneath the pebbly, sandy topsoil. The drainage problems that a preponderance of clay can cause were recognized in the nineteenth century, when the system of drainage channels, stretching for 100 kilometres, was originally constructed. It is strictly maintained. It would be rash to attribute Yquem's greatness to any single factor, but the clay mound on which the vineyards rest is not encountered elsewhere in Sauternes, where the subsoil is limestone-dominated. It cannot be coincidental that the most powerful wine of the region springs from a unique soil.

The estate employs seventy workers and craftsmen to maintain and administer the property. About twenty of them live on the estate. At harvest time up to 130 pickers undertake the skilled work of *triage*, of whom about eighty are hired each year. Yquem, like other top properties, tries to hire the same pickers year after year.

Although Yquem used to be a Sauvignon-dominated wine in the early nineteenth century, it is now planted with 80 per cent Sémillon and 20 per cent Sauvignon. In recent years the proportion of Sauvignon has been growing slightly, partly to account for the vines' shorter life span and because a small quantity is used to make the dry wine, Ygrec. The average age of the vines is about twenty-five years and the new plantations are not used for the *grand vin* until they are six years old. The estate takes cuttings from its own vines and grafts them on to American rootstocks. Pruning is very severe which ensures that yields are as low as possible – 9 hl./ha. is said to be the average – and only organic fertilizers are used. The Sauvignon is pruned so that the fruit-bearing spur has only six eyes, whereas many other estates will allow eight. No herbicides or chemical treatments are employed.

Yquem is the supreme wine of Sauternes because its harvesting procedures are more rigorous and because its special soils give wines of unusual richness and power. Without those qualities and without the concentration brought to the wine by low yields and scrupulous harvesting, Yquem would be unable to tolerate the lengthy ageing in new oak that is routine here, even in lighter vintages. The grapes are picked and placed in small wooden baskets. At times when botrytis is widespread, whole bunches or parts of bunches can be gathered; at other times, only individual berries can be picked. The whole process is carefully monitored by the *chef de troupe*, the foreman of the harvesters, who in turn takes his orders from Yves Laporte and Guy Latrille. To produce a single barrel of wine consumes the day's labour of up to ten harvesters.

The aim is always to pick with must weights of between 19 and 21°. After the *assemblage*, the balance of the wine will be approximately 14° of alcohol and 6° of residual sugar, but of course there is no formula and there are slight variations from vintage to vintage.

It may be of interest to review the harvesting of Yquem as practised in recent years. In 1982, picking began on 16 September, the earliest date since 1966; the first *trie* produced enough must to fill 200 *barriques*, but eight days later it began to rain and all succeeding *tries* had to be declassified. Some of them seemed promising initially and even after fermentation, but off-flavours in the wine caused these later *tries* to be discarded. There was a late harvest in 1984, beginning on 15 October and finishing on 18 November after five *tries*.

In 1985, an atypical year, harvesting began in early October, but since there was so little botrytis, only 6 *barriques* were made from the early *trie*. A small quantity was picked at the very end of October, but on 1 November harvesting stopped again. By mid-November there was not only no botrytis, but temperatures were dropping with the approach of winter. Any grapes that were unlikely to evolve further were picked with the intention of using them to make the dry Ygrec. However, in December temperatures rose again, botrytis appeared and picking resumed. This extraordinary vintage came to an end on 19 December, the latest harvesting date recorded at Yquem in modern times, and the result was a small quantity of excellent wine.

In 1986, harvesting began on 6 October. It began to rain on 18 October, so picking stopped. Fortunately the damp weather provoked more botrytis, and picking resumed and continued until 18 November. In 1987, it was more troublesome. Harvesting began on 30 September, as botrytis was developing. Then came the rain on 9 October; on 12 October, the pickers were able to resume work for one week. A third *trie* took place from 20 to 23 October. A fourth took place at the very end of the month, and there was a fifth from 2 to 6 November. As the grapes picked tended to be botrytized but wet, the new cryo-extraction technique was employed for the first and possibly last time at Yquem.

There was a superb vintage in 1988. A brief first *trie* occurred at the very end of September, but the main stage of picking began on 17 October. By the end of the month, the grapes were marvellously concentrated and the succeeding *tries* – 24–29 October, 7–10 November and 14–16 November, when the harvest ended – were highly satisfactory. It was equally superb in 1990, but exceptional in that the whole harvest lasted only sixteen days and was over by 10 October. Must weights shot up rapidly, so the pickers had to hurry.

In 1991, although below average, the quantity was quite high for the region, since Yquem only lost about 20 per cent of its crop to frost. No wine was bottled in 1992, but by October 1994 there were high expectations of a few lots of 1993, but no final decision had been taken.

In 1994 there were two days of picking of Sémillon and Sauvignon in September, but serious picking resumed on 6 October with Sémillon. Although the rain had ceased a few days earlier, they waited until the wind had dried the grapes. Already half the crop had been lost to rain and attendant damage.

The vinification of Yquem is classic and simple. The two grape varieties are vinified separately, and lots picked on different days are also kept apart. After a light crushing, the grapes are pressed three times in hydraulic presses, though a pneumatic press is kept in readiness should any of the hydraulic presses break down. The must is never chaptalized and is fermented in Limousin or Slovenian oak. A good day's harvesting should yield about 9 *barriques*. The largest quantity made in a single day was 18 *barriques* in 1969. The three pressings are blended, the aim being to have an average must weight of about 20°.

The cellars are heated to 20°C to ensure a steady fermentation, which usually takes one month. The *assemblage* begins in the summer following the vintage, though Alexandre de Lur-Saluces was reluctant to be too specific. Guy Latrille says there is sometimes preliminary blending of lots picked on the same day, but no final blending is done until they are absolutely certain about which lots are good enough to be bottled as Yquem. This is a crucial stage in the creation of the *grand vin*, as Yquem is probably more ruthless in eliminating unsatisfactory lots than any other Sauternes estate.

Sometimes, as in 1992, the entire production is sold off to whole-salers as generic Sauternes, and a cheapish blend that ends up on the supermarket shelves may well contain some wine discarded by Yquem. In years when noble rot is rare, lots may be rejected because they lack botrytis character. In 1973 and 1978, 85 per cent of the wine was sold off; in 1977, 70 per cent was rejected; and in 1979, 60 per cent. Even in fine years, such as 1970, 1975, 1976 and 1980, 20 per cent of the wine was not used for the *grand vin*. Given the prices it demands, Château d'Yquem simply cannot afford to release any wine that could be considered remotely substandard. The estate's reputation was damaged by the wretched 1963 and 1968 vintages, and Alexandre de Lur-Saluces does not want those mistakes to be repeated.

As the wine slowly matures in its *barriques* – each vintage may provide up to 500 – it loses 20 per cent to evaporation over three and a half years, a significant addition to the cost of production. The casks have to be topped up once or twice a week and racked every three months, giving fifteen rackings in all. Because of the long ageing process there is no need for filtration, but the wine is fined. Since 1922, all Yquem has been château-bottled.

Comte Alexandre's pride and joy is the new underground cellar, a rarity in Sauternes. It was constructed in 1987; 7 metres deep, it is vaulted and air-conditioned. The cellars can also be heated, which comes in handy with final *tries* picked in cold weather. Musts with a temperature of 5°C need a little warmth before fermentation can begin. The cellars can also be chilled later in the *élevage* process to help the wines to clarify naturally.

Yquem is one of the very few Sauternes never offered for sale *en primeur*. The wine trade loves to sell *en primeur*, as both the pro-prietors and the merchants can get their hands on some cash before the wine is even bottled. Lur-Saluces's decision not to follow this trend is expensive but justifiable. The wine is never offered for tasting at the château until it has been in bottle for six months. Visitors, including those from the wine trade, are shown the barrels, but the *pipette* remains on the wall. 'Once the wine is bottled,' says Lur-Saluces, 'we all speak the same language.' Throughout Bordeaux there is intense pressure from the wine trade and wine journalists to rush to judgement on each vintage, but each *barrique* will be ever so slightly different, and procedures such as racking and fining will also affect the aroma and flavour of the wine as it develops. Lur-Saluces is right in wishing to avoid premature judgement of his majestic wine. He admits, however, that he is in a privileged position and that most other proprietors cannot afford to take his principled stand.

A recent development has been the acquisition in 1985 of Château Pajot, an adjacent property between Yquem and Guiraud. Of Pajot's 13 ha., 8 ha. are entitled to the Sauternes appellation and have a similar soil structure. The vineyard has been replanted, but only when the vines are mature will they contribute to Yquem itself.

In this century, no Yquem has been released in the following vintages: 1910, 1915, 1930, 1951, 1952, 1964, 1972, 1974 and 1992. The average production twenty-five years ago was 82,500 bottles, but in recent years it has fallen to about 66,000. This figure is likely to rise as viticultural practices improve the performance of the vines without compromising quality. Once the vines of Pajot and another recently acquired vineyard at Bellevue, close to Château Rieussec, are included among the parcels worthy of making Yquem, the average production should increase to about 95,000 bottles. The wine is not available directly from the château. Instead it is distributed entirely through the Bordeaux wine trade.

Yquem has always been expensive, but the value of older vintages has shot up since 1985. The lean days of the early 1970s are well and truly history. Figures assembled by *The Wine Spectator* show that, between 1985 and 1989, the auction price of top vintages of Yquem trebled. Unfortunately, the consequence of such appreciation in value is that Yquem is now out of reach of all but the very rich. It is now a collector's wine, an investment, a status symbol. It always has been, it's true, but not that long ago it was conceivable that one could order a bottle in a restaurant or lash out on a few bottles of the latest vintage on release. No longer. Of course, Yquem is a wine made with the most painstaking care and with no compromises; it has never been a wine for everyday drinking. If any Bordeaux deserves cult status, it has to be Yquem. But studying the auction prices up to September 1994, it is apparent that in a good vintage, Yquem is six or seven times more expensive than any other Sauternes. Has Yquem become too expensive, or are other top Sauternes too cheap?

The answer is: both. Yet it is no secret that Yquem has not exactly been raking in the profits over recent years. Quite apart from the fanatical attention to detail and quality, Yquem has to be run along the lines of a small principality. The château and its great wine form the *locomotive* of the region, as the French like to say, tugging behind it the other *crus* which all benefit from Yquem's eminence. Yet all this costs money and, as I watched an enthusiastic group of Swiss wine lovers sipping a glass of 1988 Yquem after a tour of the cellars, it occurred to me, as it no doubt occurs daily to Comte Alexandre's accountants, that this hospitality was costing him about £10 per visitor.

For the small grower, the elevated status of Château d'Yquem is a mystery. Why, he wonders, when I sell my wine for 80 francs does Lur-Saluces charge 600 or more for his? The reader should by now realize what the answer is, but it says much about the gap between the mighty aristocrat and the humble *viticulteur* in the Sauternais that the question should ever be asked.

In 1994, it became known that under pressure from other members of the Lur-Saluces family, Châteaux d'Yquem and de Fargues were for sale. The Yquem establishment deny it, but there is ample evidence that this is indeed the case. It seems scarcely conceivable that centuries of history should be drawing to a close and it is hard to imagine any new owner will care for Yquem as conscientiously as the Lur-Saluces have done. But times change and it is entirely possible that Yquem will maintain its eminence even if in the hands of new proprietors.

Michael Broadbent records tasting the 1747 vintage, though the bottle was 'of unknown provenance'. The wine was slightly sweet, as was the 1784. Both the 1784 and the very fine 1787 were Jefferson bottles unearthed by the collector Hardy Rodenstock. Some questions have since been raised about the authenticity of the wines, but this is not a question I am able to resolve. Top vintages of the nineteenth century include the 1825, the celebrated 1847 (in 1995 a single bottle fetched $18,400 at auction), the 1848, 1858, 1861, 1864, 1865, 1868, the magnificent 1869, the 1874, 1875, 1893 (when the harvest began on 28 August!) and 1896. The oldest Yquem I have tasted was 1892; it was still lightly sweet but was drying out and clearly well past its best. Isolated tasting notes of ancient vintages can give only an approximate notion of what the wine was like at its peak, as one has to take into account such factors as bottle variation and storage conditions. With bottles over a century old, we are usually talking about very frail old ladies indeed.

As the twentieth century began, Yquem made fine wine in 1900, 1904 and 1906, but 1921 was the vintage that everyone raved about. Its extract, body and concentration of flavour marked it out as exceptional. It is, apparently, still going strong. I've tasted a very sweet but attenuated 1923, but the 1924 was a more harmonious and weighty wine. The decade concluded with two superb vintages in 1928 and 1929; the 1934 and 1937 were very fine too. Despite wartime constraints, Yquem, like many other Sauternes properties, produced excellent wines in 1943 and 1945. Another superlative vintage came in 1947 and the 1949 was not far behind. The 1955 had a tremendous reputation; those who have tasted it recently, however, note a falling off and over-prominent acidity. The 1959 is a rich wine of great vigour, though David Peppercorn finds its level of volatile acidity troubling.

The 1967 is reputed to be the best wine of that difficult decade, though it was never particularly voluptuous; its balance and vigour have, however, always charmed those who know the wine well. Yet surely the sublime 1962 is its equal? The 1971 was at first reputed to have the edge over the 1970, but in their present state of evolution, the 1970 is showing better. Both 1975 and 1976 are superb, but the 1975 is a touch more closed and may outlast the 1976, which at present is showing better than the previous vintage. The 1980 is delicious, with ample toasty oak on the nose, and fine concentration and acidity on the palate; not a blockbuster, but a beautifully made wine. The 1981 is even better; sumptuous, yet spicy and elegant. The 1983 is glorious, the best wine of a very fine vintage, but I confess to some disappointment with the 1986, which has not been showing the finesse and poise I would have expected. Of the great trio of vintages from 1988 to 1990, I have tasted only the exquisite, almost racy 1988, which was showing the extreme oakiness of a youthful Yquem. There is little doubt that all three will be great wines.

Ygrec is not a Sauternes, but there is so much confusion about what it is that I shall add a few words about it. Unlike Yquem, which is dominated by Sémillon, Ygrec, which was first made in 1959, contains about 50 per cent Sauvignon. It is not produced every year, but is an offshoot of certain vintages, especially those with low botrytis levels. Lur-Saluces stresses that it is his primary aim to produce Yquem. But in dry years there may be lots, picked with the intention of producing Yquem, that have only 16° of potential alcohol: a mighty must, but not up to Yquem standards. There may be other vines in which the development of the grapes has become arrested and the *chef de culture* may decide that the fruit, although unsuitable for Yquem, is worth saving before it rots. All these lots may be blended and the outcome is a powerful dry wine of at least 14° of alcohol: Ygrec. Like Yquem, Ygrec is fermented and aged in new *barriques*, but for thirty-six rather than forty-two months.

I recall being given a glass of 1979 Ygrec to taste blind at a dinner in 1987. 'Ah yes,' I said, admiring the golden colour and sniffing thoughtfully, 'Sauternes.' I then tasted the wine, which was completely dry. That is typical of Ygrec, since there is invariably a component of botrytized wine, as some of the lots will have been intended for Yquem. Surely this is what the fabled dry Sauternes, that was so prized in the early nineteenth century, must have tasted like.

Ygrec is an acquired taste. I happen to like it, though sometimes the high alcohol shows through, since there is no, or very little, residual sugar to balance it. In 1988 I tasted a whole range of Ygrecs: the 1960 was still spicy, creamily textured and long; the 1964 was nutty and fully mature; the 1969 was lush, alcoholic and just past its best; the 1972 had a trace of sweetness that I found cloying; the 1977 was showing some oxidation; the 1978 was firm and rich; the 1979 was superb, oaky, stylish and beautifully balanced, with a long, firm finish; I didn't care for the 1980, which was alcoholic and somewhat hard. Since 1980, the wine has only been produced in 1985, 1986 (a mere 3,000 bottles), 1988 (splendidly rich and powerful) and 1992.

Ygrec is an oddity, but a thoroughly intriguing one. Its cost will deter many people, but it is no more expensive than the most fashionable white Graves, which can't offer that mysterious combination of botrytis on the nose and a dry, rich palate.

Comte Alexandre de Lur-Saluces, Château d'Yquem, 33210 Langon, telephone: 57 980707, fax: 57 980708

6

The Premiers Crus *of Barsac*

CHÂTEAU CLIMENS

It is hard to imagine a greater contrast to the medieval majesty of Château d'Yquem than the modest compound of Château Climens. There's a small'house, a gravelly courtyard with a well, a long, low, undistinguished château with dumpy turrets at either end, and the *chais*. A sign alongside the gates proclaims this to be a *'Premier Grand Cru Classé'*, the same *folie de grandeur* that one encounters at Château Coutet. That's about it, although a few other structures nearby have been appropriated for storage and workshops. Climens is a wine rather than an estate. My first experiences of visiting Climens were not auspicious. The owners inhabited Château Bouscaut, close to Bordeaux, while Climens itself was guarded by the elderly Mme Janin, who was notorious for keeping visitors at bay. Her family had watched over Climens for a century and she herself had manned the gates for thirty years. A tasting of half a dozen vintages had been arranged for me at Climens, but when I arrived, Mme Janin disclaimed all knowledge of the appointment. Brigitte Lurton, who had made the arrangements, had departed from Bouscaut for her annual holiday. In short, nothing doing. The fault, of course, was Mme Janin's, who had either misunderstood the instructions or wilfully ignored them. The old dragon has fortunately retired.

In the fifteenth century, Climens was the property of the Roborel family. There were vines here by the mid-seventeenth century and Climens was much appreciated, especially in England, where demand was strong. At that time, red as well as white wine was produced here. The estate remained in the possession of the Roborels until 1802, when the widow of Jean-Baptiste Roborel de Climens sold the estate to Jean Binaud, a wine merchant. The most important owner of the nineteenth century was the Lacoste family, who replanted the vineyard and earned the estate its *Premier Cru* status in 1855. Subsequent owners included Alfred Ribet, who bought it in 1871.

The modern history of Climens begins in 1885 when Henri Gounouilhou, the proprietor of another Barsac *Cru Classé*, Château Doisy-Dubroca, bought the estate. Under Gounouilhou ownership the estate both grew in size and acquired a reputation that in certain vintages rivalled that of Yquem. It remained in his family until 1971, when it was acquired by Lucien Lurton, who has made a habit of collecting Bordeaux properties such as Châteaux Brane-Cantenac and Durfort-Vivens. In the early 1970s the fortunes of the Sauternes district were at a low ebb, so his decision to acquire Climens – and Doisy-Dubroca was thrown in for good measure – was regarded as crazy. In retrospect, it was a shrewd move. Lurton, who has entrusted the management of Climens to a few of his many children, changed little at Climens. Its winemaking remains simple and conservative.

Of the 30 ha. under vine, 27 are in a single parcel between the house and the *autoroute*; the remaining 3 ha. are located behind the house. The vineyards, planted entirely with Sémillon, are situated in the highest part of Barsac. This is not saying much, as the height above sea level is a mere 20 metres. The soil is classic Barsac: red sand and gravel over a limestone subsoil, with good drainage. The vines are an average of thirty-five years old. Yields vary from 9.6 hl./ha. – as in 1978 and 1991 – to 20 hl./ha. in 1990 and the maximum of 25 hl./ha. in 1986. The average yield is about 18 hl./ha., which sounds quite a lot for a *Premier Cru*, though it is hard to fault the quality of the wine here.

Christian Broustaut has been at Climens since 1969 and is now the *régisseur*. He is a plump, confident man, direct and straightforward. He gives the impression that there are no tricks to producing Climens: all you need are first-rate grapes and simple vinification. He is surely right. The grapes are picked, of course, in *tries successifs* and scrutinized in the vineyard so that any substandard fruit can be eliminated immediately. Although hydraulic presses remain in place, they are not used. Instead, Broustaut favours horizontal presses, which is surprising given their relative roughness. Only the first two pressings are used. As at Yquem, each day's crop is put separately into barrels for fermentation, so that by the end of the harvest there can be up to twenty-five different lots. No cultivated yeasts are used to begin the fermentation.

Broustaut and the Lurtons are not keen on chaptalization, but they will use it in vintages which, in their opinion, call for a slight boost: 1985 and the unreleased 1987 are recent examples. The *chai* at Climens is not high-tech. In the unlikely event that fermentation temperatures creep up to a worrying level, Broustaut will simply fling open the shutters and windows of the *chai* and allow the cool autumn air to circulate around the barrels. There is no enthusiasm here for cryo-extraction. Broustaut argues that the machinery is very expensive and of use only in poor vintages which are hard to sell anyway. And in great years, who needs it? Broustaut also worries that if harvesters know that cryo-extraction is being used, they may be less careful in their grape selection. These are persuasive arguments, at least for a medium-sized estate.

Fermentation is arrested by chilling the wine and adding sulphur dioxide. The *assemblage* takes place in the spring following the harvest and the selection is strict. In 1982, a wet vintage, two-thirds of the crop was rejected. In years such as 1983 and 1985, most of the wine ended up in bottle. The production is about 35,000 bottles on average. In 1988, 45,000 bottles were produced; in 1989 and 1990, 35,000 bottles; and in 1991, 20,000 bottles.

When one tastes Climens, it can give the impression of being quite an oaky wine. In fact, no more than one-third new oak is used, a reflection of the intrinsic delicacy of Barsac, in contrast to the greater power of Sauternes or Bommes. The wine is racked every two or three months and aged for up to two years. There is a filtration before bottling. In the past, Climens has been criticized for excessive sulphur in the wine, but that problem seems to have been rectified. Broustaut says that the total sulphur level is 280 milligrams, of which 50 are 'free'.

The brilliance of Climens, given the essential simplicity of the winemaking, must derive from the soil, the vines and the *triage*. Even in mediocre vintages plagued by poor and irregular weather patterns, such as 1973, Climens usually turns out a respectable wine and sometimes an outstanding one. The 1983 was superb, but Brigitte Lurton, who managed the estate in the 1980s, always maintained that the 1985 was almost as fine. Climens didn't harvest as late as Yquem – nobody did – but their final *trie* ended in mid-

November. There is less botrytis in the 1985, as one would expect, but it is a tremendous wine none the less. It was evident during the harvest that the 1986 would be another winner, so the interesting decision was made to release the 1984 under the second label of Les Cyprès de Climens. The 1984 was a lesser vintage, but Climens made a perfectly good and well-balanced wine that would not have been a disgrace had it been released under the château label. Those who bought the wine were able to sample a genuine if lightweight Climens at a bargain price.

Brigitte Lurton once told me that the 1986 was likely to be the greatest Climens of her experience. No one at the estate, not even the elderly Mme Janin, had ever seen anything like the onslaught of botrytis that attacked the Climens vines. Yet in the years that followed, there would be vintages that would surpass even the magnificent 1986. There was no 1987; it was all declassified. The 1988 vintage (with 13.8° of alcohol and 6° of residual sugar) was damaged by hail, but the quality of the remaining fruit was outstanding. The harvest of the 1989 (14.3° plus 4.8°) was rapid, with three *tries* between 25 September and 9 October. The 1990 (14.6° plus 7.5°) was a piece of cake, with all the grapes picked in one continuous *trie* from 17 September to 4 October.

The 1991 (14.3° plus 4.8°) was a peculiar vintage. Although the crop was a small one because of the spring frost, Climens had must weights of 19° by 15 September. The estate applied for special permission to begin the harvest, which was not supposed to begin before 25 September. Given the precocity of the Climens grapes, permission was granted and the first *trie* began on 17 September, and the third and final *trie* was completed on 9 October.

I visited Climens the day after the vintage ended in 1994 and Broustaut was all smiles. He had harvested from 21 September until 6 October and, despite the rain in September, insisted that the quality was far above his initial expectation. Yields were generous at 16 hl./ha., though some lots would not find their way into the *grand vin*, so the eventual yield would be closer to 8 hl./ha.

Climens is a superb Barsac. In its youth it is sometimes not very expressive; it is never a flashy wine and lacks the sumptuousness of Sauternes. It always has freshness, sometimes raciness, and a fine acidic backbone, which stands the wine in good stead as it ages. Climens is rich and structured, but never heavy, although it is more substantial in texture than many other Barsacs. Its gracefulness is deceptive. Pale and vigorous when young, it's a wine that demands ten years or more in bottle to display its true glory. With age, it gradually takes on weight and richness, though it is always a slow developer. Even when it becomes more honeyed with age, and thus closer to a Sauternes or Bommes in style, it never loses its quintessential elegance, its lingering length of flavour.

The oldest Climens I have tasted is the 1918, which I sampled in 1984. There were two bottles, which varied, but neither was outstanding. The 1924, however, was splendid, despite a colour as dark as oloroso sherry and a nose suggesting fruitcake; on the palate it was still sweet, elegant and spicy, with excellent length. A 1927 was slightly musty and raisiny, and had clearly seen better days. The 1928 and especially the 1929 were outstanding, the latter comparable to Yquem in its richness. A 1937 Crème de Tête was beginning to dry out in 1993, but was complex on the nose and still pleasurable to drink. Other great Climens wines of the mid-century are the 1947 (reputed to be the best Sauternes after Yquem), 1949, 1955 and 1959. The 1962 is a classic too, creamy yet perfectly balanced and very long. The 1966 shows astringency and I've never been impressed by the 1970, which lacks complexity. The 1971 is much better, with ample apricot fruit and botrytis aromas.

Poor years followed in 1972, 1973 and 1974, but Climens made some of the best wines: light, of course, but elegant and balanced. The 1973 is still attractive, but the 1974 should be drunk up. The 1975 and 1976 are both great: big, golden, honeyed wines with fine acidity and impeccable balance, wines with a long future. I marginally prefer the 1976. The 1977 and 1978, mediocre vintages, gave acceptable but one-dimensional wines. The 1979 is not exceptional, but both the plump, lemony 1980 and the smoky 1981 are excellent. The 1982 is rather light and will develop soon. The magnificent 1983 was showing rather awkwardly after ten years, but this is probably just an adolescent phase. The 1984 Cyprès was simple but delicious and is now at its best. The 1985 is elegant, with fine extract, and lemon and oak character, but it can't match the intensity and length of the 1986.

No Climens was bottled in 1987. The succeeding three vintages are all great, though in different styles. The highly concentrated and tangy 1988 is a classic Barsac; the golden 1989 is explosive in its fruitiness, and surprisingly fat and rounded for a Climens; the 1990 is a sublime wine with exquisite fruit and sweetness, mouth-watering acidity, and very good length. All three vintages will keep and improve for twenty years or more. The 1991 is one of the top wines of the vintage and very good in its own right: not especially rich, but sweet, lively and finely balanced, with ample botrytis character. The 1992 and 1993 vintages were bottled as Les Cyprès.

Bérénice Lurton, Château Climens, Barsac, 33720 Podensac, telephone: 56 271533, fax: 56 272104

CHÂTEAU COUTET

The château at Coutet is almost as modest as that at Climens. Although of ancient origin, it was remodelled in the eighteenth century, though as you walk around towards the back, its medieval core becomes more evident. Two sixteenth-century pepperpot towers remain attached to the rear of the house. At the front of the house facing the courtyard is a stout, square tower with a flat, crenellated top. The almost windowless chapel facing the main gate dates from the fourteenth century. These buildings are arranged around an irregular courtyard, and the grouping is made even more attractive by the well with an ironwork top and some fine chestnut trees. The *chais* lie on the other side of the lawns and are much larger than they appear from the outside.

Coutet's medieval history remains obscure, but there were a number of owners in the seventeenth century. It was the fashion for councillors of the *parlement* in Bordeaux to acquire estates in the Sauternais and one of them, Charles de Guérin, bought Coutet in 1643. It passed to his nephew Jean de Pichard in 1695, left the Pichards for thirty years in the mid-eighteenth century, but was returned to this wealthy landowning family in 1765. When Thomas Jefferson visited the region in 1787, he declared that Coutet was the finest of the Barsac wines. At the time it was producing 150 *tonneaux*, or 135,000 litres, so its vineyards must have been as extensive as those of Château d'Yquem. Moreover, the wine fetched a comparable price. Pichard sold the estate in 1788 to Gabriel-Barthélémy-Romain de Filhot, the aristocratic proprietor of Château Filhot in Sauternes and president of the Bordeaux *parlement*. Filhot was able to enjoy his new possession for only five years, as he was guillotined in 1794. Despite this misfortune, the estate itself was not confiscated during the Revolution. Consequently when Marie-Geneviève de Filhot married into the Lur-Saluces family in 1807, she brought as her dowry not only Filhot, but also Coutet and Piada.

From 1807 until 1922, Coutet remained in the possession of the Lur-Saluces family. During the nineteenth century it produced far less wine than when Jefferson paid his visit and it is possible that parts of the estate were sold or not replanted after outbreaks of oidium in the 1850s. In 1925, Château Coutet was bought by a company that owned a number of classified growths in Margaux, the Société Immobilière des Grands Crus de France. It was sold again in 1929, this time to an industrialist from Lyon, Henri-Louis Guy. His name lives on at Coutet as the manufacturer of hydraulic presses and his nameplate remains attached to those still in use at the château. He died soon after, and the estate passed to his daughter and her husband, a former priest called Edmond Rolland. Mme Rolland-Guy lived to a ripe old age and died at Coutet in 1977. After her death, the property was sold for over 4 million francs to the present proprietors, the Baly family from Strasbourg, whose Société Alsacienne owns hotels and other businesses. Marcel Baly has gradually relinquished the management of the estate to his sons Dominic and Philippe, and the latter maintains a flat in the château.

In an article in *Decanter* magazine (July 1986), David Wolfe observed that Coutet had indulged in some unsubtle self-promotion. He had spotted that on some labels the words '*1er Grand Cru de Sauternes*' appear beneath the name of the château. Yquem, of course, is the only wine entitled to this appellation. The upgrading is printed on the 1961 label and is still there in 1975. With the 1976 vintage, Coutet must have been overcome by a burst of bashfulness as the label modestly proclaims Coutet to be '*Premier Cru Classé*'. The promotion was presumably a quirk of the Rolland-Guy regime, and propriety was only partially restored by the incoming Balys, who retained the sign outside the gates identifying Coutet as '*1er Grand Cru Classé*'.

The soil is complex, a compound of limestone, gravel, weathered sand and alluvial deposits, all laid over a solid limestone subsoil which gives the wine its Barsac delicacy. The vineyards today amount to just over 38 ha. and they surround the château. One hectare is replanted each year, no young vines are used for the *grand vin* until they are seven years old and the average age of the vines is about thirty years. A sizeable portion had to be replanted after the devastating frost of 1956, and the present *encépagement* is 75 per cent Sémillon, 23 per cent Sauvignon and 2 per cent Muscadelle. The Muscadelle is usually picked first because of its susceptibility to grey rot. Naturally, harvesting is by *tries successifs*, and in 1983 there were eleven forays through the vineyards. The average yield is about 18 hl./ha. Up to half the wine is declassified after the harvest and the production rarely exceeds 70,000 bottles.

Coutet has had a somewhat unstable regime in recent years. In the 1980s, the *régisseur* was Claude Pascaud, whose father is the highly regarded *régisseur* of Château Suduiraut. He died young and was replaced by Jean-Luc Baldes, a stopgap measure as Baldes was keen to retire to his family estate in Cahors. In 1992, a new *régisseur*, Bernard Constantin from Loupiac, was installed. He works in tandem with Philippe Baly, the burly and energetic representative of the owning family.

The Balys have retained Coutet's classic vinification. The grapes are pressed three times in hydraulic presses and each pressing is kept separately. The advantage of these old presses is that they give exceptionally clear must and no *débourbage*, or decantation, is required. The must is fermented in *barriques*. Coutet favour a lowish temperature, about 15°C, though sometimes it is necessary to heat the cellars to keep the fermentation going. As it is, it can often continue for up to two months. Chaptalization is rare, but is employed when the must seems to require it. Fermentation is arrested with sulphur dioxide, and then the wine is racked and returned to clean barrels, which are double-stacked in the very long cellars. There are 800 *barriques* in all. Coutet is always fermented in new oak. The wine is racked every three or four months, and after the first racking it is put into one-year-old barrels; after the next racking it goes into two-year-old barrels; after the third racking it finds itself in three-year-old barrels; there's one more racking, after which the wine goes back into new oak for a further six months. The wine is blended from the time of the first racking onwards and gradually up to twenty-five lots are reduced to three. The wine is filtered *sur terre* before bottling. Although Coutet experimented with cryo-extraction for the *deuxième vin*, the Chartreuse de Coutet, between 1991 and 1993, they are still unsure about its efficacy.

Coutet is always a pale wine, which Philippe Baly attributes to the soil. It is not usually high-powered or alcoholic, and aims for grace and elegance rather than weight and lushness. There have

SAUTERNES

been vintages when Coutet gives the impression of being excessively light and lacking in extract and complexity, though the vintages at the end of the 1980s have been far more impressive. Yet older vintages of Coutet have held up marvellously after decades in the bottle, establishing beyond doubt that the potential for Coutet as a *cru*, although not always realized, is clearly superb. On the other hand, the wine does not have the consistency or the panache of its rival Climens, though it has sometimes produced vintages of equal quality.

M. Rolland must have had a romantic streak in him, for it was he who revived the special *cuvée* known, in honour of the chatelaine of Coutet, as Cuvée Madame. It appears to have been originally devised in the nineteenth century, though I have never come across an account of anyone having tasted one of those historical wines. Under Rolland, a parcel of vines that is considered the best at Coutet was consecrated each year to Cuvée Madame. The estate waits for a heavy infection of botrytis and often picks the parcel grape by grape to obtain juice of the utmost richness. The wine is aged in *barriques* for two years. The Balys have continued the tradition and regard it as a challenge.

'It's wildly uneconomical,' says Philippe Baly. 'It involves tying up the labour of forty people for a whole day just to produce two *barriques* of wine. But we like to do it, just to show what can be achieved if all constraints are removed.' It has been argued that producing Cuvée Madame detracts from the overall quality of Coutet itself, but Baly says the quantity involved is so small – up to 1,600 bottles – that if it were blended into the 'normal' wine, the difference would be negligible.

The estate tries to make Cuvée Madame every year, but the wine is not always bottled separately. It has been bottled only in 1941, 1943, 1949, 1950, 1959, 1971, 1975, 1981, 1986, 1988 and 1989. Surprisingly, none was made in 1990, perhaps because the harvest as a whole was of such a uniformly high quality. Cuvée Madame is usually given away a bottle at a time to especially favoured clients, though it is possible to buy vintages at the château. In 1994, for example, the following vintages were on sale at Coutet: the 1971 (1,600 francs), 1975 (1,250 francs), 1981 (700 francs), 1986 (500 francs), and the 1988 and 1989 at 600 francs. Given the rarity of the wine and its magnificent concentration and sumptuousness, such prices – which are about three times the price of the standard

Coutet – do not seem excessive in relation to, say, Yquem. The genius of Yquem, of course, is that it is the standard wine of that estate, not a special heroic effort.

Coutet has discontinued its production of red wine, but there is a dry white that comes from Pujols in the Graves and is rarely of much interest. Reading on the label the words '*Vin Sec du Château Coutet*', the purchaser could be forgiven for believing the wine came from Coutet vines, which is not the case. The *deuxième vin*, the Chartreuse de Coutet, is made from declassified lots not used for the *grand vin*. Sensibly priced, it has a strong following in Australia and France.

The oldest Coutet I have encountered was the 1919, which had become caramelly with age, but was still sweetish and elegant, with a fine nose of *crème brûlée* and candied oranges. The 1924, 1926 and 1929 vintages, tasted in 1990 and 1993, were all impeccable: wonderful, complex wines, exquisitely concentrated, still retaining that Barsac raciness and intensity, though of course becoming quite raisiny and barley-sugared with age. The 1934, 1937 and 1942 were excellent at Coutet, as, predictably, were the 1947 and 1949. The 1950 is surprisingly good, the 1959 unsurprisingly so. I have enjoyed a satisfying bottle of 1961, which has rich marmalade flavours; impressive, though not very elegant. The 1962 is excellent too, but the 1970 is lightweight, outclassed by the elegant, silky 1971. The 1973 was pretty in its youth, and the rich but lively 1975 is superior to the 1976. The 1979 and 1980 are sound but unexciting, but the honeyed 1981 has to be one of the best wines of the vintage. I have never much liked the 1982.

The 1983 Coutet is a mysterious wine. It has never been great, but I have had good bottles and simply awful bottles. This was not my impression alone and in 1987 I joined a group of tasters who sampled blind a number of bottles. The inconsistency was plain to all of us. The corks were printed differently and the label glues were not the same on all bottles. Yet analyses of the wines revealed no significant variations between them. The most likely explanation was that there had been different bottlings, but Philippe Baly has recently assured me that there is only one bottling at Coutet, so all the wine should be of uniform standard. The mystery remains.

Coutet made serious efforts to produce a fine 1985, beginning the harvest late, on 15 October, and continuing until 28 November. The wine is good but bland, and lacking in length. The jury is still out on the plump, dullish 1986, which may yet come through as a fine wine. But the 1988 is delicious: sweet, intense and citric, with good tangy length of flavour; not one of the great 1988s, but extremely attractive. The 1989 is succulent and creamy, probably the best Coutet since 1975, and the 1990 is also very stylish and intense. In 1991 only 12,000 bottles were produced and in 1992, 22,000 bottles. No 1993 was bottled as Coutet.

In 1994 Coutet lost 30 per cent of its production to spring frost, but the summer was excellent. Two weeks of rain required three *tries de nettoyage* in September, followed by serious harvesting in early October. By 6 October there was ample botrytis and Philippe Baly had high hopes for the vintage as long as the weather held for another ten days, by which time he hoped the harvest would have been completed.

All accounts of Cuvée Madame confirm that the wine is truly sensational, as rich and concentrated and luscious as one could hope for. I have tasted only one vintage: the plump, honeyed 1989, rich in extract and immensely long in flavour. The 1971 is reputed to be especially glorious.

For all the achievements of its top wines, Coutet remains a slight disappointment. Perhaps the momentum established by the 1989 and 1990 will be maintained and the estate will acquire the consistency it ought to have as one of the only two *Premiers Crus* of Barsac.

Bernard Constantin, Château Coutet, Barsac, 33720 Podensac, telephone: 56 271546, fax: 56 270220

7

The Premiers Crus *of Bommes*

CHÂTEAU CLOS HAUT-PEYRAGUEY

With its chunky neo-medieval tower overlooking the vineyards on a slope up on the Bommes plateau, Clos Haut-Peyraguey is visible from far and wide. In the eighteenth century' it belonged to the Pichard family, but after the Revolution, in which Pichard lost his head, it was acquired by M. Lafaurie. The Clos became the highest part of Château Lafaurie-Peyraguey, but became detached from it in 1879, when, after a family squabble, the property was divided. This portion was bought by a Parisian businessman named Grillon, who gave it its present name. In 1914, it was sold by Mlle Charlotte La Tremouille to the great-grandfather of the present proprietor, Jacques Pauly. The Paulys were the owners of Château Haut-Bommes, which is now in effect the *deuxième vin* of Clos Haut-Peyraguey. Jacques Pauly is not the sole owner of the Clos, but he controls a three-quarter share and has managed the property since 1969.

There are 15 ha. in production: 9 ha. are located between Lafaurie and Rayne-Vigneau; other parcels are close to Yquem. The *encépagement* is 83 per cent Sémillon, 15 per cent Sauvignon and 2 per cent Muscadelle. The soil is sandy gravel on a clay subsoil and the dominating exposure is to the north-east. The average age of the vines is thirty-five years and yields are about 18 hl./ha.

Pauly is thin, watchful and quiet, but clearly has firm ideas about the kind of wine he wants to make. He believes strongly in waiting for botrytis to appear in the vineyard, although the wines are not especially marked by noble rot in most vintages. The grapes are pressed in a horizontal press and natural yeasts set off the fermentation. Until quite recently, Pauly fermented all the must in cement vats. He stresses the importance of controlling the temperature of fermentation and likes to keep it at about 19°C. The fermentation takes three or four weeks. Perhaps responding to the criticism that Clos Haut-Peyraguey was one of the weaker *Premiers Crus*, in 1989 Pauly began to ferment a quarter of the crop in new *barriques* and the following year raised the percentage gingerly to 30 per cent. Chaptalization is rare, but does occur. Fermentation is arrested by chilling and adding sulphur dioxide.

The *assemblage* takes place in February. Pauly can be quite severe in his selection process. Half the crop was rejected in 1984, even though yields were relatively low at 15 hl./ha. The wine is aged up to twenty-two months in *barriques*. There are the usual rackings and a filtration before bottling. The preferred balance of Clos Haut-Peyraguey is 14–14.5° of alcohol and 4–4.5° of residual sugar. Production rarely exceeds 36,000 bottles. Pauly exports about 40 per cent of the wine and sells principally to private customers. To his credit, Pauly is one of the more accessible proprietors, and the château and its sales room can be visited every day of the week. Prices are fairly high.

Château Haut-Bommes, a 7-ha. estate between Rayne-Vigneau and La Tour-Blanche, also belongs to the Paulys, and it is the second wine of the *Cru Classé*. There is no Muscadelle here, and the wine is aged in tank as well as in barrels and bottled after eighteen to twenty-two months. The maximum production is 18,000 bottles.

Jacques Pauly declares that he is trying to make an elegant wine, *fin* rather than *liquoreux*. Fat, unctuous flavours and textures displease him. The problem is that finesse can often come across on the palate as lightness and lack of concentration. Pauly claims that his wines age very well, though I myself have no experience of wines older than 1983.

If Pauly was trying to avoid lushness, he certainly succeeded in 1983, which was lean and delicate; an attractive wine, but hardly worthy of a great vintage. The 1984 struck me as a success for the vintage, and the 1985, made from six *tries*, was sweet, racy and had good length. I don't detect much botrytis in the 1986, but it's a clean, juicy wine, well balanced and with good length. The 1987 is acceptable, given the vintage, and the 1988 is a success. It is sweet, spicy and elegant, with marked acidity, an attractive wine with fruit and vigour, but no complexity, no added dimensions. The 1989 has more fat than Clos Haut-Peyraguey usually exhibits, and bracing lemon-curd and apricot flavours. It is quite stylish, but by no means a great 1989, and its lack of length on the palate suggests it will evolve quite rapidly. The 1990 is the best wine from this estate that I have encountered; there is ample botrytis on the nose and lush, spicy fruit on the palate, with better length than the 1989. Despite an odd citric nose, the 1991 is a success, lean and with high acidity, and an excellent example of the Pauly style. Only 10,000 bottles were made. Pauly sold off much of his 1992, leaving only 9,000 bottles worthy of the château label. In 1993, when he experimented for the first time with cryo-extraction, yields were only 10 hl./ha. and half the crop was rejected, leaving 10,000 bottles.

Jacques Pauly, Château Clos Haut-Peyraguey, Bommes, 33210 Langon, telephone: 56 636153, fax: 56 766965

CHÂTEAU LAFAURIE-PEYRAGUEY

The medieval towers and crenellated walls that enclose the ivy-covered château are a reminder of the region's instability in medieval times. The oldest parts of the fortifications were built in the thirteenth century, though the château itself was largely reconstructed in the seventeenth. Within the walls, a spacious courtyard is shaded by tall trees. A hint or two about the microclimate is given by the presence of potted palms outside the house. To the right of the château are the *chais*, which were air-conditioned in 1978. In the eighteenth century, the estate was named Château Pichard after its prosperous and powerful owner, who was also the Seigneur of Bommes. After the Revolution, Pichard's estates were taken over by the state. This domaine was sold in 1794 to two gentlemen called Lafaurie and Mauros; Mauros was soon bought out by Lafaurie, who appended his name to Pichard's and eventually dropped Pichard's name altogether. Lafaurie put in hand various viticultural improvements, so that by the time of the 1855 classification the estate was placed close to the top of the list of *Premiers Crus*, immediately behind Château La Tour-Blanche.

After Lafaurie's death in 1860, the estate was acquired by M. Saint-Rieul-Dupouy, who subsequently married the widowed Mme Lafaurie. In 1865, the estate was sold to Comte Duchâtel, the proprietor of Château Lagrange; he died shortly thereafter and his widow inherited the property. It was after the Comtesse's death that the estate was divided. The portion henceforth known as Château Clos Haut-Peyraguey was detached and sold separately, possibly because the heirs could not agree among themselves on how to dispose of the estate. The new owners were called Farinel and Grédy. In 1913, additional vineyards were bought which compensated for the loss of Clos Haut-Peyraguey.

In 1917, the estate was bought by its present owners, Domaines Cordier. This fine company owns Châteaux Gruaud-Larose, Meyney and many other properties in the Médoc and Saint-Émilion. Cordier have been good stewards of the estate, although there was a bad patch in the 1970s; when it became apparent that the changes made were compromising the quality of the wine, Cordier admitted their error and reinstated traditional winemaking methods in 1978. Ever since, Lafaurie-Peyraguey has been an outstanding wine. The estate was slightly enlarged when a 4.5–ha. vineyard that was once part of Château d'Arche (which in turn had once been owned by Lafaurie) was sold to Cordier and incorporated within Lafaurie-Peyraguey.

The château is located on slopes to the north-east of Yquem, but the vineyards are more dispersed. Of its 42 ha., 40 ha. are in production: 12 ha. are planted within a walled *clos* around the château, there is another parcel of 5 ha. near Bommes, another 5 ha. near Château d'Arche on gravelly soil, 4.5 ha. behind Château Rabaud-Promis, and various other smaller parcels, mostly planted on gravel soils. The *encépagement* is 90 per cent Sémillon; the remainder is Sauvignon, with only traces of Muscadelle. In the final blend, there is a slightly higher proportion of Sauvignon in the wine. Many years ago, Sauvignon accounted for 30 per cent of the vines, but no longer.

The *régisseur*, Michel Laporte, has been at Lafaurie since 1963 and has run the estate since 1981. The Cordier executives seem to have given him a free hand – at least since 1978 – to run the estate as he thinks best and their confidence is justified by the extraordinary improvements in quality made throughout the 1980s. Laporte is fanatical about selecting only botrytized grapes. In 1985, this required eight *tries* between 14 October and 22 November; in 1984 and 1988 there were six *tries*, five in 1989 and 1990, but only three in 1983 – which confirms that the best vintages are often the easiest to harvest. Yields are variable and in the most generous vintages, such as 1988 and 1990, did not exceed 20 hl./ha. The yield in 1983 was 18 hl./ha.; in 1994, 16 hl./ha.; and in 1987 and 1989, only 14 hl./ha. The average works out at about 17 hl./ha. Like Yquem, Lafaurie-Peyraguey is seeking fruit with a must weight of 20–21°. Laporte is highly sceptical about the usefulness of cryo-extraction, arguing that it is easily subject to abuse, encouraging harvesters and winemakers to attempt short cuts.

From 1967 to 1977, when the Sauternes market was at a low ebb, Lafaurie used horizontal presses, and the wine spent most of its time in glass-lined metal tanks under a carpet of nitrogen gas and was finished off with a mere four months in *barriques*. Not surprisingly, the results were mediocre and, in 1978, Lafaurie reverted to classic winemaking. Now the grapes are pressed three times in hydraulic presses. Fermentation begins without the addition of cultivated yeasts; chaptalization is used only when Laporte considers it necessary. The must is fermented in *barriques*. The oldest barrels are four years old and, since 1985, half the barrels have been new. For Laporte, the attraction is that barrel-fermentation conserves the aromas better than tank-fermentation, which is more rapid.

Three-quarters of the barrels stop fermenting by themselves. Sometimes the wine is a touch too high in alcohol, but this is corrected by blending. Sulphur dioxide ensures the yeasts are eradicated. After a month, the wine is racked and it is fined after another month, chilled to rid it of tartrate deposits, then filtered. Now the wine is ready for its final *élevage*. It goes back into barrels of a medium toast from coopers such as Demptos and Séguin-Moreau, and is racked every three months. The wine spends a total of up to twenty-two months in cask before being bottled. There can be up to fifteen lots blended for the final *assemblage*. Up to 90,000 bottles are produced in an abundant vintage, but 70,000 is more usual. From 1992 onwards, declassified lots will sometimes be bottled as a *deuxième vin* under the La Chapelle de Lafaurie label. There are no direct sales from the château.

Lafaurie-Peyraguey is an extremely stylish wine, rich and powerful, but always with an underlying finesse that keeps it from seeming heavy or overblown. Since 1983, the oak has been marked on the nose and palate, but never in a clumsy way. It is impressive how swiftly the oak and fruit flavours become integrated and harmonious.

The oldest Lafaurie I have tasted was the 1913, with a pronounced marmalade nose and rich sweetness on the palate; but at over seventy years old it was undeniably beginning to dry out. Michael Broadbent has noted positively the 1906, 1909, 1914, 1918 and 1921 vintages too. A 1926 had caramel aromas and flavours, and was becoming astringent and piercing; concentrated, lightly sweet, but in decline. Broadbent commends the 1934, 1937, 1942 and 1945. After a magnificent 1947, the Lafaurie style seemed to become lighter and less fleshy. After the change in vinification in the 1960s, the 1975 was the only outstanding wine and some of the wines, such as the 1980, were distinctly poor. No Lafaurie was bottled in 1968 and 1974. Although the 1982 was pleasant enough, it didn't show much botrytis. The 1983 is the first of a run of great wines from Lafaurie: rich, oaky and elegant from the outset, it has stayed that way, gathering concentration and depth of flavour, although it will be a few years before the wine reaches its peak.

I have always enjoyed the 1984. It is not a vintage that could ever have produced a great wine, but the Lafaurie has some richness, intensity and length. It is arguably the best 1984 Sauternes other than Yquem, although it is not for long-keeping. The 1985 is extremely good too, distinctly oaky, showing more botrytis than many 1985s, with a compact structure, high alcohol and very good length. This is another wine built to last. In its youth, the 1986 was a touch clumsy and blowsy, but it has now settled down into a big, tangy, mandarin-flavoured wine with a velvety texture and exceptional length of flavour. The 1987 was another minor vintage, but again Lafaurie produced one of the year's top wines, its apricot fruitiness touched by noble rot and balanced by a lively acidity.

I last tasted the 1988 in 1992. Very oaky on the nose, it was very sweet and dense, but closed; its potential to develop into a classic Sauternes was plain to see, but it was revealing little in its youth. The 1989 and 1990 are both fabulous: the 1989 more rounded and opulent; the 1990 more racy and vivid, and obviously oaky. The harvest in 1989 began on 5 September, exceptionally early, but continued until 23 October; in contrast, the 1990 began on 17 September and was all over by 12 October. The 1989 showed better when young, but the 1990 is now overtaking it and I suspect it will be the greater wine in twenty years.

The 1991 is very good too, with flavours of marzipan and ripe lemons, a lean style that may peak within ten years, but most enjoyable. There's not much of it, as 60 per cent of the vines were smitten by frost. The harvest was tricky as there was considerable variation in ripening dates for various bunches. A miserable year followed in 1992 and many estates did not bottle any wine at all, but Lafaurie made an attractive, slender, finely honed wine with flavours of dried apricot and quite good length. It's not great, but it's surprisingly good, considering how wretched the weather was in 1992. When grey rot hit the vines in September 1992, Laporte treated against it, removed leaves to aerate the vines, and waited for better weather and botrytis. His patience was rewarded and he had a good quantity of usable wine. In 1993, he picked before and after the rain, finishing the last *trie* at the end of October. Laporte says the 1993 will be leaner and more elegant than the 1992. In 1994, the yields were 16 hl./ha. and Laporte was comparing the wine in quality with the 1986.

Michel Laporte, Château Lafaurie-Peyraguey, Bommes, 33210 Langon, telephone: 56 636054

CHÂTEAU RABAUD-PROMIS

Rabaud-Promis had its origins as an aristocratic estate owned from 1660 onwards by the noble de Cazeau family. In 1819, Pierre-Hubert de Cazeau sold the estate to Gabriel Deyme, who was the owner at the time of the 1855 classification. In 1864, the estate was bought by Henri Drouilhet de Sigalas. He expanded the estate and absorbed into it the whole of the 10–ha. Château Pexoto, which had been classified as a *Deuxième Cru*. For some reason, Château Rabaud retained its first-growth status, despite the incorporation of Pexoto.

In 1903, the estate was divided after Pierre Drouilhet de Sigalas, son of Henri, sold part of the property to M. Adrien Promis, who had been associated with Rabaud for some years before the sale was negotiated. In 1929, the two halves of the Rabaud estate were reunited under Fernand Ginestet, who ran the property on behalf of its co-owners: a daughter of Pierre's son Gérard, who had married the Marquis de Lambert des Granges, and the daughters of Adrien Promis. It must have seemed like an ideal solution until 1949, when the Marquis decided to buy his portion of the estate, disposing of the Promis property to Raymond-Louis Lanneluc. In 1952, the history of Château Rabaud as a single property came to an end.

It isn't clear why Raymond-Louis Lanneluc wanted Rabaud-

Promis, since under his stewardship the property was badly neglected. The wine was fermented and aged in underground tanks and
spent little or no time in barrels. For a *Premier Cru* it was little
short of a disgrace. As late as the mid-1980s, when I first visited
Rabaud-Promis, the cellars were grubby and unappetizing. So was
the wine. Rabaud-Promis tended to be bottled on demand, sitting in
underground tanks until somebody placed an order. The wines of
the early 1970s were so dreadful that they had to be sold under a
different label.

In 1972, a young man called Philippe Dejean, whose family owns
vineyards in Loupiac, married M. Lanneluc's granddaughter Mich-
elle and began to work at the estate in 1974. In 1981, the Dejeans
were able to buy out the other Lanneluc shareholders and took over
the management of the property, but a shortage of money meant
that improvements had to be made slowly. The Dejean family live in
the château, which is a modest but charming eighteenth-century
house by the Bordeaux architect Victor Louis. The house, its grassy
courtyard, its workshops and outbuildings are surrounded by vineyards, and there are few more delightful vistas in Sauternes than
looking out of the windows at sunset on to the rows of vines that
creep up to the very walls.

There are 33 ha. of vineyards at Rabaud-Promis, with an *encépagement* of 80 per cent Sémillon, 18 per cent Sauvignon and 2 per
cent Muscadelle. The vineyards are a combination of very old and
very young vines. The soil has a high gravel content, but is under-
pinned by a layer of clay and limestone, which helps to give the
wine considerable structure and longevity. The average yield is 18
hl./ha., as in 1988. Dejean was able to harvest 25 hl./ha. in 1990,
but that was exceptional.

Among the many innovations at Rabaud-Promis was the instal-
lation in 1988 of two pneumatic presses to replace the older horizontal presses. The grapes are not crushed before pressing. In the
bad old days the must was fermented in those underground vats;
Philippe Dejean later acquired some 50-hl. steel tanks and thereafter the wine was fermented partly in those tanks and partly in
barrels; since 1989, all the wine is *barrique*-fermented. Since 1988,
one-third of the barrels have been new oak, though Dejean lowers
the proportion in lighter years. The must is occasionally chaptalized, but most lots that require chaptalization end up in the *deuxième vin*. The wine is racked every four months and bottled about

thirty months after the harvest. It does not usually spend the entire period of *élevage* in wood, but also reposes in steel tanks to retain the wine's freshness. The maximum production is 80,000 bottles.

The second wine is essentially a declassification and Dejean does not produce it on a regular basis. In 1989 and 1990, for instance, there was no second wine. Two labels are used: Domaine de l'Estrémade and Château Bequet, and the two wines are usually identical.

Rabaud-Promis is a rich wine, fat without being heavy. In its youth it has a freshness that makes it pleasurable to drink young, though of course the top vintages will benefit greatly from bottle maturation. Perhaps because of its history, the wine has been somewhat underrated. Certainly since the 1986 vintage, the wine has been beautifully made, proving yet again that those who made the 1855 classification knew what they were doing. Rabaud-Promis is now one of the most reliable wines of Sauternes.

In 1990 I tasted the 1918 vintage which, although frail, left enough clues to suggest what a charming and voluptuous wine it must have been at its peak. The 1924 seems to have retained more weight and power, and I was greatly impressed by the sweet, lush 1948, the first of the trio of fine vintages that saw the last appearance of Château Rabaud alone on the label. Good wines were made in 1955, 1961 and 1967. The viscous but cloying 1975 aged rapidly and wasn't particularly attractive when young. The 1981 has a good reputation and the 1983, though not complex or elegant, was a fine, spicy wine. The 1985 is good and the 1986 considerably better; it's plump but supple, with charm and a fair amount of honeyed opulence. It should keep very well. Dejean made a fine 1987 from minimal yields of 7.5 hl./ha. and the wine is more concentrated than one would have expected from the vintage.

The 1988 is simply wonderful, with a smoky, elegant nose lightly touched by oak, ample botrytis on the palate, which is finely tuned, complex and long. The 1989, picked throughout October, is a great wine, packed with flavours of dried fruits, quite forward, with the oak well integrated and masses of extract. After this pair the 1990, tasting of ripe apricots and with an oaky nose intense with botrytis, doesn't seem quite complete. But it is also the youngest wine and still rather closed. In 1990, some lots were very rich and difficult to ferment and had to be blended with less rich batches in order to keep the fermentation going. These three vintages form a brilliant trio and the 1988 is surely one of the top wines of that classic year.

The 1991 is racy but one-dimensional. The 1993, according to Dejean, is marginally better than the 1992, but at the time of writing no decision had been made about whether either vintage would be released as Rabaud-Promis.

Philippe Dejean, Château Rabaud-Promis, Bommes, 33210 Langon, telephone: 56 766738, fax: 56 766310

CHÂTEAU RAYNE-VIGNEAU

In Gascon dialect, 'Vignau' refers to a spot well suited for vine-growing and Gabriel de Vignau was the owner of this fine hilltop site in the early seventeenth century. His son Étienne married Jeanne Sauvage of Yquem, and Vignau might have eventually ended up in the Lur-Saluces portfolio had Jeanne's nephew Hyacinthe not sold the estate in 1742 to a Bordeaux wine merchant, Jean Duffour. His son Bruno inherited the estate in 1774. He was a high-ranking court official but managed to survive the Revolution and, by the time of his death in 1817, he had amassed 160 ha. in the Graves. In 1834, the estate was bought by Catherine Marie de Rayne, the widow of Baron de Rayne. By this time the modern spelling of Vigneau had been adopted for this substantial estate with its 60 ha. of vines. The standing of the property was high: in the 1855 classification it was third in the pecking order of *Premiers Crus*, immediately below Lafaurie-Peyraguey. After the baroness's death, the property passed to her brother, Vicomte Gabriel de Pontac, a member (as indeed was she) of the famous family who owned some of the finest vineyards in Bordeaux. Gabriel was succeeded by his son Albert, who created the double-barrelled name of the estate in homage to his late aunt. After Albert's death, the property was managed by his son-in-law, the Vicomte de Roton, who became the mayor of Bommes. Roton lived to the ripe old age of ninety-eight, and his son François now lives in the flamboyant nineteenth-century château that stands proudly on the hilltop.

François de Roton no longer has any connection with the vineyards that surround his home. In 1961, the vineyards and cellars were acquired by a Bordeaux wine merchant called Raoux. After ten years he sold the property to the Mestrezat company, which has a substantial portfolio of estates throughout the Bordeaux region, of which the most celebrated is the Pauillac estate of Château Grand-Puy-Ducasse. The Mestrezat team recognized that Rayne-Vigneau had become run down and would require substantial investment. The first problem to be tackled was the state of the vineyard, which had to be replanted. New barrels were unknown here. Jean Merlaut, whose father Jacques had bought Mestrezat in 1970, took the keenest interest in Rayne-Vigneau and is largely responsible for its renovation.

It is not hard to understand why Rayne-Vigneau, even in its run-down condition, should have been considered a great prize by Mestrezat. Those who know the region and its soil intimately declare that potentially the *terroir* at Rayne-Vigneau is the finest in the Sauternais after Yquem. It is certainly most unusual, as the 73-metre-high hill is studded with precious and semi-precious stones, including sapphires, opals, amethysts and agate, as well as oysters and other fossils, all deposited, presumably, by glaciers during the Pliocene epoch. Even today it is possible to walk between the rows of vines and spot the occasional gleaming stone.

The Merlaut family may be the driving force behind the estate, but the man on the spot is the worldly Patrick Eymery, who has been the *régisseur* since 1982. Previously he had been at Château Guiraud. Under Eymery's supervision, new *chais* have been built and filled with rows of the latest stainless-steel tanks and, in another portion of the cellars, rows of 800 *barriques*. There is a cold chamber for cryo-extraction and no fewer than three pneumatic presses. It doesn't look as romantic as Coutet or Lafaurie-Peyraguey, but it must be a joy to work in such hygienic and modern surroundings.

The vineyards are extensive, 80 ha. in all, but they are still young, with most vines under twenty years old. The soil is unusually stony, a gravelly sand with a clay subsoil, and the drainage is excellent. Sémillon accounts for 80 per cent of the vines; the remainder are Sauvignon. Eymery is strict about selecting parcels to be used for Rayne-Vigneau. The young vines, and that means any vines up to eight years old, as well as those planted at the foot of the hill are used only for the *deuxième vin*, the Clos l'Abeilley and for the Sauvignon-dominated Sec de Rayne-Vigneau, a fresh dry white wine. The density of plantation varies from 5,000 to 7,000 plants per ha., and the vines are pruned *à cot* to six to eight eyes. The average yield is 18 hl./ha. Eymery's harvesters seek a must weight of

18–19°, to give a wine with a balance of 14.5° of alcohol and 4° of residual sugar, a wine that will retain some Bommes elegance.

Until 1988, horizontal presses were in use; now pneumatic presses do the job, and the must sinks by gravity into 45-hl. subterranean tanks for its *débourbage*. The must is chaptalized when necessary, and fermented partly in stainless steel and partly in *barriques*. In 1990, one-third of the wine was *barrique*-fermented. Fermentation is stopped with sulphur dioxide. All lots are kept apart until March, when the blending process begins. Since 1986, the wine is aged in barrels, of which half are new each year, for eighteen to twenty-four months. As the selection proceeds, up to half the lots may be declassified. The wine is racked every three months and chilled to precipitate the tartrates. There is a single fining and a filtration *sur terre* just before bottling. The maximum production is 110,000 bottles, and the second wine, Clos l'Abeilley, varies from 30,000 to 80,000 bottles, depending on the vintage. There are no direct sales from the Château.

Some of the early experiments in cryo-extraction were made here and the cold chamber was used during the 1987 vintage. It wasn't necessary in 1988 and 1989, of course. The 1989 was an easy vintage here. There were four *tries* from 20 September to 31 October, and by May the following year the *assemblage* was complete. In 1990, there were only three *tries*; some of the lots had potential alcohol of 28°. Cryo-extraction was employed again in 1992, but the resulting wine was blended into Clos l'Abeilley. The cold chamber was used in 1993 too, but no Rayne-Vigneau was bottled as the grapes were insufficiently ripe. Eymery is not opposed to cryo-extraction, but doubts that it is capable of producing wine suitable for a *grand vin*.

Patrick Eymery's commitment to quality is evident. Yet perhaps the wine is lighter than it should be. He admits to seeking a style that is elegant and not too *liquoreux*, but there are times when one feels the splendour of the site and the costly sophistication of the winemaking should result in wines with a little more richness and depth. Part of the explanation, no doubt, lies in the relative youth of the vineyards, and when a greater proportion of older vines can be used, the wine will surely gain in concentration and profundity.

I have not had the privilege of tasting truly venerable wines from Rayne-Vigneau, but there have been ecstatic tasting notes on the

1893, 1904, 1911, 1919, 1923, 1927 and 1928. I have tasted the 1939, a bottled labelled 'Crème de Tête', and it was sensationally good: a fruit salad of oranges, peaches and barley-sugar on the nose, and rich *rôti* fruit on the palate. It tasted twenty years younger and was by no means fading. The 1949 was superb, but then the reputation of Rayne-Vigneau took a nosedive, with only occasional successes, such as the 1959. Throughout the 1970s the wines were heavily sulphured, lacked botrytis and were marred by a coarseness that made them far from pleasant. My own notes begin to register some excitement only with the 1983, a vigorous wine that lacked richness, but had considerable elegance and length of flavour. There was a good 1985, but the 1986 was a touch disappointing. It was perfectly correct, but it lacked complexity and depth, and was one-dimensional for the vintage.

A huge leap in quality is evident in the 1988 vintage. Here there is abundant botrytis, spicy, peachy fruit, excellent concentration and verve, resulting in a wine of great stylishness and length of flavour. The 1989 had a similar balance – 14° of alcohol and about 5° of residual sugar – but is richer and more up-front in its fruitiness, though somewhat underpowered for the vintage. The 1990 is a brilliant wine, oaky on nose and palate, voluptuous without a trace of heaviness, impeccably balanced, creamy and intense. I have not tasted the 1991, but the 1992 is sweet and supple, better than expected and should evolve quite rapidly.

Patrick Eymery, Château Rayne-Vigneau, Bommes, 33210 Langon, telephone: 56 766163, fax: 56 013010

CHÂTEAU SIGALAS-RABAUD

The division of the Rabaud estate – its history has been recounted in the entry for Château Rabaud-Promis – became final in 1949, when Marquis René de Lambert des Granges disposed of the portion belonging to the daughters of Adrien Promis. The Marquis and Marquise owned the estate outright until 1972, when a company was formed which included their four sons, one of whom, Comte Emmanuel de Lambert des Granges, has managed the estate since 1982 and lives with his family in the small seventeenth-century château. Sigalas-Rabaud is the smallest of the *Premiers Crus*, some 14 ha. planted on gravelly clay slopes with a south and south-east exposure. This slope, or *croupe*, has soil that is quite similar to that of its neighbour Lafaurie-Peyraguey. The vines are 85 per cent Sémillon, the remainder Sauvignon, and their average age is thirty-five years.

The general practice at Sigalas-Rabaud is to harvest relatively early. Lambert des Granges says this is because the gravelly soil is precocious, its stoniness retaining the warmth of the sun and helping to ripen the fruit. He often defoliates in the early autumn to increase the bunches' exposure, both to assist the ripening and to ensure any attacks of botrytis are efficacious. Average yields are about 17 hl./ha. Although Lambert des Granges says it's essential to wait for botrytis, his former *régisseur* Jean-Louis Vimeney took a more cynical view, telling me in the 1980s that there came a point when it was counter-productive to keep waiting and it was better to pick overripe fruit without botrytis than no fruit at all. This is true as a practical proposition, but his willingness to compromise was not reassuring.

The vinification is slightly unusual. It begins in a highly traditional way, with a crushing and two pressings in hydraulic presses. Then the wine is fermented in tanks, and aged both in tank and in *barriques*. Vimeney was not keen on barrel-ageing, and I suspect that Comte Emmanuel's decision in 1988 to age almost half the wine in new oak hastened Vimeney's departure in 1990. He was replaced by Eric Combret, who is more comfortable working with *barriques*. The Comte would like to have an even higher proportion of new oak, but cannot afford to do so at present. None the less, he is not trying to make an oaky wine. Above all else, he prizes freshness and aroma, and to achieve this he not only ages some of the wine in stainless-steel tanks, but also bottles the wine early, about eighteen months after the vintage. He himself likes Sauternes when it's young, rather than elderly and maderized.

The maximum production is about 40,000 bottles, as in the copious 1990 vintage. Older vintages are still for sale direct from the château, where there is a tasting corner in the *chai*. Since 1957, the *chai* has been curiously decorated with large paintings in praise of vine and wine, which I have never managed to admire as much as visitors are expected to. Sigalas-Rabaud is following the lead set by Château Guiraud in bottling its more recent vintages in 50-cl. bottles.

Comte Emmanuel is short, garrulous and feisty, rarely seen without a cigarette in hand or mouth, and entirely unconcerned that he may be seen as out of step with his more ambitious neighbours. Still, the wine is very good. The balance is finely tuned, and

Sigalas-Rabaud invariably has charm and finesse; in very ripe years it has richness and concentration too, and is never heavy. Comte Emmanuel is a stickler for quality and doesn't believe in second wines. Yet I don't recall tasting a mind-blowing Sigalas-Rabaud and some of the other Bommes *Premiers Crus* are far more impressive. The modesty of Sigalas-Rabaud is highly satisfying on its own terms, but not when compared with its peers and neighbours.

In late 1994, Cordier, who already own Château Lafaurie-Peyraguey, took a minority shareholding in Sigalas-Rabaud, and will oversee vinification and sales and marketing. Michel Laporte of Lafaurie-Peyraguey will henceforth manage the estate. It will surely be fascinating to see if and how the distinctive Sigalas style will change.

I have not tasted older vintages of the wine, but those who have applaud the overall quality of the wines even in the mostly dreary decades of the 1960s and 1970s. The wines I have tasted from the 1980s have tended to be very good but light. I found a lemony freshness and elegance on the 1983, but not a great deal of botrytis. The 1985 was delicious in its youth and the 1986 tangy and charming, pleasingly aggressive. In 1987, Comte Emmanuel tried cryo-extraction, as he was to do again in 1993, though he has no cold chamber at the estate. The sleek, racy 1987 proved similar in style to the 1985, but less succulent and robust. The 1988 is a terrific wine, still rather closed on the nose, but with gorgeous ripe fruit on the palate and fine balance. It doesn't appear to have great structure, but that impression could be deceptive, as Sigalas-Rabaud does keep well. Both the 1989 and 1990 are very powerful wines, with almost 15° of alcohol and about 6° of residual sugar. The sweetness is particularly evident in the 1990, which has an almost minty intensity. I marginally preferred it to the 1989, but it will be a few years yet before their characters emerge more definitively. Sigalas-Rabaud produced only 6,000 bottles of the 1991, but it is exquisite and surprisingly honeyed. It is almost as sweet as the 1990, but far less powerful. It's a forward wine, but I would not be surprised if it aged well. Its success is surely due to the very severe selection exercised in this vintage. The 1992, of which only 8,000 bottles were produced, is much simpler and lacks length. It should be enjoyed while it has its youthful fruit and spiciness. No 1993 was bottled. In 1994, the harvest began with a *trie de nettoyage* during the rain, and picking began on 4 October.

Comte Emmanuel de Lambert des Granges, Château Sigalas-Rabaud, Bommes, 33210 Langon, telephone: 56 766062

CHÂTEAU LA TOUR-BLANCHE

Château La Tour-Blanche first achieved celebrity when, according to legend, its owner M. Focke travelled to Germany in the 1830s and returned with the secret of making wine from nobly rotten grapes. The story, alas, is nonsense, as botrytized grapes were cherished in Sauternes back in the eighteenth century, but it helped put La Tour-Blanche on the map. So did the 1855 classification, which rated the estate's wine as the finest after Yquem.

Not much is known about the estate before M. Focke's day. It takes its name from one of Louis XVI's court officials, Jean Saint-Marc du Latourblanche, but his connection with the estate, and the nature of its agricultural activities in the eighteenth century, remain obscure. By the time of Focke's death in the 1850s, the estate had 35 ha. under vine. His widow sold the property in 1860 to a consortium, which twenty years later sold it to Daniel Osiris. Osiris was an umbrella tycoon, but he was serious about his wine, and after his death in 1907 he left La Tour-Blanche to the state, stipulating that it be used as an agricultural school. The bequest was implemented in 1909 and is honoured to this day.

The French government, as proprietors of La Tour-Blanche, weren't sure what to do with the vineyards, so from 1925 until 1954 they were leased to Domaines Cordier, the owners of Château Lafaurie-Peyraguey and numerous other estates in the Bordeaux region. Cordier were entitled to half the crop which, one assumes, was either sold or marketed separately from the château-labelled wine.

There is a clear separation between the wine estate and the college, although some students may occasionally find themselves involved in the winemaking. Until the arrival of the dynamic Jean-Pierre Jausserand as director in 1983, it was tempting to speculate that La Tour-Blanche's mediocrity was attributable to the incompetence of the students let loose on it. Since 1983 it hasn't been appropriate to joke about La Tour-Blanche, as under Jausserand and his *maître de chai* Jean-Pierre Faure the wine has become very good indeed.

A single parcel of 30 ha. of vines slopes down from a height of 67 metres near the château to the Ciron valley. Towards the top of the slope, gravel dominates the soil, which as it descends becomes more suffused with sand and clay. The clay in the soil seems to delay the ripening, which is significantly later than at other Bommes estates, such as Lafaurie-Peyraguey or Sigalas-Rabaud. In 1994, the château acquired an additional 4 ha. close by, bringing the total area under vine to 34 ha. The *encépagement* is recorded very precisely as 77.8 per cent Sémillon, 19.5 per cent Sauvignon and 2.7 per cent Muscadelle. The density of plantation is 6,000 vines per ha., slightly fewer than is customary. The yields used to be high, and even in 1983 they were the maximum of 25 hl./ha., though more recently they have varied from 8 to 18 hl./ha. The average age of the vines is about thirty years and about half the plants are over twenty years old.

The harvesters aim to pick only grapes with a potential alcohol of at least 19°. The winery is well equipped, with a cold chamber for cryo-extraction, air-conditioned cellars and, since 1987, pneumatic presses. The first pressing, although copious, is not always used, at least not for the *grand vin*, as the must is not considered rich enough. If the third pressing shows any trace of bitterness, it too is discarded. The must used to be fermented in temperature-controlled steel tanks, but under Jausserand's directorship barrel-fermentation has been employed. La Tour-Blanche is never chaptalized, which is why high must weights are so essential. The fermentation is arrested with sulphur dioxide. The *grand vin* spends up to two years in barrels and is racked every three months. Jausserand favours fine-grained oak and orders barrels from four different coopers; the toastings vary. Many of the casks are from Limousin, Allier or Châteauroux oak. The proportion of new oak has been rising steadily. The 1988 was aged in 50 per cent new oak. From 1989 onwards, the entire crop has been fermented in new oak, as at Yquem, even in vintages which were never released, such as 1992. The *assemblage* takes place quite late in the evolution of the wine and as many as eighteen different lots may be blended. Up to 60,000 bottles of La Tour-Blanche are produced.

Rejected lots are either sold off or bottled as the *deuxième vin*, Mademoiselle de Saint-Marc (known until 1986 as Cru Saint-Marc). Any must that requires chaptalization is also destined for the second wine, and is fermented in steel. Not a great deal of Mademoiselle de Saint-Marc is made: about 15,000 bottles. The château also produces a white wine with the simple Bordeaux appellation. Called Osiris after the estate's benefactor, it is made from botrytis-affected must that, presumably, like the Mademoiselle, is not up to *grand vin* standard. Osiris, of which only 6,000 bottles are produced, is available primarily in Belgium.

No one can dispute the strides made here under Jausserand's direction. Not only have technical improvements been made in the cellar, but pruning has become more severe and *triage* more rigorous. However, some accuse Jausserand of moving too fast, of making exaggerated claims for his wines before they have stood the test of time. The *prix de sortie* or opening price of the 1988 vintage was 78 francs. The 1989, which was fermented in costly new oak, was first offered at 125 francs, a very steep increase that some Bordeaux *négociants* found unpalatable. Jausserand points out that La Tour-Blanche's pricing structure started from a lower base than most other *Premiers Crus*, thanks to the dim reputation of the wine before his arrival. He also declares that he will bring the price down if he feels a vintage shows any decline in quality. Indeed, the 1990 *prix de sortie* was marginally lower at 115 francs, and the 1991 came out at 90 francs; Jausserand estimates that the 1994 will be similarly priced.

La Tour-Blanche at its best is rich and weighty, a full-throttled Bommes that is easily mistaken for Sauternes. Jausserand is right in thinking that the structure of the wine can survive a lavish use of new oak, and the vintages of the late 1980s are undeniably successful. Sightings of very early vintages have been rare, but I have seen positive notes on the 1869, 1921 and 1927. I have twice tasted the 1923. The second encounter, in 1990, was the more impressive, as the earlier bottle was a touch oxidized. The second had evolved aromas of barley-sugar and caramelized orange, but the wine was vigorous and elegant on the palate, and still moderately sweet. It wasn't going to improve, but it was still extremely healthy. The 1931 was lean and acidic, but stylish and long, and not as good as the 1934, which was still fresh and concentrated, with honeyed botrytis on the nose and only a slight raisiny quality on the palate to suggest its advanced age. The 1935 and 1939 were pleasant, but in decline. The 1945 and 1947, which I have never tasted, must have been glorious, and good wine was made in 1962. No La Tour-Blanche was bottled in 1963, 1964 and 1968, showing greater restraint and wisdom than Yquem during this period. The 1970s proved to be a lacklustre decade and the watery, ungainly 1975 was especially disappointing. The 1976 was marginally better, but should be drunk up. The sulphur dioxide must have been added with a heavy hand, as I found the 1977, 1978 and 1981 scarcely drinkable, hot, clammy wines with no charm and little future.

The 1983 also shows excessive sulphur and lacked weight and complexity in its youth. I have not tasted the wine since 1988, so perhaps it has filled out with age and lost its initial pungency and coarseness. The 1985, harvested in seven *tries*, is very sweet but one-dimensional, but with the 1986 there are distinct signs of improvement. Soft and lush, it lacks flair and is very good rather than great. The 1987 is very good for the vintage, a pretty, well-made wine with a pleasing hint of embonpoint. Its abrupt finish suggests that it should not be kept too long.

The 1988 is impressive and improving from year to year. It remains closed on the nose, but is rich and ripe on the palate, with a pineapple tanginess and intensity. With 5.6° of residual sugar, it is distinctly sweet, but not unbalanced. The 1989 is more powerful, packed with ripe apricot flavours and with very good length. Yet I prefer the 1988, which is more classic and tightly structured. The exceptionally sweet 1990 (it has 7.2° of *liqueur*) is superb: the oak doesn't dominate the fruit, which is rich and concentrated and in perfect balance; a wine with a great future. The 1991 is lean but attractive, with candied flavours and plenty of acidity; it should develop quite rapidly into a savoury and vivacious bottle. There isn't much of it, only 5,000 bottles; La Tour-Blanche lost 90 per cent of its crop to frost, the yield was a trifling 3 hl./ha. and much of that was declassified. In 1992, the late ripening here meant that by the time the grapes were ready to pick, the rain was falling. Château Rieussec was already picking its second *trie* when La Tour-Blanche was attempting its first. Jausserand was unhappy with the quality and there will be no La Tour-Blanche from either 1992 or 1993.

The wines may be bought directly from the estate. About 35 per cent of production is exported.

Jean-Pierre Jausserand, Château La Tour-Blanche, Bommes, 33210 Langon, telephone: 57 980270, fax: 57 980278

8

The Premiers Crus *of Sauternes,*
Preignac and Fargues

CHÂTEAU GUIRAUD

It is quite surprising that the 1855 classification could designate only one wine, other than Yquem, as a *Premier Cru* from Sauternes itself. Guiraud is a very large estate that has had mixed fortunes during this century, but at its best it is a splendid and highly individual wine.

You won't find Guiraud's name in the 1855 classification because at that time the estate was known as Château Bayle. No one has definitively established the derivation of that original name. In the early eighteenth century, the property was owned by Marie-Catherine de Mons and her husband. In 1730, the estate passed to their daughter and subsequently to her brother Joseph; he in turn left it to his nephew. In 1759, it passed out of the family when it was sold, as were so many Sauternes estates, to the family of a Bordeaux wine merchant. The new owner was Pierre Guiraud and his family retained the property until 1846, when it was purchased by a consortium. It was not until the early nineteenth century that references testify to the high quality of the wine from Guiraud. The estate changed hands a number of times until 1867, when it was acquired by the wealthy Bernard family; they expanded the vineyards to more or less their present size and built the grandiose but dignified château with its mansard roof. Under the Bernards' management, the wines became first-rate and fetched high prices. The Bernard daughters married into the Irish Maxwell family, who took on the stewardship of the property from 1910 to 1932, when it was sold at auction to Paul Rival.

Rival's home base was in Provence and he would commute to Guiraud in his private plane. His commitment to his new possession soon diminished and Rival was profoundly disturbed by the damage inflicted by German troops during the Second World War. He became a recluse, the château was never properly repaired, the cellars became grubbier with each passing year, and the quality of the wine inevitably deteriorated. He put the château up for sale and after protracted negotiations with various would-be purchasers, including the Champagne house of Roederer, he finally sold the estate in July 1981.

The new owner was Frank Narby, an Egyptian-born shipowner who had settled in Canada. He installed his son Hamilton as manager of the estate. Hamilton was appalled by the condition of the property when he moved in. Under Rival the wine had been aged in cement vats, and the *barriques* that remained were ancient and unusable. Hamilton sold them off for 30 francs each. The handsome château was restored and the public were welcomed to the estate, as they still are. The Narbys could afford to sink a small fortune into Guiraud and Hamilton always insisted he wasn't so much interested in making a profit as in challenging the supremacy of Yquem. Given the condition of the vineyards and cellars, it would clearly be a while before Guiraud was in a position to do so, but the estate had had a fine reputation at the turn of the century and, as the only Sauternes *Premier Cru*, if any wine should have been capable of rivalling Yquem, it was Guiraud.

Hamilton Narby was a charming, slightly raffish young man who brought some badly needed fresh air and dynamism into the Sauternais. Not only did he resuscitate Guiraud with considerable energy, but he also opened a stylish restaurant in the village which still exists under new management as Le Saprien. To be fair to his neighbours, there was no resentment that I could ever discern at his energetic attempt to revive the splendours of Guiraud. Unfortunately, in 1986 Hamilton had a row with his father which led to his departure two years later. The estate was placed under the management of the very capable Xavier Planty, who had been *régisseur* ever since the Narbys acquired the property. Planty, who was formerly the *régisseur* at Château La Gaffelière in Saint-Émilion, is still there, though the Narby family keeps a close interest in Guiraud and all its workings. Hamilton's younger brother Jeremy, an anthropologist based in Switzerland, visits Guiraud as often as he can.

The renovations at Château Guiraud are still not complete. The present *chais* can accommodate 230 *barriques*, but work is under way to expand it so that it can house 400 *barriques* by the time the 1995 vintage begins.

The soil is typical Sauternes, consisting of sand, gravel and a little clay, resting on a varied subsoil of clay, limestone and fossils. The gravel is quite thick and there have been problems with drainage. Where vines have been replanted, the drainage system has been repaired or installed, but older sections of the vineyard can suffer from excessive humidity, which can damage the vines. The red grapes Rival had planted here, mostly Merlot, were grubbed up by Narby. The replanting has been extensive, so, as at Château Rayne-Vigneau, the vines are on average much younger than they ideally should be. At present, 85 ha. are under vine and yields are kept low at an average of 14 hl./ha.

The *encépagement* is quite unusual, as 35 per cent of the vines are Sauvignon, which Paul Rival had planted because of its relatively high yields. In the 1970s, the proportion of Sauvignon had been much higher, but the Narbys' replanting programme has redressed the balance to some extent. The remainder is Sémillon, with just a few rows of Muscadelle, which isn't used for Guiraud as Planty doesn't care for the variety here in Sauternes, though he admits it can be a useful component in a Preignac or Barsac. Planty is not displeased by the high proportion of Sauvignon, which he particularly likes when botrytized. 'In poor vintages,' he says, 'it's not much use, but in outstanding years it's wonderful, adding smoky flavours to the wines.' Most estates in the region pick Sauvignon quite early, to give the blend aroma and freshness. Planty disagrees and says that many estates pick Sauvignon early as an insurance policy; they want to avoid risk, but they are missing out on the elegance that nobly rotten Sauvignon can bring to the blend. Excess Sauvignon is used to make a dry white wine called 'G'.

Grapes are not picked until they have reached a potential alcohol of at least 18°. The *grand vin* is never chaptalized. There is no cryo-extraction, despite the early experiments carried out here. Xavier Planty acknowledges its usefulness, but finds no compelling reason to employ it regularly at Guiraud. Since 1990 the grapes have been pressed in pneumatic presses. After a brief *débourbage*, some of the must is fermented in stainless-steel tanks. To kill the yeasts, the wine is chilled to -4°. Increasingly, however, Guiraud is being fermented in *barriques*. In 1988, one-third was barrel-fermented; by 1990, the proportion had risen to 45 per cent; in 1992, the whole crop, which was not much, was fermented and aged in *barriques*. In lighter years such as 1984 and 1992, the wine was aged in barrels for eighteen months, but in top vintages such as 1989 and 1990, the wine spent thirty months in *barriques*, of which almost half were new.

The wine is racked every three months and progressively blended to give three or four super-lots, which will eventually compose the *grand vin*. Sometimes the blending process is simple; in 1990, the *assemblage* was over within three months. In a trickier vintage such as the sodden 1987, eighteen months elapsed before the final blend emerged. The wine is chilled to precipitate tartrate crystals and there is a single filtration before bottling, which takes place three years after the harvest. The maximum production is about 120,000 bottles.

The wines are sold directly from the property, which is open to the public seven days a week. In the hall of the château stands a table with a bowl containing soils from various parcels of the Guiraud vineyards. A tasting is usually offered in one of the stylishly panelled reception rooms on the ground floor. Even in 1994, vintages dating back to 1976 were still for sale. Guiraud is one of the most expensive Sauternes, and prices rose steadily once the Narbys arrived and began to invest in the property. In 1980, the *prix de sortie* had been 48 francs, rising to 60 francs in 1981 and 65 francs in 1982. With the fine 1983 vintage the opening price leapt to 90 francs, and the 1985 was probably overpriced at 135 francs. In 1994, the superb vintages of the late 1980s are available from the château at between 220 and 240 francs. Perhaps as a way of stimulating sales, Guiraud was the first estate to start bottling its wines in 50–cl. bottles, I imagine on the grounds that a half-bottle is too small for a dinner party of four or five, and a whole 75–cl. bottle is too much (not with my dinner guests). Planty says the innovation has proved a commercial success.

The oldest Guiraud I have tasted is the 1921, which was becoming maderized. There was *crème brûlée* on the nose, a common feature of venerable Sauternes, and still plenty of concentration and vivid fruit on the palate. But the acidity and alcohol were poking through and the wine was in decline. Some celebrated wines were made at Guiraud in the first decade of the twentieth century, but I have never tasted them. The 1929 was renowned and there were a few good wines made by Rival, for all his lack of commitment to the estate, in 1942, 1959, 1962 and 1967. I never much liked the 1975, a modest wine from a great vintage. The 1976 was probably over-botrytized and took on a very deep and later mahogany colour with alarming rapidity. By 1993, the wine was baked and peachy on the nose, but was coarsening on the palate and the alcohol, always marked, was becoming obtrusive.

The 1979 was attractive when young, but showed a worrying flabbiness. Sulphur marred the 1981, leaving the wine harsh and bitter for many years. Like many other estates that harvest late, Guiraud was caught out in 1982 and 60 per cent of the crop had to be rejected. The final blend was caramelly, but lacking in generosity – a disappointing wine. With the 1983, Guiraud at last turned the corner and produced a splendid wine. The grapes were heavily botrytized and the average must weight was 19.7°; the first *tries* were the best. It was rich and toasty and concentrated from the outset, and by 1994 had developed real complexity: the nose was floral, nutty, slightly petrolly, while on the palate there were hints of woodsmoke and grilled nuts. It is probably nearing its peak. The 1985 was good, but lacked botrytis and complexity. Like other estates, Guiraud had to labour mightily in 1985; eight *tries* continued into early December, although fewer than half the grapes found their way into the *grand vin*.

In 1986, Guiraud produced a richly fruity wine from four *tries*, now showing tangerines, peaches and vanilla on the nose. Unfortunately the balance was not perfect, and the wine seems to lack acidity and class. I suspect it will evolve quite swiftly. The 1988 is delicious. It had an orangey opulence in its youth, but bottle-age has allowed its elegance and richness of extract to emerge. The Sauvignon keeps this powerful wine vivid and fresh, and its exemplary length suggests it will be very long-lived. The massive 1989 has a slightly odd nose, with the petrolly tones that I often discern with Guiraud. The palate, however, is incredibly rich, extracted and persistent, and has the smokiness that Planty attributes to heavily botrytized Sauvignon Blanc. The 1990, picked in a single *trie* from 11 to 25 September, is even better, richly botrytized on the nose and with a tremendous attack on the palate; the fruit is super-ripe and opulent, the oak beautifully integrated, the length superb and the finish bracing. This is a wine for the long haul, unlike the sappy, apricotty 1992 which, thanks to the vagaries of this difficult vintage, contains 75 per cent Sauvignon. Only 21,000 bottles were produced. No 1991 was bottled.

Guiraud is now hitting its stride. Xavier Planty is fully aware of the occasional defects in the wines, which are attributable not to any lack of skill on his part, but to the youth of the vines and to a breadth and power in the wine that outweighs its finesse in some vintages. Hamilton Narby's great ambition to challenge Yquem has not yet been realized, but Guiraud is certainly worthy of its classification, which was not the case during the Rival years.

Xavier Planty, Château Guiraud, Sauternes, 33210 Langon, telephone: 56 636101, fax: 56 766752

CHÂTEAU RIEUSSEC

Château Rieussec is the only *Premier Cru* in Fargues, although the vines come right up to the boundaries of Yquem and Sauternes. A tall, rather ugly tower gives a fine view over the vineyards, as Rieussec is on one of the highest slopes in the Sauternais. Topographers bicker about whether the hill at Yquem or Rieussec is higher.

Until the Revolution it was a monastic possession, owned by the same Carmelite order after which the Graves estate of Carmes-Haut-Brion is still known. After the Revolution, it was appropriated by the state and sold off to a gentleman named Mareilhac. Its wine does not seem to have enjoyed much of a reputation and was regarded as a second growth in the early nineteenth century. Between 1846 and 1872, a small part of the estate was purchased by Monsieur Maillé, who owned the *Deuxième Cru* Château Pexoto and sold the wine under the name of Pexoto-Rieussec. After the owner of Rieussec, Charles Crespin, bought back those vines from Pexoto (which was soon to be absorbed in the Rabaud estate), he acquired the exclusive right to sell his wine as Château Rieussec.

The property was inherited in 1892 by Paul Defolie, who instigated improvements and expanded the vineyards by acquiring a neighbouring property. New proprietors followed thick and fast in the early twentieth century. They included the Vicomte du Bouzet and his American brother-in-law P. F. Berry. Monsieur Gérard Balaresque was the owner from 1957 to 1971, when Albert Vuillier bought the estate. Vuillier, the owner of a chain of supermarkets, was always committed to Rieussec and lived at the château. When he took over, the vineyards had deteriorated and many parcels had to be replanted; there was no new wood in the *chai*. In 1984, Château Rieussec was purchased by the Lafite-Rothschild group and Charles Chevallier was installed as director in the following year. Vuillier lingered on at Rieussec for a while, finally leaving his much-loved estate in 1986. The *régisseur* is Bertrand Latastère, who has worked at Rieussec since he was fifteen years old.

In 1949, Cocks & Féret recorded the area of white vines at Rieussec as 50 ha. Today, the area under vine is 75 ha., all entitled to the Sauternes appellation; 72.5 ha. are in production. Part of the reason for this seeming expansion is that vineyards planted with Sauvignon that used to have the simple Bordeaux appellation were reclassified as Sauternes vines in the 1980s. In addition, the estate has leased the 8–ha. parcel called Clos Pilotte which adjoins Château de Fargues. The soil on this large estate is varied, as one would expect; there is plenty of gravel, and a subsoil dominated by limestone and clay.

The vines at Rieussec, which on average are about thirty years old, are precocious and usually ripen up to a week earlier than those at Yquem. The *encépagement* is 89 per cent Sémillon, 8 per cent Sauvignon and 3 per cent Muscadelle. The density is 7,000 vines per ha. Average yields are quite high, at 22 hl./ha., but usually about half the wine is rejected during the *assemblage*. Chevallier says that harvesting has become much more selective since the mid-1980s. This is probably in response to the criticism I sometimes heard that Rieussec was less than fanatical in its grape selection and took the easier alternative of simply eliminating lots later on if they didn't seem up to standard.

Thanks to the Rothschild investment, Rieussec is very well equipped. The grapes are pressed in pneumatic presses and chaptalized when necessary. After a *débourbage*, the must is fermented in stainless-steel tanks at a temperature of 20–21°C. Sulphur dioxide is added to kill the yeasts when the wine is balanced. Rieussec used to spend eighteen to twenty months in *barriques*, of which half were new. Château Lafite-Rothschild has a full-time cooper, who supplies and maintains the *barriques* at Rieussec. Since 1988, Chevallier has been leaving the wine slightly longer in wood, up to twenty-four months. This has been possible since the enlargement of the *chai de barriques*, allowing two harvests to be kept there for at least two years. The *chai* was air-conditioned in 1989.

Rieussec is no longer sold *en primeur*, so there is no rush to create the final blend of the *grand vin*. The wine is chilled to get rid of any tartrate crystals, filtered *sur terre* (a relatively light form of filtration through ground, fossilized shells) and filtered again immediately before bottling. Many rejected lots end up in the *deuxièmes vins*, Clos Labère and Château Mayne des Carmes. The wines are not necessarily identical, but the estate insists they are of the same quality, the two labels being used for different markets.

Rieussec has been undergoing an identity crisis. The wine always used to be described as aromatic, elegant, understated, yet powerful. Under Albert Vuillier's direction the style changed: the wine became darker, richer, heavier and more *rôti* or raisiny in flavour. Many drinkers enjoyed this lush, unctuous style, with its honeyed botrytis character, but it was not the traditional Rieussec. Now Chevallier is trying to restore the finesse of Rieussec without sacrificing its generosity of fruit.

The oldest Rieussec I have tasted was the 1926, a good vintage overshadowed by the 1928 and 1929. The wine was drying out, certainly, but still had good concentration, and the sweetness was being replaced by a nutty austerity that was by no means unpleasant. The 1959 was marvellous. It always had a tremendous attack on the palate, and an elegance that survived an onslaught of apricot and barley-sugar flavours; it had wonderful length too. The 1961, 1962, 1967 and 1970 were good if not great; they were mostly simple wines that lacked flair and excitement. The 1971, however, was lovely, a big, ripe, peachy wine that never became heavy or unbalanced; its tangy, clean finish suggests it still has plenty of life left in it.

The 1975 was a typical Vuillier wine: deep gold in colour, with aromas of marmalade as well as peaches; lush, orangey, caramel flavours on the palate and, in recent years, a nagging acidity on the finish that indicates it may soon fall apart. The 1976 was similar, very forward and distinctly raisiny; a little of this goes a long way and the wine is probably already past its best. The 1979 is far too alcoholic, soupy and coarse, and is already cracking up. But I find the 1980 charming; it is no heavyweight, but finely balanced and rich in botrytis flavours.

The 1982 Rieussec is surprisingly good, despite a curious banana and raisin nose; on the palate it is plump, with good fresh acidity and spiciness, and by 1993 it had gained in complexity and balance. The 1983 is a great Rieussec, though some years ago it was evolving so fast that I feared it would go the way of the geriatric 1975 and 1976. But this rich, honeyed, fruit-salady wine is holding up well; perhaps it has a touch too much alcohol and there's not much elegance here, but no one could complain about a lack of fruit, concentration or botrytis. The 1984 was good for the vintage, but is now ready to drink. The 1985, picked in seven *tries*, is average for the year: little botrytis, a slight soapiness on the palate and insufficient fruit to balance the alcohol.

The peachy, oaky 1986 is another sumptuous wine, lush and almost oily on the palate, powerful rather than elegant, but silkily textured and highly extracted. The final *trie* in 1986 was not used for the *grand vin*. The 1987 was one of the best wines from that modest vintage. The 1988, made from eight *tries* which continued until 18 November, struck me as somewhat coarse and dour in its youth, but by 1994 it had settled down into a deep, oaky wine, perhaps still a little burly and inelegant, but with ample botrytis and very good length. The 1989 was all picked in October. It was forward in its youth but has since closed up, which is no bad sign. It has a fine golden colour, peaches and botrytis on the nose, delicious fruit, and fine concentration and length. Even the second wine, Clos Labère, was excellent in 1989, though less high-powered than the *grand vin*. I have tasted the exceptionally sweet 1990 only from cask, but it seemed highly promising. Because of the precocity of its vines, Rieussec was able to start harvesting on 2 September and completed the harvest on 4 October. Rieussec made a small quantity of 1992, some 20,000 bottles, which was not wildly interesting, but will be a satisfactory wine for the short term. It was picked before the rain and the yield was a minute 3 hl./ha. Fermentation was stopped at 13.5° of alcohol to keep the wine fresh and light; like the 1991, it was only aged for eighteen months in oak. There were four *tries* in 1993, but only 30 per cent of the normal crop was picked.

Maximum production is just over 100,000 bottles, the quantity produced in 1988, 1989 and 1990. There are no direct sales from the château. Rieussec also produces a dry and rather costly white wine – half Sémillon, half Sauvignon – called 'R', which used to be somewhat coarse, but has improved greatly in recent years. Since 1990, Charles Chevallier has stopped ageing the dry wine in oak, and the vintages of the 1990s are fresher and cleaner.

Charles Chevallier, Château Rieussec, Fargues, 33210 Langon, telephone: 56 622071, fax: 56 762782

CHÂTEAU SUDUIRAUT

It's not every château in the Bordeaux region that can boast of gardens laid out by Le Nôtre, who designed the park at Versailles. Mature cedars and other magnificent trees dominate the park. The château is also splendid, a broad structure dating from about 1670 that replaced an earlier mansion destroyed by fire. Small pepperpot turrets add an oddly medieval touch to an otherwise classical façade. The pediment over the entrance bears the arms of the Suduirauts (boar heads) and the Du Roys (ermine). Iron gates close off the courtyard, but there is no longer a family behind the gates seeking some privacy. Château Suduiraut is uninhabited and the property of an insurance company.

During the late eighteenth century a family called Suduiraut owned the estate. After the Revolution, one of the Suduiraut daughters married a gentleman named Du Roy. The tag 'Cru du Roy' was added to the label, later altered to 'Ancien Cru du Roy', until the late 1980s, when the line was sensibly dropped. I am sure I am not alone in having long interpreted this slogan as implying that the estate used to be a royal domaine. Nothing of the sort. After the sale of the property in the mid-nineteenth century to the Guillot family, it passed through many hands until in 1940 it was acquired by an industrialist from northern France, Léopold Fonquernie. He made significant improvements to the estate and at first imposed rigorous standards on its harvesting procedures. After his death his five daughters took command, which made life none too easy for Pierre Pascaud, the able *régisseur*, who could never be quite sure from whom he should take his orders. This slightly unhappy situation came to an end when in 1992 the French insurance company AXA bought a majority share in the property, which had apparently been appraised at the astonishing figure of $38.5 million. Pierre Pascaud has a new spring in his step.

Acquisition by an insurance company sounds like a kiss of death, but AXA owns a number of Pauillac classified growths such as Châteaux Lynch-Bages and Pichon-Longueville-Baron, and the wines, especially from the latter, have greatly improved under their regime. Behind the bland name of the company is the dynamic figure of Jean-Michel Cazes, who is interested in quality above all else.

Château Suduiraut, the sole *Premier Cru* of Preignac, is a large estate, with 62 ha. under vine, of which two are renewed each year. The estate actually encompasses just over 100 ha. entitled to the appellation, but authorization has not been granted to plant them as yet.[23] Should that occur, Suduiraut will become as large an estate as Yquem. The vineyards surround the château and reach as far as the hamlet of Butoc. They are at the southern edge of Preignac and close to those of Yquem. But the soil is lighter and poorer than that of Yquem; it is essentially sand and gravel. The *encépagement* is the conventional 80 per cent Sémillon and 20 per cent Sauvignon, and the average age of the vines is about twenty-five years, though some are in their seventh decade. The vines are planted to a high density, about 7,000 per ha.

Since 1978, the *régisseur* is the proud, confident, amiable Pierre Pascaud, now assisted by his son Alain. Before his arrival the estate replaced most of its *barriques* with cement tanks; the wine spent only one year in wood. Suduiraut was not the only *Premier Cru* to offend in this way; exactly the same thing was happening at Lafaurie-Peyraguey. But even worse, there was virtually no selection during the *assemblage*. Indeed, one wonders whether there was any *assemblage* to speak of. Some of Suduiraut's distributors were not slow to spot the consequent deterioration in the quality of the wine, so perhaps it was commercial pressure that eventually persuaded Léopold Fonquernie to return to traditional winemaking. Whatever the reason, Pascaud sensibly restored barrel-ageing on coming to Suduiraut. The wines showed an immediate improvement in quality.

Pascaud has always favoured relatively early harvesting. He claims that this is because of the precocity of the vines which derives from the microclimate. Not everyone is convinced by the argument and there is some suspicion that the early harvesting

23 Before new vineyards can be planted, even where a right to plant exists, old vineyards must be grubbed up so that the overall area under vine does not increase. Hence the odd practice of some Sauternes estates of purchasing vineyards in the Graves or Médoc and then uprooting them as a preliminary rigmarole before planting new vineyards in Sauternes.

has more to do with expediency than microclimate. The policy has certainly led to some atypical vintages at Suduiraut. Pascaud also insists that Suduiraut is not one of the heavier wines of Sauternes because of its meagre sandy soil, yet most top vintages from here have been extremely rich.

Pierre Pascaud readily admits to chaptalizing up to 2° when the grapes are insufficiently rich. Yields are moderate, usually between 15 and 18 hl./ha. The fermentation used to take place in stainless-steel tanks, but Pascaud has reverted to barrel-fermentation for the best lots. Until 1992, only the 1988 had been partly barrel-fermented. No doubt with the approval of Jean-Michel Cazes, *barrique*-fermentation will become more common.

The wine is racked in the early spring and if it is sufficiently limpid, it is then decanted into barrels, 30 per cent of which are new oak, where it stays in *barriques* for up to two years. It is widely believed that the advantage of barrel-fermentation over barrel-ageing alone is that it permits a better integration of oak and wine. Pascaud, however, believes the *élevage* of the wine has more influence over its eventual character and quality than how it has been fermented. It is filtered and bottled about two and a half years after the harvest.

Like Château Coutet, Suduiraut will, in outstanding vintages, release a special *cuvée* of extreme richness. Suduiraut made an outstanding 1982; the estate's policy of early harvesting was in their favour and superb grapes had been picked before the rainfall that interrupted the harvests in early October. (Pascaud recalls that Pierre Meslier spotted the Suduiraut harvesters at work by 16 September and ordered the Yquem team out into the vineyards on the following day.) The best lots were picked on 26 September and 4,800 bottles were released as a Crème de Tête with about 7° of residual sugar. Another Crème de Tête was produced in 1989. The quantity was slightly larger, at 6,000 bottles, and the grapes were picked on 16 October. The wine was aged, but not fermented, in new oak for thirty-eight months. No Crème de Tête was made in 1990 because the overall quality of the fruit was so high and because botrytis spread too rapidly; Pascaud didn't want to do anything that would detract from the harvesting. Pascaud is under no pressure to make a special *cuvée* in every fine vintage. If the circumstances arise which permit it, well and good.

To the argument that such *cuvées* inevitably diminish the average quality of the regular bottling, Pascaud replies that 6,000 bottles out of a total of 150,000 aren't going to make a great difference. Jean-Michel Cazes, on taking over Suduiraut, shared the doubts about making such wines, but has subsequently changed his mind.

Suduiraut has long been one of the most expensive Sauternes. In 1994, the 1989 was available from the château at 250 francs; the Crème de Tête from the same vintage cost 750 francs. Suduiraut was much criticized by the wine trade for the high opening price of its 1989; for the 1990 the price came down slightly and at the château bottles are sold for 230 francs. Suduiraut is much coveted on the international market and about 70 per cent of the production is exported.

Suduiraut at its best is a glorious wine. It pleases the eye too, as good vintages soon develop a golden and then coppery glow. In 1949, Cocks & Féret remarked on the high proportion of *vins de tête* that had traditionally been used at Suduiraut, which accounted for its richness. There is flowery peachiness on the nose, and usually rich, honeyed fruit on the palate, which has finesse as well as power. When Suduiraut is great, it is classic Sauternes. It showed well in the outstanding vintages of old: 1893, 1899, 1928 and 1959. The 1967 was the last great vintage before the estate's bad patch in the first half of the 1970s. The 1970 is very sweet but lacks complexity. The 1975 was good, but lacked freshness and vigour, and is now becoming tarry. The deep gold 1976 is richer, with *confit* aromas, a chewy marmalade flavour and sufficient freshness to prevent the wine becoming blowsy. The velvety 1979 is smoky on the nose and harmonious on the palate, but overshadowed by the 1982, one of the outstanding wines of the vintage. The average must weights of the grapes were about 19.5°. Even so, it doesn't show much botrytis on nose or palate and has soft, sweet lanolin flavours rather than honeyed richness. The 1982 Crème de Tête, which I have not tasted, is said to be superb.

The 1983, picked in four *tries* between 26 September and 10 November, is good but not as exceptional as one has a right to expect from a *Premier Cru* in an outstanding vintage. It simply lacks complexity, intensity and depth, and when I tasted it blind in 1987 and again in 1992, it seemed more like a Barsac than a Preignac. In 1985, to make good wine, estates had to wait and wait in order to obtain nobly rotten fruit. It seems that Suduiraut, as usual, picked too early, completing the harvest after five *tries*, whereas many other estates had to comb the vineyards eight or ten times to obtain fruit of sufficient quality. The 1985 shows little botrytis, little elegance and little length. A Crème de Tête was made from grapes picked in late September.

What went wrong in 1986? It should have been a classic vintage for Suduiraut, but the wine is a severe disappointment: citric, rather than peachy; light and lean, rather than rich. Fortunately the 1988, picked in seven *tries* from 25 September to 8 November, shows a vast improvement. This is what Suduiraut should be like: yellow-gold in colour, an oaky apricot nose and lively peachy flavours on the palate. In 1994, it was still rather closed and adolescent, not yet in harmony, but it should evolve well. The 1989 is richer, opulent but not heavy, and with firm extract and surprising elegance for the vintage. It is more open than the 1989, but will age very well. The 1989 Crème de Tête is fabulous: sumptuous botrytis on the nose and almost syrupy on the palate, densely peachy and honeyed, and immensely concentrated; a very great Sauternes.

The 1990 is another monster: very high in alcohol and rich in residual sugar. Yet it is finely balanced wine, well structured, with rich, oaky flavours and dried-apricot intensity. All the elements are in harmony – oak, alcohol, acidity – and its superb length suggests that it will be a great Suduiraut. Pascaud believes it is the best Suduiraut since 1959. Suduiraut was the only top estate in the Sauternais to announce that it would bottle no *grand vin* from the 1991, 1992 and 1993 vintages, although 50,000 bottles of a second wine, Castelnau de Suduirat (a new departure for the château), were released from the 1993 vintage. No doubt the mighty resources of AXA make such high-minded dedication feasible.

Pierre Pascaud, Château Suduiraut, Preignac, 33210 Langon, telephone: 56 632729, fax: 56 630700

9

The Deuxièmes Crus *of Barsac*

CHÂTEAU BROUSTET

In the early nineteenth century, Broustet was joined with Nairac and was known both as Broustet and as Broustet-Nérac. Both estates were owned by Bernard Capdeville. In 1855, the joint estate was classified as *Deuxième Cru*. After Capdeville died in 1861, the estate was split and Château Broustet was acquired by his daughter, who was married to the owner of Château de Myrat, Henri Moller, while Château Nairac was inherited by the other sister. Mme Moller ran the estate for a while as Myrat-Broustet. Broustet was sold as a separate 10–ha. estate to the Fournier family of Saint-Émilion in the late 1880s; they prized the property more for the Gabriel Supau cooperage based here than for its wine. Until 1994, the estate remained in the hands of the Fourniers' great-grandson, Eric Fournier, who managed the property. As Fournier lives at Château Canon, the splendid Saint-Émilion estate, the day-to-day supervision of Broustet was entrusted to the *maître de chai*, Roland Faugère. In 1992, one of Eric Fournier's brothers wanted to dispose of his share of the Fournier estates and so Broustet was put up for sale. In 1994, the property was finally sold to Didier Laulan of Château Saint-Marc, which adjoins Broustet, although the stock remained the property of the Fournier family.

The château at Broustet is a modest house flanked by the air-conditioned *chais*. The 16.5 ha. of vineyards surround the buildings in a single parcel. The soil is varied: near the railway line there is gravel and sand, whereas further west there is clay and red sand over limestone. The average age of the vines is twenty-five years and the *encépagement* is slightly unusual because of the significant proportion, some 7 per cent, of Muscadelle, as well as 68 per cent

Sémillon and 25 per cent Sauvignon. Of the 10 ha. of Muscadelle vines planted in 1910, half still survive. It's a tricky variety to handle, as botrytis (and other less desirable ailments) can attack the bunches early. But Fournier recognized that the proportion of Muscadelle gave Broustet much of its character, so he was keen to retain it in the vineyards. Average yields are 18 hl./ha.

Under the Fournier regime the grapes were pressed in horizontal presses, but in 1991 Fournier installed a gentler pneumatic press. After an overnight *débourbage*, the must was fermented in small, 2,500–litre stainless-steel tanks. The idea was that each tank is roughly equivalent to a single day's harvest, so lots could be separated. There was chaptalization in less ripe vintages, but never by more than a single degree. In vintages such as 1982, 1983 and 1985, when other estates did chaptalize, Broustet did not. Fournier liked a good deal of alcohol, so he allowed the fermentation to continue until the wine acquired about 15°; the wine was then chilled, sulphured and filtered before going into *barriques* for ageing. There was a change of approach in 1988, when Fournier began fermenting some of the wine in *barriques*, of which 30 per cent were new. For the lesser, lighter vintages of 1991 to 1993, he reverted to tank fermentation and Laulan followed suit in 1994.

The *assemblage* took place in the spring after the harvest. The wine spent about sixteen months in oak and was filtered again before bottling. Wine not considered good enough for the *grand vin* was bottled as the second wine, Château de Ségur. The maximum production of Broustet is about 36,000 bottles. There are no direct sales from the château.

This is how Fournier made Broustet; gradually Laulan is sure to introduce changes. The style of Broustet is distinctive, not only because of the unusually high proportion of Muscadelle, but also because of its high alcohol. Broustet has at least 14.5°; sometimes, as in 1989, considerably more. Consequently there is less residual sugar in average vintages. Eric Fournier probably had tradition on his side, as this is how much Barsac used to be vinified in the nineteenth century. There must be a following for this powerful but somewhat ungenerous style, but it has never appealed to me. Nor has the quality been as fine as one feels it should be. This is surprising, given that Château Canon is one of the greatest wines of Saint-Émilion, and the reason may well have been that Fournier never lived at the property.

I have not tasted older vintages of Broustet and they hardly ever seem to appear at auction. The 1947 is reputed to be first-rate. No wine was bottled in 1974, 1976 and 1977. I found the vintages of the early 1980s soft, waxy and rather flabby, with little length of flavour and no charm or finesse. Since the leading attraction of Muscadelle is its aromatic pungency, one would expect to find the aromas flowery and seductive, but all too often they seem deadened by sulphur and somewhat dour. The 1986 was an improvement, but even in this fine vintage there were wet-wool aromas masking the peachiness and an abrasive quality to the palate. The 1988 is an excellent Broustet, though the alcohol is too apparent. It has an apricotty nose, plenty of richness and spice on the palate, but what it lacks is finesse, which a top Barsac should always have. None the less, it is a very good wine and it has a future.

The 1989 certainly shows plenty of new oak on the nose. It seems to have more charm and extract than the 1988, but it's quite heavy too and doesn't have the sensuousness one would hope for in a 1989. The 1990 has 15.5° of alcohol, betrayed by a rather hot finish. The nose is promising, with ample oak and botrytis, but the palate is frankly dull and less concentrated than most 1990s. The wine had not been long in bottle, so it may well have been excessively closed when tasted. No Broustet was bottled in 1991 and only 10,000 bottles will be bottled from the 1992 vintage.

Didier Laulan, Château Broustet, Barsac, 33720 Podensac, telephone: 56 271687, fax: 56 271505

CHÂTEAU CAILLOU

Whenever I drive up to Château Caillou I think I have arrived in Toytown. The nineteenth-century château tries to be imposing but fails completely, as its two flanking turrets are too slender for the body of the building. In the centre of the façade is a large clock, which seems to have been imported from a railway station in Nevada. In the middle of the lawn in front of the château, a gigantic bottle made from cement points its neck ominously at the façade like a cannon. It used to have the Caillou label painted on it, but the feet of various generations of Bravo children have obliterated it.

The estate had a fine reputation in the early nineteenth century and was mentioned by André Jullien in 1816 in the same breath as Coutet, Climens and Doisy; indeed, he called it a *Premier Cru*.

From the late eighteenth century, Caillou was owned by the Sarraute family, who sold it in 1909 to Joseph Ballan, whose daughter married into the Bravo family. In 1990, the formidable Mme Bravo died. Now the third generation of Bravos, the energetic jazz-loving Jean-Bernard and his sister Marie-José Pierre, manage the estate, though relations between the two are far from cordial. Jean-Bernard is assisted by his young *maître de chai* Xavier Pallu, who succeeded the impressively named Jean de Tocqueville in 1991. The property has expanded since it came into the hands of the Bravo family; today 13 ha. are under vine in south-west Barsac, not far from the *autoroute*, and bordered in parts by pine and acacia woods. The vineyard is a single parcel and the soil is typical Barsac: clay and limestone, and a particularly stony subsoil. As at many other Barsac estates, Sémillon dominates with 90 per cent of the vines, the remainder being Sauvignon. Their average age is twenty-five years and they are not planted as densely as at many other estates. Here at Caillou there are 5,500 vines per ha. The average yield is 17 hl./ha.

The vinification is slightly unusual. The grapes are pressed in a sophisticated horizontal press, which Bravo says he finds preferable to pneumatic presses, which give too squeaky-clean a must. The must is fermented in stainless steel and aged in barrels, of which 20 per cent are new each year. (In 1991 he fermented part of the crop in new oak, calling the wine Cuvée Spéciale; part of the 1992 was also barrel-fermented.) Caillou is not usually bottled until two and a half years after the vintage, though in lesser vintages, such as 1992, it is bottled after eighteen months. The style used to be quite alcoholic, but has moderated in recent vintages.

As at Suduiraut and Coutet, special *cuvées* are produced at Caillou, but with greater frequency and with a smaller gap between the price of the two wines. At Caillou the policy is an extension of the Crème de Tête bottlings commonly made fifty years ago from the most botrytized lots. The oldest Caillou I have tasted was a Crème de Tête from 1943. The last Crème de Tête to be thus labelled was the 1975. Since then, the special *cuvée* has been called Private Cuvée. At Coutet, a special parcel of vines is responsible for producing Cuvée Madame; at Caillou the *cuvée* is a selection of the best lots from a particular vintage, and those wines are given a longer ageing in barrel, usually thirty to thirty-six months. Production varies: in 1990 it was 3,000 bottles, and is never more than

6,000. The production of the regular Caillou is up to 40,000 bottles. Private Cuvée has been made in 1981, 1983, 1985, 1986, 1988, 1989 and 1990.

Declassified wines are sold under the labels Château Petit Mayne or Haut-Mayne, two other Barsac properties owned by the Bravo family. Each is only 3 ha. in extent, and their wine is vinified and aged at Caillou. These second wines are identical in terms of quality and style. A third label, Les Tourelles, is used for wines that are *moelleux* rather than *liquoreux* and these are sold only in super-markets or export markets.

One of the attractive features of Château Caillou is its welcome for visitors. Caillou is the least intimidating Sauternes estate, and wines are available for tasting and purchase. The Bravos have delib-erately conserved stocks of older vintages, which are still for sale. In 1994, the oldest vintage available was the 1921. Of course, these older vintages are expensive. The 1976 was priced at 360 francs, the 1975 at 480, the 1967 at 710 and the 1961 at 980. The oldest Private Cuvée for sale is the 1981 (295 francs). The regular 1990 was priced in 1994 at 160 francs, and the Private Cuvée was 230 francs.

Caillou is never among the most impressive or stylish Barsacs, but they do age well. The 1943 Crème de Tête was still going strong in 1984, though I doubt it has improved further. The colour was remarkable, with no browning after forty years in bottle, and there were attractive marmalade aromas; the wine was still extremely sweet, though there was little depth of flavour. The 1947 Crème de Tête was still fresh, yet more evolved on the palate with barley-sugar and orange tones. It wasn't great, but it was very attractive and at its peak after forty years. The 1973 regular bottling, admit-tedly from a modest vintage, was slightly oxidized and clearly tiring. The 1975 Crème de Tête has a great deal of lemony elegance. I found it bland in 1986, but delicious and spicy, though not very complex or rich, in 1994. It is entirely possible, at estates such as Caillou, that there are considerable bottle variations; some wines may have been bottled relatively young, others kept in cask for too long.

The 1976 and 1979 are disappointing, sweet but hollow and too alcoholic. No 1980 was bottled. The 1983 is lean and citric and has little botrytis; pleasant enough, but modest for the vintage. A remarkable *cuvée* was produced in 1985 from grapes picked on 14

December; it was bottled in January 1989, but unfortunately never commercialized. The 1986 is dull and loosely structured; there is botrytis here, cru the thinness of the wine suggests that yields were high. There was a light vintage in 1987, and Caillou's wine is pleasant, lively and sweet; no complexity, but enjoyable young. A great vintage followed in 1988, but the Caillou wine is slight; it is pretty, but lacks concentration and botrytis. This same lack of depth mars the 1989, which is certainly sweet and peachy, but has little complexity. I much preferred the 1990, which is plump and apricotty, and quite stylish. In 1994, the 1990 Private Cuvée was oily and lumpish, though there was plenty of richness and weight; it doesn't have the elegance that Caillou often has in good vintages, but its excellent length suggests that it will settle down and develop into a fine wine.

The standard 1991 (3,000 bottles) showed no botrytis character, but was lemony and stylish. I prefer the 1991 Cuvée Spéciale (1,000 bottles), oaky on the nose – this was barrel-fermented – and richer and more concentrated, with better length. In 1992, some 5,000 bottles were produced, and the wine is assertive and spicy, with quite good length; a great deal of 1992 was declassified, which accounts for the good quality of this wine. No Caillou was bottled in 1993. In 1994, 80 per cent of the crop was lost to spring frost and the eventual yield was a derisory 4 hl./ha., which will give about 1,500 bottles.

Jean-Bernard Bravo is no parochial proprietor. He is worldly and knowledgeable about wine. So it always comes as a surprise that Caillou is not better than it is. Even in top vintages, the wines lack *liqueur*. He says that he does not seek to make a particularly opulent wine; he wants *nervosité*, good acidity and vivacity: '*Un vin jeune et gai et vif.*' The wine has a strong following, so clearly he is pleasing his customers.

Jean-Bernard Bravo, Château Caillou, Barsac, 33720 Podensac, telephone: 56 271638, fax: 56 270960

CHÂTEAU DOISY-DAËNE

The 1855 classification lists as a *Deuxième Cru* a single estate called Château Doisy. It is now three estates, each deservedly with *Deuxième Cru* status. In fact, the unified estate had already been divided by the time the classification was made. What happened remains obscure. An Englishman named Daëne bought one section of about 7 ha.; the Védrines family, who had inhabited Barsac as landowners from at least the early eighteenth century, retained the other, though the management of the vines seems to have been undertaken by the Dubosq family, who are named by Paguierre in 1828 in his listing of Barsac estates. A third section, now Château Doisy-Dubroca, was acquired by Mlle Faux. Clive Coates has pointed out that the Château Doisy of the 1855 classification refers only to M. Daëne's portion, so one could question whether the other two Doisys are entitled to their status.

M. Daëne died in 1863; by 1879, the proprietor was M. Bilot, followed by Jules Debans and M. Dejean, who was associated with the Bordeaux wine merchants Cazelet. In 1924, the modern era at Château Doisy-Daëne began when the estate was acquired by Georges Dubourdieu. It passed to his son Jean and then to his grandson Pierre, the present owner. He inherited the estate as long ago as 1945, though he says he was involved in winemaking here from 1942 onwards. Pierre expanded the estate slightly in the 1960s when he bought part of Château Doisy-Dubroca.

Pierre Dubourdieu is one of the most remarkable and idiosyncratic characters of Bordeaux. He has not the slightest regard for fashion or convention, but is obsessed with the art of vinification. Each of his wines, and he makes more dry wine than Barsac, is crafted into the style that he wants. In an age when the role of the winemaker is being played down so that we can pay greater homage to the *terroir*, Pierre Dubourdieu resolutely remains a manipulator. Fortunately he is a brilliant one and all his wines are superbly made, though whether one likes their style is a matter of personal taste. One senses that for Pierre Dubourdieu, winemaking is an intellectual and technical challenge, a way of finding the best means to specific ends.

When I first met him he told me he disliked Sauternes, a somewhat startling confession from the owner of a leading *cru*. 'As far as I am concerned,' he said airily, 'a single glass of Yquem is plenty for me. I don't make Sauternes,' he added, 'I make Doisy-Daëne.' For all that, Doisy-Daëne is a very fine Barsac.

The Dubourdieus own 55 ha. in all. Doisy-Daëne and another Barsac property, Château Cantegril (which belongs to his wife's family), constitute 16 ha. each; the remaining vineyards are in the Graves. At Doisy-Daëne, the grapes planted are 90 per cent Sémillon and 10 per cent Sauvignon, planted to a density of 7,000 vines per ha. In practice, the Barsac is made solely from Sémillon. The average age of the vines is thirty-five years and the sandy clay soil over limestone ensures good natural drainage.

Pierre and his oenologist son Denis, who gives a helping hand and a helping brain when not preoccupied with his own estates, are pioneers of the new style of dry white Graves: the grapes, when healthy, are macerated before fermentation, and the wines are left on the lees and stirred, which gives the wine greater aromatic power and structure. Dubourdieu used to make a splendid wine called Saint-Martin from late-picked grapes, aged in new *barriques* for a year; the Sauvignon-dominated Doisy Sec is aged on its lees in partially new oak. The aim, says Dubourdieu, is to produce digestible white wines with modest alcohol that can be enjoyed young, but at the same time have depth and complexity. Sadly, Dubourdieu stopped making Saint-Martin in 1989 for reasons connected with his relations with his distributors, but he hopes to revive production before too long.

Dubourdieu is an innovative winemaker, but traditional in his approach to harvesting for sweet wines. He practises up to seven *tries* and seeks botrytized grapes. Unfortunately, from his point of view, botrytis robs the eventual wine of freshness and vigour, so his vinification is directed at preserving those qualities. He respects botrytis, but does not seek grapes with exceptionally high must weights. For his purposes, 17–18° of potential alcohol is sufficient, except in the greatest vintages, such as 1989 and 1990, which allow rich grapes to be vinified without giving the wine undue heaviness. The bane of much winemaking in Sauternes is the excessive use of sulphur dioxide and this Dubourdieu works hard to avoid. He also dislikes chaptalization and for this reason regards cryo-extraction as a godsend. Indeed, he claims to practise it in all vintages, not only in damp ones.

The grapes are pressed in a horizontal press and selected yeasts are added to begin the fermentation. The fermentation used to take place in stainless steel; since 1988, he has reverted to *barrique*-fermentation. Fermentation is arrested by chilling the wine to 2°C, at which temperature it remains for up to three weeks. The wine is then aged in *barriques* from the coopers Séguin-Moreau; one-third of the barrels are new each year and the wine remains in wood for up to two years, sometimes slightly less. (From 1955 to 1975,

Dubourdieu aged the wines in tank.) The *chai de barriques* is chilled to no more than 12°C to prevent too speedy an evolution; the last thing he wants in his wines is any trace of oxidation that would mar its essential freshness. Before bottling, the wine is fined and given a sterile filtration. I have read elsewhere that the wine is filtered repeatedly, but Dubourdieu says this is not the case and the wine is only filtered once. The vinification process allows him to keep sulphur-dioxide levels low, and even in rich vintages such as 1989 and 1990, when you need to use more sulphur because of the risk of secondary fermentation, he was able to keep the levels of total sulphur below 250 milligrams per litre.

Dubourdieu experiments tirelessly. In 1978, a year when botrytis was virtually absent, he covered some of his vines with clear plastic sheeting until Christmas, when he harvested the shrivelled grapes. I haven't tasted the wine, but Clive Coates in his journal *The Vine* describes it as follows: 'The nearest thing to Dubourdieu's wine I have tasted recently was a Vin de Paille made by Chapoutier in 1985. The Vin de Noël has naturally high alcohol, very little botrytis flavour, is fat, oily and slightly oxidised on the nose, even a little burnt and spirity, but on the palate it is fresh, supple, complex and intriguing.'

In 1990, when must weights were astonishingly high, Dubourdieu made 2,400 half-bottles of a wine he justifiably called l'Extravagant de Doisy-Daëne. The grapes were picked in mid-November (some three weeks after the end of the last *trie* here and elsewhere), by which time they had attained 42° Baumé. When the fermentation finally ended, the wine had a balance of 15.5° of alcohol and 23° of residual sugar. Pierre Dubourdieu allowed me to gaze with admiration on a bottle, but understandably didn't pull the cork, as he is selling each half-bottle for 500 francs.

The style of Doisy-Daëne is very consistent. It is light, but not deficient in flavour; it is invariably stylish, but rarely opulent; its most remarkable characteristic is a great purity of flavour. That is precisely what Dubourdieu is aiming for and he usually achieves it. 'For me,' he says with typical dogmatism, 'the taste of honey in Sauternes is an abomination.' Although Doisy-Daëne is fairly light, it ages well as a consequence of the reductive winemaking, which deters any oxidation that could age the wine too rapidly. The maximum production is 60,000 bottles and the wines can be bought directly from the château. Almost half the wine is exported.

Pierre Dubourdieu affects a certain gruffness and does not have a high opinion of journalists and wine writers. None the less, he has always been generous in allowing me to taste his wines. A famous vintage occurred here in 1943 when the grapes had an average must weight of 21°. It spent four years in barrels. In 1986 it was just beginning to fade, but was still a gorgeously intense figgy wine, though fresher on the nose than the palate. Subsequent vintages that were outstanding include the 1945, 1953, 1961, 1962 and 1970. The 1970 was rich, but had tremendous vigour on the nose and palate, concentrated and classy, and long in flavour. Neither this wine nor the 1971 was barrel-aged, and in the 1971 it shows on the less complex palate, though the wine has charm and freshness; the nose, suggestive of mango and banana, is atypical. A tasting organized by the Gault-Millau journal acclaimed, of all vintages, the 1972, which I have not tasted.

The 1975 is perhaps too light for the vintage, although it is impeccably balanced. The 1976 is richer, more *rôti*, with flavours of tangerine and apricot, and, unlike some 1976s, not tiring in the least. The 1980 is a disappointment; the 1981 has a better repu-tation, though I have not tasted it; and the 1982 is one of the best from this difficult vintage: it has a fresh pineapple nose and surprising plumpness, as well as elegance on the palate. The 1983 is very fine: not enormously botrytized, rich but not viscous, stylish and with good length – very Doisy. The 1984 was never very interesting, but I certainly liked the 1985 in its youth; how well it has aged, I do not know. I confess to some disappointment with the 1986. After an awkward youth it has developed into a plump, melony wine, soft and gentle, but not very concentrated.

The 1988, made after seven *tries*, is quintessential Doisy-Daëne: sweet, delicate, racy, with delicious pure fruit and great elegance. It should age into a classic Barsac. The 1989 is much fatter, nicely concentrated, charming and long. I suspect it is too voluptuous for Dubourdieu's personal taste, but I like it greatly. The 1990, like most wines from this vintage, is high in alcohol (14.8°) and residual sugar. I tasted it from cask and again in 1994, when it was still far too youthful to judge, but it was evidently well-structured, elegant and packed with fruit; its impeccable length suggests the wine will age very well. The 1991 is light, sweet and citric, a wine of much charm. Only 25,000 bottles were made and there will be no 1992 or 1993, just as there was no Doisy-Daëne in 1956, 1963, 1965, 1968, 1974 and 1977.

Pierre Dubourdieu is approaching his late seventies, though with his slight build he doesn't look it. It is typical of the man that, in 1994, he was busy building himself new subterranean cellars at Doisy-Daëne. It is this restlessness and drive that infuses the wines from this estate and keeps them so vigorous and interesting.

Pierre Dubourdieu, Château Doisy-Daëne, Barsac, 33720 Podensac, telephone: 56 271584, fax: 56 271899

CHÂTEAU DOISY-DUBROCA

After the division of Château Doisy in the mid-nineteenth century, Mlle Faux became the owner, for a short time, of the portion now known as Château Doisy-Dubroca. The Dubroca family acquired the estate in 1880, when one of the Dubroca daughters married a gentleman called Gounouilhou, who acquired Château Climens in 1885. The fates of Châteaux Climens and Doisy-Dubroca have been linked ever since. In 1949, Cocks & Féret identified the owner of the estate as Marcel Dubroca. When in 1971 Lucien Lurton acquired Climens, he also became the owner of Doisy-Dubroca.

The estate is tiny, a mere 3.8 ha., planted solely with Sémillon. The average age of the vines is twenty-three years and the soil is typical of Barsac, with its red sand and gravel on a limestone base. The vines face south-east and enjoy excellent drainage. The buildings on the estate are somewhat dilapidated, and since the Lurtons don't seem committed to restoring them, other Barsac proprietors have long had their eye on the property. Pierre Dubourdieu of Doisy-Daëne, which adjoins Doisy-Dubroca, did buy some parcels of vines in the 1960s, but Lucien Lurton shows no willingness to sell him the rest of the property, even though the total production from Doisy-Dubroca is a mere 9,000 bottles, a drop in the ocean when set against the production of the Lurton portfolio of estates throughout Bordeaux.

The wine is made by the Climens team, under the direction of Christian Broustaut. Consequently, the vinification is identical to that at Climens. Only the first two pressings are used, and the wine is fermented in barrels and aged for about two years.

Doisy-Dubroca is a wine that used to be seen quite frequently in Britain, but since the early 1990s it seems to have disappeared from the market-place. Its relative obscurity means that it has been underrated. It is not as powerful, sleek and magnificent as Climens, but its style is very similar and its cost much lower, though it is by no means as cheap as it used to be.

As at Climens, the vintages of the 1970s were remarkably good, including difficult years such as 1972 and 1973. The 1976 is said to be exceptional, but the oldest I have tried is the delicious 1979, which was holding up extremely well in 1994, with a lightly honeyed nose, and fine balance and breed on the palate. The 1980 had a nose suggestive of glue, but was quite rich and intense on the palate with ample acidity. The 1981, never particularly rich, has opened up well with bottle-age and is now an intense, assertive wine with *crème brûlée* flavours; medium-bodied, but with good length. Fine acidity is a hallmark of Doisy-Dubroca, and gives elegance to the dense and concentrated 1983. The 1985 was marked by a marzipan nose and an absence of botrytis; although unctuous in texture, it never showed much fruitiness.

The 1986 is better, a rather citric wine, but not a lean one; both oak and botrytis are abundant, but it is typically Barsac in its clean elegance and length. The 1988 is quite similar in character, but even better; it is immensely ripe, but doesn't have the sheer power of the Climens from the same year. The 1989 has good grip and a tangy acidity, but could use more concentration of flavour; none the less, it is excellent and more forward than most vintages of Doisy-Dubroca, which tends to be reserved when young. I have tasted the 1990 only once, in 1993, when it was still very closed.

Climens is the glamorous wine; Doisy-Dubroca is the equally good-looking if less striking and conspicuous younger sister.

Château Doisy-Dubroca, Barsac, 33720 Podensac, telephone: 56 307240

CHÂTEAU DOISY-VÉDRINES

The Védrines family first came to Barsac in the early eighteenth century, and their property remained in the family until 1846. It was probably at about this time that the Doisy estate was split up, though it is not clear whether the vines that now comprise this estate remained in the possession of the Védrines or the Dubosq family, who were managing the estate at the time. In 1851, the estate was acquired by the Boireau family, who were coopers in

Barsac. Doisy-Védrines passed into the hands of one of the family's descendants, Mme J. Teyssonneau, who also owned another Barsac estate, Château Ménota. Her daughter married into the Castéja family, in whose hands the property remains to this day. Pierre Castéja first moved here in 1947 with his family. The château is a charming late-sixteenth-century *manoir*, which has been sympathetically restored. Photographs and paintings of racehorses line the walls, as Pierre Castéja admits to a passion for the turf, which had to be curbed after the responsibilities of marriage and parenthood were assumed. The Castéjas own the *négociant* firm of Roger Joanne, and Pierre readily admits that his allegiance is to the Médoc as much as to the Sauternais. In 1964, to compensate for the poor sales of Sauternes at that time, he also planted red grapes in the vineyard.

Château Doisy-Védrines is today by far the largest of the three Doisy estates, with 27 ha. in production. It is said that the vines are planted on the highest plateau in Barsac, but that is not saying a great deal in this flat commune. The *encépagement* is 80 per cent Sémillon and 20 per cent Sauvignon Blanc. The exposure is to the south-west, and the density 6,500 vines per ha. The average age of the vines is now more than twenty-five years. Yields are very low and *triage* is scrupulously practised. Castéja wants must weights of 19° and anything below 17° is immediately sold off to wholesalers. There were four *tries* in 1989 and 1990, but in the very difficult 1993 vintage there were eight. A large cold chamber has been installed, but although Castéja used cryo-extraction in 1987, he didn't bottle the small quantity of wine he made.

The grapes are pressed in pneumatic presses. Fermentation begins in stainless-steel tanks, but after a week the must is transferred to *barriques*. There they stay for eighteen months. The proportion of new oak has been creeping up. In 1988, 65 per cent of the wood was new and since 1989 he has used nothing but new *barriques*. The cellars are air-conditioned, so the wine can evolve slowly and prudently in barrel. The wine is fined, filtered and bottled about twenty-two months after the harvest. The average production is about 36,000 bottles, which is not a great deal considering the size of the estate. About 90 per cent of the wine is exported.

Doisy-Védrines is the richest of the Doisy wines, but it rarely attains the finesse of the other two. Indeed some vintages don't even seem typically Barsac and could easily be mistaken for Preignac or Bommes, such is their depth of colour and fullness of body. It is quite different from high-alcohol wines such as Caillou and Broustet; Doisy-Védrines rarely exceeds 14°. The wine has always been dependable, but it has expressed its full potential only in recent vintages.

Old vintages of Doisy-Védrines have not come my way, but I have seen good accounts of the 1927, 1949, 1962 and 1967. The 1970 is sumptuous, tasting of peaches and oranges, yet still fresh and lively, and with good length. Castéja admits that if the estate had been as well equipped in those days as it is now, he could have made a truly great wine in 1970. As it is, the 1970 is extremely good. The fine 1975 is decidedly *confit*, with aromas of dried apricots and an elegant smokiness on the palate, but it is now becoming dry and should be drunk soon. The 1978 is rather fat and alcoholic. The 1981 is mediocre, but the supple 1982 has been evolving well, despite its initial blandness and lack of botrytis.

The 1983, made after eight *tries*, also has a *confit*, dried-apricot character, but is imbued with far more Barsac raciness and delicacy. No 1984 was bottled. The late-picked 1985 was good, but not exceptional for the vintage. If the 1983 was very much a Barsac, the rich oaky 1986 is very Védrines, with power and body balanced by good acidity and length. It has been slow to develop, and will undoubtedly improve further. The 1988 has a sweetness and intensity of mouth-watering fruit that is irresistible; the oak is expressed by vanilla undertones rather than tannic structure, but the wine will surely evolve into a very stylish Védrines.

Like the 1988, the 1989 is not especially alcoholic (about 13.5°). Even in cask this was an exceptionally delicious wine, and it has been getting better and better. By 1994, it was showing lush botrytis aromas, a rounded but not heavy palate, and a creamy texture. Good as the 1988 is, this is surely the best Védrines for many a year. The 1990 is its equal, but not better; less opulent, it has a touch more spiciness and elegance, and exceptional length. There was no 1991 bottled. The 1992 is distinctly lightweight and short. Only 20 per cent of the wine made in 1993 will be bottled.

Pierre Castéja, Château Doisy-Védrines, Barsac, 33720 Podensac, telephone: 56 271513, fax: 56 272676

CHÂTEAU DE MYRAT

In a region of charming little châteaux, Château de Myrat, built in the 1720s, is one of the most delightful, a small but lofty mansion with a mansard roof, flanked by lower pavilions and situated in a small park, which is surrounded by a single parcel of vines. The château was built on the foundations of a much older building. According to Pierre Dubourdieu, before 1855 Myrat was allied with Château Cantegril, since one of the seigneurs of Cantegril had married a daughter of the Myrat family. There is evidence from letters written by one of the Bordeaux merchants responsible for the 1855 classification to suggest that Château de Myrat might have been classified as *Premier Cru* had not vines belonging to the estate also been planted at nearby Château Cantegril. In the mid-nineteenth century, it was owned by a family called Perrot and then by Henri Moller, who also acquired Château Broustet through his wife's family. For a while the wines were sold as Château Myrat-Broustet. In 1893, the estate was sold and subsequently bought from the Martineau family in 1939 by the de Pontacs, who still own it. The de Pontacs have one of the greatest names in Bordeaux, for their ancestors owned Château Haut-Brion and other estates. The proprietor, Maximilien de Pontac, restored the property and replanted the vineyard, but sold most of its production to Bordeaux wholesalers.

In 1855 Mirat, as it was then spelt, was ranked as the best of the *Deuxièmes Crus*, so it was especially sad when in 1976 Comte Maximilien decided to uproot the vines, even though there had been some memorable vintages of Myrat: the 1922 was much admired, as were the 1928 and 1948. All estates suffered from the slump in the Sauternes district in the 1960s and 1970s, but Comte Maximilien was the only proprietor of a classified growth to take the extreme step of grubbing up his vines.

He died in April 1988. His heirs, Jacques and Xavier, had to act fast if they were to save Myrat from extinction. Only a certain amount of time can elapse during which vines can be replanted if the estate's classification is to be retained, and they planted 150,000 new vines in the nick of time: 88 per cent Sémillon, 8 per cent Sauvignon and 4 per cent Muscadelle. Xavier de Pontac claims that the soil on which Myrat's 22 ha. are planted is the finest in Barsac after that of Climens.

In the *chais*, the old hydraulic presses survive, standing proudly in their large wooden troughs. At Myrat, pressing begins in a horizontal press, but is completed in the hydraulic presses. The wine is fermented and aged in *barriques*, half of which are new, for eighteen months. The *assemblage* takes place in the spring following the harvest.

That, at any rate, is the formula. But the reality is that since the replanting, Myrat has produced virtually no Sauternes. The first crop was in the superlative 1990 vintage, but the still-infant vines were not entitled to the Sauternes appellation and had to be sold as Bordeaux AOC. The wine was charming, and had both botrytis and *nervosité*, a raciness often encountered in Barsac; inevitably, given the youth of the vines, the wines lacked concentration and richness.

The great frost in 1991 meant that Myrat could produce only 6,000 bottles, although the estate is capable of producing up to 60,000. The wine was disappointingly simple and dilute. The 1992 evidently lacked ripeness, but Xavier de Pontac decided to release 6,000 bottles as Myrat, the rest having been sold off to wholesalers. As a vintage, 1993 was slightly better than 1992 and by October 1994, Xavier de Pontac was expressing pleasant surprise at the quality of the best lots. In April 1994, Myrat was one of the corners of Barsac to be severely damaged by frost. The only hope for the 1994 harvest was that there would be a small crop from the *contre-boutons* that grow after the vines recover from the initial shock which killed the developing buds. The evening after the frost, Xavier de Pontac played host in the *chais* as 100 classic-car enthusiasts drove past his blackened vines to a reception he had organized. There was nothing in his cheerful demeanour to suggest that he and his brother were facing disaster for the fourth year in a row. The harvest began in early October in good conditions and it seemed probable that Myrat would produce a small quantity of good wine.

Xavier de Pontac is a delightful man. Short, chubby, chain-smoking, usually dishevelled, he has a rueful wit and charm that make him one of the most popular proprietors in the region. Even his commercial rivals must hope, as I do, that the climate will be kinder to Myrat in the 1990s than it has been hitherto, so that his commitment to his reborn estate can be repaid in the form of a good and abundant harvest of fine Barsac.

Comte Xavier de Pontac, Château de Myrat, Barsac, 33720 Podensac, telephone: 56 271506

CHÂTEAU NAIRAC

Like Château de Myrat, though in less dramatic fashion, Château Nairac was reborn. For many decades the estate had been neglected, until in the early 1970s Nicole Tari and her then husband Tom Heeter acquired the property and transformed it into one of the finest estates in Barsac.

Its history has been traced to the seventeenth century, when it was owned by André Duranceau. Subsequent owners were Jérome Mercade, his daughter-in-law Elizabeth Prost, who expanded the vineyards, and, from 1777, Élysée Nairac. The Nairacs, who were merchants and shipowners and probably slave-traders, purchased this Barsac estate as their country retreat. In the 1780s they commissioned a new mansion from the architect Jean Mollié, a pupil of Victor Louis, who transformed Bordeaux into the most handsome city of south-west France. Over the past twenty years, both the château and its gardens have been restored, with the original designs used as the basis for the renovation.

Élysée Nairac, unlike his more aristocratic neighbours, was able to enjoy his new estate after the Revolution, although some of his relatives fled to Holland and thence to Mauritius, where many Nairac descendants still live. When Elysée Nairac died in 1791, two of his daughters, Henriette and Julie-Émilie, managed the property. After Henriette's death the estate was sold to Bernard Capdeville, who already owned Château Broustet and other estates. Nairac at that time was probably only 8 ha. in extent. The two estates were combined and the wine was marketed either as Broustet-Nérac or simply as Nérac. It was in its double-barrelled form that it was classified as a *Deuxième Cru*.

Capdeville died in 1861 and Broustet was inherited by one daughter, who was married to Henri Moller, the proprietor of Château de Myrat; Nairac was inherited by her sister Georgina, who was married to Pierre Gustave Brunet, the owner of Château Piada, also in Barsac. When phylloxera ravaged the vineyards at Nairac, Brunet replanted the estate entirely with red vines. Georgina Brunet died in 1906 and the estate passed to distant relatives before being sold to Jean-Charles Perpezat. The new owner proved more conscientious than the Brunets and the estate was soon producing sweet wine again, as the red vines were gradually replaced with white. After the catastrophic frost of 1956, the vineyards had to be entirely replanted. Perpezat was a member of the wine merchants Mas et Mostermans, and the name J. Mas is given as the proprietor of Nairac on labels of the 1950s, when small quantities were bottled for the owners' consumption. Ten years later, the Perpezats sold the estate to Bordeaux councillor Dr Jean Seynat, but he neglected the vineyards and the wine, sold off in bulk, lost what reputation it had.

In the early 1970s, Nicole Tari and Tom Heeter came on to the scene. She was the daughter of Pierre Tari, the dynamic proprietor of Châteaux Giscours and Branaire-Ducru in the Médoc. Heeter had arrived at Giscours from Ohio to study winemaking; a romance led to marriage and the young couple looked around for a wine estate of their own. After protracted negotiations they acquired Château Nairac in August 1971 for 800,000 francs. The mansion had been uninhabited for decades and the couple began the slow job of restoring it room by room. Two years elapsed before they could move in, but winemaking had begun as soon as the deeds changed hands. Their first vintage was in 1972.

By this time the vineyards comprised 15 ha. Like the vines, the *chais* had been neglected. The transformation was swift. Although inexperienced, Heeter immediately turned out a series of excellent Barsacs, even from the mediocre vintages of the early 1970s. Disaster struck in 1977 when frost, a frequent problem at Nairac, damaged 85 per cent of the vines; and again in 1981, when the Garonne flooded and the cellars were under 1.5 metres of water. To this day, the curtains in the ground-floor rooms are stained where the water lapped at them. Fortunately the vines were not affected; indeed, they may have benefited from the silt deposited by the floodwaters.

Thereafter all went well until the latter half of the 1980s, when the Heeter marriage foundered. The 1986 Nairac was the last vintage made solely by Tom Heeter and he moved out the following year. A young winemaker from the Loire, François Amirault, was installed at Nairac and in 1987 Tom Heeter tutored him in the Nairac style. One change initiated by Amirault was the gradual alteration of the *encépagement*, with slightly more Sauvignon being planted. In 1993, Amirault left to become *régisseur* at Château de

Fargues.[24] By now Nicole's son Nicolas was keen to take over the reins, having already been working at the estate for two years.

The vineyards of Nairac, which were built up piecemeal over the decades, are dispersed. Behind the château lie 9 ha., 3 ha. border the *route nationale*, 2 ha. adjoin Climens. The last parcel is classic Haut-Barsac soil; the larger parcels nearer the château have more alluvial soil and little clay. The vines consist of 90 per cent Sémillon, 7 per cent Sauvignon Blanc and 3 per cent Muscadelle. Heeter always obtained a larger crop from the Sauvignon, as he wanted it to be an emphatic component in the wine, giving it freshness to balance the onslaught of new oak. The vines today have an average age of thirty years, the density is 6,600 vines per ha., and yields are low, usually 13–15 hl./ha., and rarely exceeding 20.

Harvesting at Nairac was exceptionally severe, though Heeter liked to pick the Sauvignon relatively early. The grapes were pressed twice in hydraulic presses. On the recommendation of Emile Peynaud, the great Bordeaux oenologist who acted as a consultant here, he added Vitamin B1 to the must as a way of replacing vitamins destroyed by the action of botrytis. Apparently this allowed him to lower the amount of sulphur dioxide during the early stages of vinification. In the 1980 Nairac, for example, the total sulphur-dioxide content is only 238 milligrams per litre.

The must was put into barrels, of which at least half were new, and chaptalized when considered necessary. The fermentation was protracted, sometimes as long as two months. If the temperature was too high for comfort, Heeter would simply hose down the

24 In 1994, unaware that Amirault had been lured away by Alexandre de Lur-Saluces, I spotted him by chance in the offices at Yquem. Comte Alexandre confirmed that it was indeed Amirault, who was now looking after Château de Fargues. But I was puzzled because he kept referring to him as François, while the Comte couldn't understand why I kept referring to him as Max, the name under which he had been known at Nairac. Amirault later explained to me that while at Nairac his co-workers had always called him Max even though he kept reminding them that his real name was François. Once at Fargues, he could reclaim his real name. So François it is. I tell this story so that those who knew him from his Nairac days will realize that Max and François are one and the same.

cellars and the evaporation would lower the temperature. Like Christian Broustaut at Climens, he found the common-sense solutions were the most effective. In practice, it was usually necessary to heat the cellars rather than cool them. After fermentation, the wine remained in oak for up to three years. At first it was racked every three months, but once the wine was clear there were greater gaps between rackings. There was a bentonite fining only if required for clarification, but the wine was filtered before bottling.

There are those who criticize Nairac for being over-oaked. It's a matter of taste, though I didn't usually find the oak obtrusive, since the wine was usually so concentrated. Heeter, who enjoyed working in the *chai* more than in the vineyard, adored oak and experimented like crazy, trying different woods from different coopers in different toastings. He kept the various lots separate for as long as possible, so as to have as many ingredients as he could for the eventual *assemblage*.

It is a great tribute to Tom Heeter that this brash American, largely self-taught, speaking heavily accented French, managed to produce a series of wines that put many classified growths to shame. Perhaps his wines were not sufficiently Barsac, though they nearly always had underlying raciness and vigour, however rich and concentrated the flavours, and however intense the oakiness. Since his departure, François Amirault and Nicolas Tari-Heeter have broadly maintained his style of winemaking, though arguably in a more moderate fashion.

Nairac is the Sauternes I know best. I have always been encouraged to taste new wines from the cask, so that I could get the clearest impression of all the lots made in any single vintage. So although I have tried not to weary the reader with exhaustive data for every vintage at every château, I will record as much information here as I was able to note at the time, so that those interested in the details of harvesting and *assemblage* can appreciate the intricacy of the process from one vintage to the next.

The only pre-Heeter Nairac I have tasted is the 1955, generously opened for me by Nicolas Tari-Heeter. It was a splendid wine, with a nose of caramelized orange and honey, and on the palate, which was beginning to dry out, there were rich flavours of bitter orange (not disagreeable); the wine was well balanced, reasonably concentrated and clean on the finish.

The first Heeter Nairac, the 1972, was wisely bottled young,

after eighteen months in *barriques*. Only 7,400 bottles were produced. The wine had a smoky nose, with a whiff of tobacco as
well as oak; on the palate it was rich, and had good balance and
concentration. But after fifteen years it peaked and is now in
decline.

The 1973 (14° of alcohol plus 3.7° of residual sugar) survived
much better than its predecessor. It was always lively, charming and
clean, and is still surprisingly distinguished, with a nutty, oaky nose
acquired after thirty months in barrels, and an elegant spiciness on
the palate. In 1994 it was lean, but in remarkable health, still going
strong after most 1973s had faded away.

Heeter was undeterred by a dreadful year in 1974 (14.2° plus
3.4°) and wrested fruit from the vines after eleven *tries*. Only
14,400 bottles were produced, as 70 per cent of the wine was
declassified. Much of it was bottled in magnums, as Nicole Tari
decided the wine would come in handy at receptions. It was always
somewhat dilute and light-bodied, with an alcoholic finish. I doubt
that it is ageing gracefully.

I have always admired the 1975 (14° plus 3.9°), one of the classic
wines of the vintage, greeny-gold in colour, impeccably oaky on the
nose, and on the palate immensely stylish and long. The botrytis is
evident yet understated; it has never dominated the wine.

The 1976 (14° plus 4.35°) was plumper, more luscious, ever so
slightly blowsy on the palate when I first tasted it in 1986. Sampled
again more recently, the wine has come together beautifully,
delivering sumptuous apricotty richness and concentration of flavour. It doesn't have the vigour of the 1975, but it is more sensuous
and, again, the oak is finely judged. The wine spent three years in
barriques.

After his heroic efforts in 1972 and 1974, Tom Heeter took it
easy in 1977 and 1978 and declassified the lot. Even in 1979 (14.1°
plus 3.7°), a far better vintage, 60 per cent was declassified. In its
youth it was lush, very oaky, perhaps overblown and lacking in
acidity, but a delicious mouthful. It has evolved quite rapidly.

A more abundant vintage followed in 1980 (14° plus 4°); 25,500
bottles were produced. This was always one of the successes of the
vintage, a wine of great charm and lemony elegance with botrytis to
give it complexity. It has evolved very slowly, thanks to its fine
balance, and there is no rush to drink it up.

The flood in 1981 meant that many of the best lots were

destroyed by the muddy waters. If this wine has a fault, it's a certain austerity and hardness, with the oak for once obtrusive. I have not tasted the 1981 (14° plus 3.6°) in many years and perhaps with bottle-age it has become more harmonious.

Nairac began picking quite early in 1982, on 21 September. This was just as well, considering the heavy rain that was to interrupt the harvest on 2 October. It was bottled in October 1985. When young, the 1982 (14° plus 3.9°) was pleasant, quite waxy, flavoury, but lacking in fleshiness and grip, an honourable rather than distinguished effort. When tasted in 1990, it had developed a bizarre nose and candied flavours on the palate, which had become meaty and quite coarse. Clive Coates' notes from 1992, while more positive than mine, also mention a 'fruit-salady flavour'. However, by 1994 the wine had become peachy on the nose, with lanolin aromas, and soft and unctuous on the palate, though its low acidity suggests it is now at its peak.

The 1983 (14.2° plus 4.3°) was bottled in September 1986. It always had impressive complexity, with aromas of apricots, toasted almonds and tobacco leaf, as well as honeyed botrytis; on the palate it was less opulent, more citric and restrained, with an almost fiery acidity giving the rich wine the necessary Barsac *nervosité*. It is not among the greatest 1983s as it lacked harmoniousness; there has always been something slightly wild and dangerous about it. But it is unquestionably very good.

Heeter says he made an acceptable 1984, but because the vintage had such a poor reputation he sold off the whole crop. In 1985, hail reduced the crop by about half. By picking until 25 November, he harvested grapes with good botrytis. In its youth the wine (13.6° plus 4°) was dominated by oak rather than noble rot; it was undoubtedly well structured, but lacked complexity.

Frost reduced the crop again in 1986, by about 30 per cent. But it was an easy vintage, with ample noble rot. Four *tries* were picked between 13 October and 15 November. The wine was aged in 60 per cent new oak for thirty months. Perhaps the problems within the Tari-Heeter household affected their concentration on the wine-making, but the 1986 (13.5° plus 4.6°) has always been problematic. The new oak has been very marked, as well as a dieselly tone on nose and palate. The usual Nairac finesse was missing and the balance was awkward. Perhaps it will come round eventually.

Once again, frost reduced the crop by about 30 per cent in 1987

(13.5° plus 4°). That, together with the damp autumn weather, kept yields down to a miserable 5 hl./ha. Amirault managed to pick the Sauvignon and Muscadelle before the rain began on 5 October. He began picking the Sémillon on 20 October and there were three *tries* until 13 November. The later *tries* gathered botrytized grapes. By the end of the harvest, Nairac had 70 *barriques*, but half were later rejected. They certainly varied in style and quality when tasted from cask. The wine turned out to be rather light and simple for Nairac, with tangerine flavours beneath the light oakiness.

An easier vintage followed in 1988 (13.6° plus 5.2°), especially after 18 October, when there was an explosion of botrytis in the vineyard. There were three *tries* of Sauvignon, beginning on 13 October, giving healthy grapes with good acidity. The first *trie* of Sémillon began on 14 October and continued for a week, giving whole bunches of botrytized fruit. But the second *trie*, from 31 October to 2 November, had to be picked grape by grape. The third *trie* of Sémillon from 3 to 10 November brought in half the crop, with must weights of about 18.5°. Yields were about 14 hl./ha. But quantities were small: some 68 *barriques* that eventually translated into 18,000 bottles. All the wine was fermented in new oak, but only half was aged in new oak; no barrels were older than one year. Half the wood was from Allier, the remainder Limousin, which always imparts a strong flavour to the wine. The 1988 is a Barsac with fine typicity and intensity; closed and oaky in its youth, like most Nairacs, it should develop well. But in its youth it seemed to lack the brilliance of the very best 1988s.

The warm, humid September in 1989 brought on an early attack of noble rot. Amirault launched the first *trie* on 19 September. Over the next four weeks there were three more *tries* which continued until 18 October. Half the crop was harvested from 9 to 14 October. Again, all the must was fermented in new oak, but aged in half new oak, the remainder in one and two-year-old wood. The yield was relatively big, at 17 hl./ha. In March 1990, the *assemblage* began when the Muscadelle, which had been vinified separately, was blended with the Sauvignon. The various *tries*, tasted from cask, had very different personalities and it was hard not to be overwhelmed by the sumptuousness of the third Sémillon *trie*. The most concentrated vintage of the 1980s may have been 1989, but was surpassed in elegance by the 1988. The 1989 (13.7° plus 5.3°)

yielded 24,000 bottles of rich, oaky Barsac, well structured though perhaps low in acidity, a wine with a very good future.

An exceptionally precocious vintage ensued in 1990. Amirault began picking on 12 September and finished on 10 October. Noble rot was abundant but uneven. There had been some frost at Nairac, so some bunches were second-generation and were considerably less ripe than the first generation, which had must weights of up to 25°. Amirault was quite pleased to have less-ripe bunches to moderate such excessive lusciousness and many lots were blended early to achieve a better balance. In cask, the young wines were exceptionally delicious. Because of the richness of the wine, it was kept in oak with a light to medium toast for thirty months. Nicole Tari was exceptionally pleased with the 1990 (13.8° plus 6.7°) and, unlike other proprietors who gently lowered prices for this vintage, she raised hers. She released 24,000 bottles. The wine was rich and very sweet, but also classically Barsac, with its lemony intensity, its vigour and length. It will age slowly, but beautifully.

In 1991, botrytis came early, but before the grapes were ripe – such grapes as had survived the frost. Warm, dry weather after mid-September helped and the first *trie* began on 23 September. Two days later it rained for four days. Picking resumed from 2 to 4 October. Another *trie* beginning on 16 October proved disappointing. Dry weather returned on 19 October, and more grapes were picked from 22 to 25 October and on 29 October. After all this effort, there were only 19 *barriques* to show for it, a yield of under 3 hl./ha. New oak was not used for this vintage. Ironically, the 1991 (13.8° plus 4.8°), all 4,000 bottles of it, was excellent; not especially weighty, but a lively, spicy Barsac for medium-term drinking.

In 1992, the first *trie* began on 20 September when early botrytis developed on the vines. Six days later it rained and picking could resume only on 7 October. Rain later in the month stopped the harvest until early November. It started to rain again on 11 November and the harvest was abandoned with a third of the grapes still on the vine. Over six weeks of picking yielded 12 *barriques* (2,900 bottles); all the wine was aged in new oak. The wine proved somewhat unstable and was bottled after only eighteen months, in February 1994. The 1992 (13.4° plus 5.2°) had a deep colour from the outset; a light, honeyed nose and considerable concentration; but in its youth it had an aggressive acidity and some bitter-orange flavours that will need time to harmonize.

By October 1994, no decision had been made about the 1993, which had been vinified entirely in new oak. There had been no chaptalization and the wine had taken up to four months to ferment to 13.5°. There was enough wine for only 2,500 bottles.

Wines can be bought directly from the property. While Nicolas Tari-Heeter is looking after the winemaking, his mother continues her crusading work, persuading restaurateurs to match Sauternes with food and to serve the wine as an aperitif.

The various changes at Château Nairac since 1986 have not helped the wine. It remains a very fine Barsac, but it has lost some of its flair. Not much has changed since Tom Heeter left. Certainly the same rigorous standards of harvesting and selection have been maintained. But the inexplicable magical touch that could turn a moderate vintage such as 1980 into a superlative wine is now missing. Now that Nicolas Tari, with his intense personal commitment to maintaining quality at Nairac, has assumed responsibility for the winemaking, the wine is likely to return to its former brilliance. Even in 1994, when the pressure to produce some saleable wine must have been intense, he made no compromises: his *triage* in the vineyard and severe rejection of barrels unworthy of the Nairac label will reduce the production to a few thousand bottles only. But, he insists, they will be first-rate.

Mme Nicole Tari-Heeter, Château Nairac, Barsac, 33720 Podensac, telephone: 56 271616, fax: 56 272650

CHÂTEAU SUAU

This has to be the most obscure classified growth in Sauternes, partly because the wines are made well away from the vineyards. They had a following in England in the nineteenth century, but are rarely seen these days. The estate was named after Élie de Suau, a courtier during the reign of Louis XIV. His daughter married Marquis Pierre de Lur-Saluces and it was their descendant Claude Henri Hercule de Lur-Saluces who sold Suau in 1793. Later it came into the hands of M. Pédesclaux, a Bordeaux wine broker who owned the *Cru Classé* of that name in Pauillac. By 1845, it was the property of the Marion family. At the end of the nineteenth century, it was owned by the estate manager for Lur-Saluces, Emile Garros. When the 8 ha. of vineyards were sold to Daniel Biarnès in 1960 by the resplendently named Mme Pouchappadesse *née* Garros, her family retained the château.

Daniel's son Roger Biarnès is self-consciously hale and hearty, very much the *vigneron* without pretensions to the status of landed gentry. I have the impression that he regards Suau, classified growth or not, as one of the portfolio of wines that emerge from Château Navarro. If you like sweet wines, then he can offer you Château Suau. About half the wine is exported.

The vineyards are located in a single parcel between the railway line and the *route nationale*, quite close to the stadium that lies south of the village. The average age of the vines is about twenty years and their density is 6,000 vines per ha. The *encépagement* is 80 per cent Sémillon, and 10 per cent each of Sauvignon and Muscadelle. The soil is gravelly and sandy, with clay that is quite heavy for Barsac. Yields are quite high, averaging 20 hl./ha.

The wine is vinified in temperature-controlled tanks with natural yeasts. In recent years he has begun ageing the wine for about eighteen months in *barriques* and is trying to increase the proportion of new oak each year. The wine is chilled to precipitate tartrate crystals and bottled thirty months after the harvest. There tend to be two or three different bottlings, which is worrying, as there can be variations in the wine as a consequence of the time it has spent in wood. The maximum production is 25,000 bottles.

There is no *deuxième vin* here, but Biarnès also produces a Sauternes called Domaine du Coy, which is located between Yquem and Guiraud. The *encépagement* is the same as for Suau, but the vines are slightly older. The vinification is identical, but Domaine du Coy is aged for a shorter period and sells for about 25 per cent less than Suau. The maximum production is about 15,000 bottles. The Biarnès family is well equipped to receive visitors and sell wines directly, and Château Suau has the merit of being probably the cheapest classified growth.

On the other hand, it is not a very rewarding wine. When a proprietor says, as does Roger Biarnès, that he doesn't like syrupy wines and wants a style that is powerful, but with *nervosité*, I can be reasonably certain that I won't care for his wines, that they will be quite alcoholic and lean, with little botrytis character. Suau is what Bernard Ginestet calls a 'modern Barsac whose easy style contrasts strongly with the massive classical wines'[25] – code words to describe a sweet wine for folks who don't really like sweet wines.

I haven't tasted older vintages of Suau and have yet to read anything complimentary from those who have (except for the ever-tactful Ginestet). So I was surprised to find the 1989 and 1990 perfectly agreeable wines, lightish, simple, not very concentrated, and sweet, lively and grapy, with reasonable length. The 1990 is the better of the two and at almost one-third of the price of Suduiraut, not bad value. Of course, neither is up to the standard one expects from a *Deuxième Cru*. Biarnès bottled wine in all three of the difficult vintages from 1991 to 1993, wines he modestly describes as 'correct'.

Roger Biarnès, Château Navarro, Illats, 33720 Podensac, telephone: 56 272027, fax: 56 272653

25 Bernard Ginestet, *Sauternes*, p. 175.

10

The Deuxièmes Crus *of Sauternes,* *Preignac and Fargues*

CHÂTEAU D'ARCHE

This estate is named after the Comte d'Arche, the *président* of the Bordeaux *parlement* who bought the property in 1727. The estate remained in the family's possession until the Revolution; after the family fled, the state sold it off in 1791 to M. Dublanc, of whom nothing is known. Château d'Arche did not survive intact and it was divided up. The new owners were the Lafaurie family, who remained proprietors of part of the property until the 1920s; a certain M. Dupeyron, who faded away in the 1870s; and M. Comet, who sold his wines as Château d'Arche-Vimeney. At the time of the 1855 classification, Lafaurie is listed as the owner, but another proprietor who comes into the picture in 1860 is Pierre Méricq, who may have owned the château itself. It is all rather confusing.

In 1893, Pierre Méricq sold the estate, or his portion of it, to Grégoire Dubédat. Under Dubédat's ownership, the estate was expanded. In 1925, another of the proprietors, Mlle Dubourg, married Armand Bastit Saint-Martin, who took over the estate. Bastit Saint-Martin was to become a powerful figure, a banker and senator, and he continued the expansion of Château d'Arche, gradually buying out the other owners. In 1950, he acquired what was called Château d'Arche-Lafaurie (which was used as the name of the second wine until 1980) and in 1960 he acquired, as tenant rather than proprietor, the former 4.5 ha. of Château d'Arche-Vimeney. Château d'Arche was now restored to its pre-Revolutionary boundaries, more or less.

After Armand Bastit Saint-Martin's son Henri died prematurely in 1980, the senator decided to give up his management of the estate. He leased it to Pierre Perromat, while the d'Arche-Vimeney vineyard was sold to Cordier, who have absorbed it into Château Lafaurie-Peyraguey. Senator Bastit Saint-Martin died in 1983. His family still inhabit the modest Louis XV château.

Jean Perromat is an influential man in the region. He is the former president of INAO (l'Institut National des Appellations d'Origine), the all-powerful body that administers the complex system of appellations and other regulations governing French viti-culture. He is now a banker and lives on the other side of the Garonne, leaving the daily management of Château d'Arche in the hands of his *régisseur*, Serge Banchereau, who by 1994 was on the verge of retirement. When he leased the property, Perromat announced that he was planning to make the best wine possible from these fine vineyards. It was certainly the case that Senator Bastit Saint-Martin's wine had not been especially distinguished. Perromat has not endeared himself to many of the other proprietors in the region. He is reluctant to participate in regional organiza-tions and promotional activities, and has given the impression that he considers his wine far better than its *Deuxième Cru* status implies. Nor did he endear himself to me by agreeing to see me, urging me to be punctual and then failing to turn up.

Château d'Arche's vineyards, quite close to the village of Sauternes, are among the highest in Sauternes. About 29 ha. are under vine, planted with 70 per cent Sémillon, 29 per cent Sauvig-non and a few Muscadelle vines. The excellent soil is gravel and marl over a clay and gravel subsoil. The average age of the vines is thirty years. Jean Perromat took all the necessary measures to improve quality: he pruned short and demanded more rigorous *triage*, so that average yields are about 15 hl./ha.

The grapes are pressed in hydraulic presses and the must used to be fermented in stainless steel. There is an initial selection after fermentation and then a final *assemblage* eighteen months later. At least half the wine is aged for up to twenty months in oak, of which up to 40 per cent is new. Since 1993, the wine has been chilled to precipitate the tartrate crystals, and there is a fining and filtration before bottling. The resulting wine is a powerful, full-bodied Sauternes. Occasionally, as in 1985 and 1986, a second wine is produced under the label of Cru de Braneyre, the original name of the estate.

I sense that standards have been slipping in recent years. The wine is bottled earlier than it used to be and there are various bottlings according to demand, which is always a bad sign as it can lead to a lack of uniformity in each vintage. Visiting the estate unannounced during the 1994 vintage, I was surprised to find Serge Banchereau absent for a few days and Jean Perromat, as usual, not there either. Under such conditions, who can ensure that high standards are maintained?

The oldest d'Arche I have tasted is the 1936, which was very dark in colour and beginning to maderize, leaving the wine with some sweetness and richness, but with excessive acidity. But 1936 was a weak vintage, so it was remarkable that the wine was still alive, let alone drinkable. The first of the Perromat vintages I tasted was the 1982, a mighty wine with 15° of alcohol. It was only lightly botrytized and that alcohol did show through, but it did indeed have the power and concentration that Perromat was aiming for.

The 1983 is a splendid wine, with ample botrytis, a creamy texture and elegant acidity. It was always forward; it continues to drink well and should improve further. The 1984 was good for the year, as was the 1985. Curiously the 1986, which should have been superb, was never very exciting; it seemed to buckle in the middle and fade away. The 1988, made after four *tries*, I tasted only when it was very young; I was not overwhelmed, but would rather reserve judgement. I was quite surprised to find it being bottled in May 1990. When I asked why, the *régisseur* shrugged and said, '*Le client est roi*.' The golden 1989 is a big, lush wine, perhaps too luscious for its own good, its botrytized flavours giving the wine a distinct heaviness. Only 24,000 bottles were produced in 1989, as hail damaged the vineyards. I tasted the 1990 from cask and was hugely impressed: a big, sweet, peachy wine with spicy acidity, plenty of lively oak and very good length.

The average production is about 35,000 bottles, much of which is exported. In 1994, a range of vintages were available for purchase at the château, the 1983 a bargain at 136 francs, and the 1988, 1989 and 1990 priced at 130 francs. It seems astonishing that at such relatively low prices the wines are slow to sell.

Jean Perromat, Château d'Arche, Sauternes, 33210 Langon, telephone: 56 766655

CHÂTEAU FILHOT

Château Filhot is the most southerly estate of Sauternes, pressed against the pine woods of the Landes. It is often visited by people with no interest in wine because, together with Château de Malle, it is one of the most imposing châteaux in the region.

The vineyard was established early in the eighteenth century by the Filhot family, who came here in 1709. There had surely been vines here in previous decades, but they were probably wiped out by the frost of 1705 and replanted. Before the Filhots' arrival, the estate was known as the Maison Noble de Verdoulet. About thirty years later, the Filhots began to build the handsome two-storey château that stands today, though pavilions were added in the 1840s in a style that blends well with the original *corps de logis*. The architect of the chapel and possibly of other original portions of the château was Pierre-Alexandre Poitevin. The landscaped park was laid out by Louis-Bernard Fischer, who designed the Jardin Public in Bordeaux. The courtyard, with its pond and fountain and stone lions, is exceptionally fine. To the west of the château, beyond the farm buildings, is an exceptionally large and well-preserved *colombier* or pigeon loft. The vineyards themselves must have been extensive and Filhot soon became a highly regarded wine. When Thomas Jefferson visited in 1787 and assessed the wines of Sauternes, he ranked Filhot immediately after Yquem, and the two wines fetched the same price.

In 1788, Gabriel-Barthélémy-Romain de Filhot made an important acquisition, buying Château Coutet from the Pichard family. To this day, the labels of the two estates are very similar. The purchase was poorly timed, with Revolution imminent. Indeed, neither Filhot nor his wife, who were ardent Monarchists, could escape the guillotine in 1794. The estate was confiscated, but eventually returned to the family. In 1807, Filhot's heiress Marie-Geneviève married Marquis Antoine-Marie de Lur-Saluces, the owner of Yquem, and when the property, by now badly run down, was eventually restored to her, Lur-Saluces found himself in possession of Châteaux d'Yquem, de Fargues, Coutet, de Malle, Piada and Filhot! From the 1830s, wine from Filhot was often sold rather grandly as Château Sauternes, but it seems that this wine was essentially a generic Sauternes, for all the pretensions of its title.

The Lur-Saluces family maintained the vineyard at Filhot and added to it by incorporating the adjacent vineyard of Château Pineau de Rey, between Filhot and Château Commarque. (The vines at Pineau de Rey no longer produce Sauternes.) By 1855, the château too had been expanded and the wine's reputation was consolidated after it was classified. Later in the century the vineyard, which had consisted of 120 ha. in its heyday, declined in area as the whole estate became increasingly neglected. In 1935, Marquis Bertrand de Lur-Saluces decided to dispose of some of his lesser properties and sold Filhot to his sister Thérèse Durieu de Lacarelle, who had married the Comte Étienne de Lacarelle, whose name still appears on the label. By this time the vineyards had dwindled to a mere 20 ha., so the Lacarelles began some replanting. Their daughter married the Comte de Vaucelles, whose son Henri has been managing the estate since 1974.

Henri de Vaucelles worked in industry before he was persuaded to take on the responsibilities of Château Filhot in 1974. Initially he seems to have been dismayed by the poor condition of the estate, which is still the largest in the Sauternais. You can still see vestiges of former tobacco-drying sheds and cattle sheds, all moribund by the time the Comte took over. He likes to point out that the roofs at Filhot alone amount to 2 ha.

Today there are 60 ha. under vine, with about 53 ha. in production. There are no vineyards close to the château; instead they lie to the north-west, between Châteaux Lamothe and Commarque. The soil is sandy gravel and clay on a subsoil of limestone. The vines planted are 60 per cent Sémillon, 35 per cent Sauvignon and 5 per cent Muscadelle. The vineyards, perhaps because of their proximity to the pine woods, are colder than others in the region and prone to frost. This is Henri de Vaucelles' explanation for the high proportion of Sauvignon in his vineyards, as he says the variety is better adapted to cooler climates. The harvest usually begins later here, a week behind Barsac. Yields are generous; in 1983, for example, there were 23 hl./ha. The production in a good vintage is about 150,000 bottles.

Comte Henri is generous with information about everything except his winemaking. Grapes are certainly picked by *tries successifs* – there were six *tries* in 1985 and five in 1988 – although he is wary of harvesting too late for fear of oxidation, a problem that other proprietors do not seem too worried about. The must is chaptalized when necessary, then fermented in fibreglass vats. There is virtually no *barrique*-ageing, though from time to time a few barrels have been glimpsed in the *chais* and some of the 1985 was aged in wood. Henri de Vaucelles says he opposes wood-ageing because he wants to avoid using too much sulphur dioxide and to ensure that levels of volatile acidity are kept low. These surely are rationalizations, as such technical problems have largely been solved. So the wine stays in fibreglass vats for about two years before being bottled.

The fact is that Henri de Vaucelles is a passionate student of the history of the region, but far less interested in producing a wine of high standards. Not that Filhot is a bad wine; it is just evident that it could, in most vintages, be so much better. Vaucelles is an economic historian trapped into being an estate manager. He likes nothing better than to welcome visitors and regale them with his theories about international commerce. A typical theme might be the Swedish market for agricultural products through the ages. I recall standing with him in the courtyard at Filhot while he expounded, speaking rapidly as he always does; it began to rain, my jacket collar went up, but he continued his lecture, quite oblivious to the fact that we were both becoming drenched.

There is no doubt, on the basis of old vintages, that Château Filhot is capable of producing outstanding wine. I tasted the 1896 in 1982 and it was still aromatic and attractive, though clearly drying out and past its best. Vintages such as 1904, 1914, 1929 and 1947 were all said to be first-rate at Filhot. In 1990, the 1934 was still well balanced and healthy, with orange-peel flavours. The 1945, tasted in 1994, was superb, with aromas of ripe lemons and stewed apricots, and a powerful raisiny palate, intense, refined rather than fat, and with excellent length – proof, if it were needed, that Filhot can produce great wine. Filhot seems to have virtually disappeared from the marketplace in the 1950s and 1960s, and no wine was bottled in 1963–5 and 1968. The 1970 was good, but the 1971 was rather light and citric, with a lean finish. The 1975 was modest for the vintage, but the 1976 was surprisingly rich and pineappley and honeyed. It is now past its best, but still enjoyable. The grapes clearly had a great deal of noble rot, which is not always the case at Filhot, even in ripe vintages.

The 1978 is insipid and soapy, the 1979 delicate and lightly honeyed. The 1980 now tastes washed out and was never up to much. The 1981 is slightly richer and more complex. In 1982,

Filhot made a pleasant, softish wine of medium length, but the 1983 was lean and mean for the vintage. The 1985 is a simple wine which finishes short.

In 1985, Henri de Vaucelles found himself with an unusual collection of grapes. On 20 November, his harvesters came back with Sémillon and a little Muscadelle that had been partially frozen during the night. Since the wine had very different flavours from those normally associated with Sauternes, Vaucelles decided to give the wine some barrel-ageing and bottled it separately as Vin de Grande Gelée. It's a curious wine, high in alcohol at 15°, only lightly sweet, but with a sprightly acidity. It reminds me of Jurançon. It is an agreeable wine, but I doubt that it will have much of a future and, like Jurançon, it will remain much as it is now for many years to come.

The 1986 was surprisingly delicious when young, almost racy, and the best Filhot since 1976. Tasted in 1994, it showed less well, but was still good, with botrytis on the nose and a fresh, spicy palate with very good acidity. Not the most lush or complex 1986, but a good wine. The 1988 lacked flair: a ripe, elegant wine, but with no structure and insufficient concentration. The 1989 is more lush, but also lacks concentration and weight. It's a pretty wine, but in a sensational vintage such as this, that's just not good enough.

The 1990 is sweet and peachy, but hardly outstanding for the vintage. In this vintage Vaucelles also produced a Crème de Tête, which is excellent: very ripe apricot fruit on the nose and a sumptuous, spicy palate with excellent length. This is splendid, as indeed the best lots from 1990 should be, and it's sad that this should be so much the exception at Filhot. The 1991 is quite successful for the vintage. Yields were only 5 hl./ha. and 30,000 bottles were produced. There is just a little more than 1992, which yielded 40,000 bottles. In 1994, Henri de Vaucelles had not made up his mind about the 1993, which was richer than 1992 but suffered from 'chemical instability', whatever that may mean.

Filhot is reasonably priced and widely distributed. Produced in large quantities, it allows wine lovers who might not otherwise encounter Sauternes to sample a competent example at a fair price. But it is hard to imagine anyone undergoing a conversion to great Sauternes on the basis of tasting a bottle of Filhot. The basic problem here is the absence of serious selection. There is no *deuxième vin*, so the temptation must be to bottle as much wine as possible under the Filhot label. The 1990 vintage shows that with greater selectivity, fine wine can be produced.

Comte Henri de Vaucelles, Château Filhot, Sauternes, 33210 Langon, telephone: 56 766109, fax: 56 766791

CHÂTEAU LAMOTHE

This is one of the most ancient sites in the region and was a fortress in the eighth century. Vestiges of the fort and of the house built here in the late sixteenth century still survive. It had many proprietors throughout the nineteenth century, including a British merchant called Jacques Dowling, who bought the estate in 1814. At the time of the 1855 classification, the owners were the Baptiste family; the estate was divided at some point during their tenure. Some time in the twentieth century, the part of the Lamothe estate that was to become Château Lamothe-Despujols was acquired by the neighbours at Château d'Arche, the Bastit Saint-Martin family. Senator Bastit Saint-Martin was trying to restore the original property at Château d'Arche, so in the course of his acquisitions he disposed of part of Château Lamothe in 1961 to the Despujols family. The remaining part of the Lamothe estate, then known as Château Lamothe-Bergey, was eventually sold in 1981 to the Guignard family, who, in time-honoured fashion, appended their name to the estate to distinguish it from the Despujols'. In 1989, Jean and Stanis Despujols handed over the running of Château Lamothe to their son Guy.

This is a high corner of Sauternes and some of the vines slope steeply to the south-west. The soil is gravel and sand over a subsoil of clay. This is a small estate of only 7.5 ha., but the vines are old, some forty years on average, and the viticulture is said to be along organic lines. The *encépagement* is 85 per cent Sémillon, 10 per cent Sauvignon and 5 per cent Muscadelle, and the density of the vines is 6,500 per ha. Yields have always been high, averaging 20 hl./ha.

There are up to five *tries*. After pressing in a horizontal press, the must is fermented in 5,000–litre vats without the use of cultivated yeasts. The wines are aged in vats for one year, then spend a further year in *barriques*, of which few are new.

In 1992, Guy Despujols introduced a second label, Les Tourelles de Lamothe. The maximum production of the *grand vin* is 22,000 bottles. The château is open to visitors and the family operate the Caves des Lauréats opposite the church in Sauternes, where their wines can be tasted and bought together with other wines of the region. Prices are moderate. In 1994, the 1990 vintage was priced at 125 francs, the 1992 at 95 francs.

The wine has been undistinguished for some time. I have tasted the 1924 vintage, which retained flavours of caramel and bitter orange, and still had reasonable length, though it was past its best. Reports of the vintages of the 1970s suggest they were thin and sulphury. More recently, the 1983 was very sweet and quite rich, pleasant enough but with no complexity. The peachy 1986 is soft and plump but, again, not complex and distinctly short. The 1989 has good fruit, but lacks concentration and structure; it is bland and has little length.

The 1990 marks a turning point for Lamothe. It is a fine wine, ripe apricots and botrytis on the nose, sweet and lean, and stylish on the palate. It is not particularly structured and is unlikely to develop much complexity, but given its straightforward, upfront style, it is well made and successful. I assume this reflects the innovations undertaken by Guy Despujols. No wine was bottled in 1991. Lamothe has better hopes of its 1993 wine than its 1992, which had peculiar marzipan aromas, but was sweet and clean on the palate, though thin on the finish. There was a loss of about 10 per cent to frost in 1994, but the Despujols are satisfied with the quality of the wine.

Guy Despujols, Château Lamothe, Sauternes, 33210 Langon, telephone: 56 766789, fax: 56 766377

CHÂTEAU LAMOTHE-GUIGNARD

This section of the Lamothe estate became detached in the nineteenth century. The owner of the united estate at the time of the 1855 classification was named Baptiste. This section was inherited by a son-in-law of the Baptistes and then in 1905 was sold to Charles Joseph Bergey, who left the estate to his daughter, Mme Tissot. The property was now known as Château Lamothe-Bergey. In 1958, Armand Bastit Saint-Martin, the proprietor of Château d'Arche just to the north of here, was offered the estate after Mme Tissot's death. He bought it, but instead of reuniting the two Lamothe properties, both of which he now owned, he leased out

Lamothe-Bergey. Three years later, in 1961, he sold the Lamothe property he had owned first to the Despujols family. Twenty years later, in his old age, he decided to dispose of his other properties. Château d'Arche was leased by Pierre Perromat and the remaining section of Château Lamothe was sold to the Guignard brothers in 1981.

The Guignards are an important winemaking family in the Graves. The two brothers Pierre and Jean are the owners of a good estate in the southern Graves, Château Roquetaillade-La-Grange, and of Château Rolland in Barsac. Jean's sons Philippe and Jacques were keen to enter the profession with property of their own and decided to buy this section of Lamothe, henceforth known as Lamothe-Guignard. They immediately set about renovating the buildings and, just as importantly, replanting some of the vineyards. The *chais* were in poor shape, since during the regime of Bastit Saint-Martin, the wine had been made at Château d'Arche.

The 16 ha. here are said to be on better land than those of Château Lamothe next door. The château and *chais* are situated at the top of a slope from which vines descend to the Ciron valley. The vineyards fall into two sections: one on a gravelly plateau facing Sauternes, the other on limestone and clay slopes with a limestone subsoil. This latter section faces north and north-west and overlooks the Ciron valley, giving a fine view on to the ruined castle of Budos on the far side of the valley. The density of plantation varies: 6,600 vines per ha. on the flatter sections, 5,000–5,500 on the slopes. The varieties planted are 90 per cent Sémillon, 5 per cent Sauvignon and 5 per cent Muscadelle. Yields are on average 17 hl./ha.

Like other newcomers to the band of classified growths in Sauternes, the Guignards have made a remarkable impact in a very short time and they are clearly determined to make wine worthy of the estate's status, something which has not been done here for a very long time. The brothers divide the responsibilities between them. Jacques looks after the vineyards, while Philippe takes care of vinification and commerce. Philippe, the only brother I have met, is quiet, conscientious and prefers to let the wines speak for themselves.

After the usual *triage*, the grapes are pressed in hydraulic presses and fermented either in small steel tanks with a capacity of 3,000–5,000 litres or in *barriques*. The quality and nature of the vintage determines the method of vinification. In 1990, half the crop was fermented in *barriques*; but the following three vintages were fermented in tanks, as the grapes were harvested in cool weather and the Guignards do not have the equipment to warm the *chais* to keep the fermentation going. Fermentation is usually arrested with sulphur dioxide, though some tanks do stop by themselves. Early the following year, after racking, the wine is put into *barriques*, of which one-third are new, for twelve to fifteen months. In weak vintages, such as 1992 and 1993, no new oak was used. The wine is fined shortly before bottling, which takes place about twenty months after the harvest.

The first vintage of the reborn Lamothe-Guignard was the 1981, which was reasonably successful, given the fact that the Guignards were still finding their way. Both the 1982 and 1983 were very good, the emphasis being on elegance rather than power. Lamothe-Guignard is not an ultra-rich wine and is not especially luscious, but there is always abundant fruit and concentration kept in line by firm acidity and a bewitching elegance. The 1985 lacked botrytis, as do most wines from that vintage, but it is sweet and spicy, and has good length.

The 1986 is a bit peculiar. When I first tasted it blind in 1988 I noted its 'Germanic' nose. Two years later, Michael Broadbent's tasting note records 'Very Germanic nose'. There was no collusion. Four years later the wine had changed, but it was still rather odd, with aromas of talcum powder and lanolin. Unlike most wines from Lamothe-Guignard, it was clumsy and lacked complexity. But it is improving with age, which is encouraging. The 1987 was very good for the year, fairly light, with good botrytis character; an early developer. The 1988 is marked by Sémillon on the nose; on the palate it is firm, concentrated and oaky; a slow developer. It is very good, if unexciting, but it does seem less botrytized than many other wines from this vintage.

The 1989 is irresistibly opulent, with rich, honeyed fruit and ripe, peachy flavours. The grapes had a potential alcohol of 22°, so the richness is hardly surprising. It's not exactly subtle, but that is typical of the vintage. Its length of flavour and good acidity suggest it will have a fine future. Excellent though the 1989 is, it is overshadowed by the wonderfully concentrated 1990. This is a wine that has everything: fruit, acidity, botrytis, structure, elegance. It is easily the best wine the Guignards have produced here and confirms that the estate is one of the rising stars of Sauternes.

No wine was bottled in 1991, but the 1992 yielded 20,000 bottles and Philippe Guignard is reasonably satisfied with the wine. It's good for the vintage, but the dilution and lack of structure are inescapable. This is a wine that will be agreeable young. Guignard also expects to bottle some of his 1993, though here too severe selection was necessary.

In under a decade the Guignard brothers have put this hitherto unknown estate on the map and, incidentally, confirmed the wisdom and experience of the merchants who devised the 1855 classification. Nor have the brothers allowed their success to go to their heads. Prices remain modest, and visitors are welcome to taste and buy at the estate.

Philippe and Jacques Guignard, Château Lamothe-Guignard, Sauternes, 33210 Langon, telephone: 56 766028, fax: 56 766905

CHÂTEAU DE MALLE

From the *route nationale*, signposts point the way to the only *monument historique* in the Sauternais, a compact mansard-roofed château flanked by turrets with domed towers. This exquisite house is flanked by low pavilions, adding to its expanse; on either side, courtyards conceal the *chais*. The château was built in the early seventeenth century for Jacques de Malle, a prominent figure in the Bordeaux *parlement*, but his family had been established in Preignac for some generations. The name of the architect has never been discovered. The property remained in the family until 1702. In that year, Jeanne, the daughter of Pierre de Malle who was the last male descendant of the family, married into the Lur-Salúces family, but the couple continued to live at the château. While the main branch of the Lur-Saluces family lived at Yquem after Louis-Amédée married into the Sauvage family in 1785, Louis-Amédée's younger brother Alexandre remained at Château de Malle, as did his descendants.

Claude-Henri de Lur-Saluces lost his head to the guillotine in Bordeaux in December 1793. His sixteen-year-old son Alexandre escaped from the château and fled to Spain, but returned later to become a parliamentarian under the Royalist banner. Henri de Lur-Saluces inherited in 1855 and his son Pierre in 1885. This was quite a large estate at the time, with about 50 ha. under vine. It was the only Preignac estate to be classified *Deuxième Cru* in 1855.

After the death of the unmarried Pierre de Lur-Saluces, Château de Malle passed to his great-nephew Comte Pierre de Bournazel in the mid-1950s. He was the son of Henri de Bournazel, who was known as the 'Red Cavalier' because of his daring military exploits as a cavalryman. By the time Comte Pierre took over the estate, it was severely neglected and the château itself had been uninhabited for two decades. Bournazel was an engineer, not a landowner, but resolved to take on the responsibilities of restoring and managing the historic estate. The disastrous frost of 1956 must have been immensely discouraging. It wiped out what was left of the vine-yards – they were one-third of the size they had been in the previous century – so they had to be entirely replanted. He studied winemak-ing, installed an up-to-date winery and, with the help of his ener-getic wife Nancy, restored the château. In 1959, he founded the Commanderie du Bontemps de Sauternes et Barsac, one of those promotional growers' organizations that every appellation feels compelled to have, if only as an excuse for dressing up in medieval robes and devising lavish dinners.

In 1980, the Bournazels considered the château to be sufficiently habitable for them to move down with their children from Paris. The restoration, aided by grants from the government, has been exemplary. Termites had destroyed much of the fabric of the house, but its magnificent mahogany bookcases and parquet floors sur-vived relatively unscathed. Portraits of the Lur-Saluces family gaze down from the walls; seventeenth-century *trompe-l'oeil* cut-outs loll against the fireplace in the main hall. The gardens too, originally laid out by the Lur-Saluces, have been restored to their original exquisite Italianate design, studded with rows of statuary on plinths.

Pierre de Bournazel died in 1985. Since then his widow Nancy has run the estate with dignity and efficiency, even taking the trouble to study oenology, as her husband had done before her. The house and its gardens are open to the public from Easter until 15 October and the estate's wines are available directly from the château at reasonable prices.

The vineyards form an oblong single parcel surrounding the château and pass through three communes: Preignac, Fargues and Toulenne. Not all of these 52 ha. are entitled to the Sauternes appellation; 25 ha. produce only Graves. The soil is sandy and rests on a subsoil of clay and gravel. The *encépagement* is 70 per cent Sémillon, 25 per cent Sauvignon and 5 per cent Muscadelle. The vines are over thirty years old now and Pierre Dubourdieu of Château Doisy-Daëne, a friend of Bournazel's, recalls helping to plant them.

More recently, changes have been made to the vineyards. Two hectares are being replanted because they consist of clones too productive to give good wine. The estate is moving towards a more organic style of viticulture, avoiding herbicides and other treatments whenever possible. However, Nancy de Bournazel is not dogmatic about it and if she feels treatments are necessary, she will authorize them. Yields are kept low and average 15 hl./ha.

The winemaking is supervised by the intelligent Alain Pivonet, who has been the *maître de chai* here since 1983. The grapes are pressed in a pneumatic press and since 1986 the must has been fermented half in new oak and half in one-year-old oak. The wine is then aged in *barriques* of which one-third are new. The ageing period depends on the vintage. In 1987, the wine was aged for twelve months; in 1991, for eighteen months; but in exceptional vintages, the wine spends up to two years in oak. The *assemblage* usually takes place after about six months of wood-ageing, between the second and third racking.

There is a second wine, Château de Sainte-Hélène, which may contain rejected lots from the *grand vin*, but also contains wine made from young vines. The production of De Malle does not exceed 50,000 bottles; Château de Sainte-Hélène varies from 5,000 to 10,000 bottles. Other wines produced at the estate include an excellent oaked white Graves, Monsieur de Malle, and the Sauvignon-based Chevalier de Malle.

Despite the great investments made at Château de Malle over past decades, the wine has until recently been uninspired. It was usually well made but light, lacking character and depth of flavour, always pleasant, but rarely exciting. The latest vintages, however, have shown a great improvement.

Because of the neglect of the vineyards during the time of Pierre de Lur-Saluces, older vintages are rarely encountered. I recall a 1938 that had become fiercely acidic with old age, and the light and rather dull 1962. The 1979 was rather citric, but the 1981 was surprisingly rich and rounded when young. The 1983 was a sulphurous brew and the 1985 was merely sweet, but equally marred by sulphur. The 1986 has drawn varying notes from me, some highly uncomplimentary; the best bottles have been plump and rounded, but lacking in concentration, complexity and persistence of flavour. The 1987, of which 60 per cent had to be declassified, is none the less not well balanced and the alcohol is too prominent; a premature whiff of caramel on the nose suggests the wine will develop fast.

The 1988 harvest continued until 25 November and the labour paid off. The wine is a great improvement on the 1986: not as concentrated as it should be, perhaps, but ripe and creamy, finely balanced and with good length; the nose of apricots and honey is delightful. The 1989 is a bigger, fatter wine, with almost 15° of alcohol and 5° of residual sugar. Insects diminished the Sauvignon crop in 1989, so the wine is lusher than is usual at De Malle. The 1990, which has 7° of residual sugar, is even better, a golden wine with real elegance; even the 1990 Château de Sainte-Hélène is excellent. Some lots in 1990 had must weights of 30° and Pivonet had considerable difficulty persuading the must to ferment. The 1991, made after a single *trie* in the third week of September, is remarkably good too, one of the best wines of the vintage, a mouthful of ripe lemon and crisp acidity. Only 10,000 bottles were produced. No wine was bottled in 1992 and 1993.

Since 1988, the features that usually made De Malle disappointing have diminished greatly. No longer is there a hot, rasping tang of sulphur dioxide, nor does the wine fade away from lack of concentration. After decades in the doldrums, De Malle is once again a wine to look out for.

Comtesse de Bournazel, Château de Malle, Preignac, 33210 Langon, telephone: 56 623686, fax: 56 768240

CHÂTEAU ROMER DU HAYOT

There is no point looking for Château Romer du Hayot. It was demolished when the *autoroute* was built. However, the vineyards which lie to the east of Suduiraut were left intact and the wine is made at Château Guiteronde in Barsac, which is also owned by André du Hayot. It is the sole *Deuxième Cru* in Fargues.

The estate had many owners in the nineteenth century: notably M. de Montalier, who prefixed his name to that of Romer, and

Comte Auguste de la Myre-Mory (related by marriage to the Lur-Saluces family). In 1881, after the death of the Comtesse de la Myre-Mory, the estate was divided among five heirs. In 1937, two-thirds of the property, some 12 ha., was bought by the mother of André du Hayot; the other third remained the property of Roger Farges. Shortly before his death in 1977, Farges leased his vines to André du Hayot, who vinifies and markets the entire production of the estate.

The soil is gravel over clay and limestone, and the area under vine is 16 ha., planted with 70 per cent Sémillon, 20 per cent Sauvignon and 10 per cent Muscadelle. The average age of the vines is thirty-five years and their density of plantation is 6,500 per ha. All vinification takes place at the very modern installations at Château Guiteronde under the supervision of André du Hayot and his *maître de chai*, Jacques Bedouret. Du Hayot is not an easy man to track down and as I have never managed to obtain an appointment with him, I chose to walk unannounced into his office in search of up-to-date information. He was cagey at first, but soon warmed up and showed me round the winery, which has an industrial feel to it, moderated by the stylish *chais*.

Romer du Hayot is a frankly commercial wine. Yields are quite high at 20 hl./ha. on average. The grapes are pressed in horizontal presses. The must is fermented in stainless steel, cold-stabilized, filtered and aged for two years. Until 1980, all ageing took place in tanks, but since André du Hayot air-conditioned his *chais*, he has been leaving some of the wine in *barriques*, of which one-third are new, for twelve months. The average production is 50,000 bottles. Second wines are released under a variety of labels, such as Château Andoyse du Hayot, but they are all the same wine. André du Hayot does keep stocks of older vintages, which he releases from time to time in small quantities. The bottles are stacked in a special cellar behind the *chai de barriques* and it is interesting to observe how the colours deepen as the wines get older.

The wine, not surprisingly, is light and lacking in concentration. They are soundly made, but unexciting. The 1982 was good; rich, but not overblown. Other good vintages include 1986 and 1990. No wine was bottled as Château Romer du Hayot in 1974, 1977 and 1984. The wine is rarely encountered in Britain, nor do I recall seeing it very often on French wine lists. Much of it seems to go to those avid wine drinkers, the Belgians.

THE *DEUXIÈMES CRUS* OF SAUTERNES, PREIGNAC AND FARGUES

André du Hayot, Château Guiteronde, Barsac, 33720 Podensac, telephone: 56 271537, fax: 56 270424

11

Other Wines of Barsac

CRU BARRÉJATS

It may be premature to write about an estate that produced its first vintage only in 1990, but the energy and commitment of its founders, Mireille Daret and Philippe Anduran, is so infectious that I am confident this tiny property will go from strength to strength. Dr Daret's grandfather was a Barsac cooper who owned a small vineyard. The wine had always been sold to wholesalers, but in 1989 Dr Daret decided she would make and market the wine herself and gradually expand the estate, which consists of three small parcels located between Climens and Caillou. So they are all on the excellent soils of Haut-Barsac; moreover the vines are mature, with an average age of thirty years. There are only 2.6 ha. under vine at present, and the *encépagement* is 85 per cent Sémillon, 10 per cent Sauvignon and 5 per cent Muscadelle. Rigorous standards of viticulture are practised, with very severe pruning and no herbicides employed.

The grapes are crushed, then pressed in a vertical press in the tiny shack that passes for a *cuverie*. The must is then fermented in new Allier or Vosges oak and aged for up to eighteen months. The *chai de barriques* can be heated to keep the fermentation going. When it is completed, the wine is sulphured and chilled to 5°C.

I first encountered the wine in 1993 and was impressed by the vigour and elegance of the 1990. The 1991 was also a great success; the grapes were *confit*, but the frost meant the yields were only 9 hl./ha. The wine is very intense, though the oak is very marked on nose and palate, and will need some time to become integrated. There will be about 4,000 bottles of the 1992, but no 1993 will be bottled.

Production, of course, is minute, with only 1,220 bottles in 1990 and 2,400 in 1991. But the wine is overpriced, with each vintage selling for 180 francs, higher than some *Premiers Crus*.

Dr Mireille Daret, Clos de Gensac, Mareuil, 33210 Pujols, telephone: 56 766906

CHÂTEAU DE LA BOUADE

See Clos Mercier (p. 161).

CHÂTEAU BOUYOT

This 13.5–ha. estate has been in the hands of the Jammu-Fonbeney family since 1936, but the wines have been estate-bottled only since 1985. Its vineyards, located in numerous parcels between Coutet and Myrat, are well located on a variety of soils. The *encépagement* is 95 per cent Sémillon, 3 per cent Sauvignon and 2 per cent Muscadelle. The wine is aged in *barriques* for twelve months and about 15,000 bottles are produced. The only vintage I have tasted was the 1990, which was good, but hardly outstanding for the year.

Bertrand Jammu-Fonbeney, Château Bouyot, Barsac, 33720 Podensac, telephone: 56 271946, fax: 56 272364

CHÂTEAU CANTEGRIL

This 16–ha. property belonged to the parents of Pierre Dubourdieu's wife; her father, who was born in 1900, still farms 2 ha. separately. Cantegril is an ancient property and there was a castle here in the Middle Ages. The estate once belonged to the powerful Duc d'Épernon, then to the seigneurs of Cantegril, one of whom married a daughter of the Myrat family, who built the present château of that name. The castle was destroyed in the eighteenth century and Château Cantegril was rebuilt in the mid-nineteenth century as a tall, handsome house overlooking a courtyard. In 1854, Cantegril was separated from Myrat and bought by M. Ségur-Montagne, changing hands many times before being acquired by Charles Rodberg, the Belgian consul in Bordeaux.

The *encépagement* is 90 per cent Sémillon and 10 per cent Sauvignon. The vinification is identical to that at Doisy-Daëne, though harvesting begins earlier here. Dubourdieu says that if he reversed the policy, Cantegril would actually produce more concentrated

wine than Doisy-Daëne. Since 1988, Cantegril has been aged in
barriques.

My experience of this wine is very limited, but the vintages I
tasted from the early 1980s were straightforward and well balanced, and the 1981 seemed particularly successful.

Pierre Dubourdieu, Château Doisy-Daëne, Barsac, 33720 Podensac, telephone: 56 271584, fax: 56 271899

CHÂTEAU CLOSIOT

This small estate of 8 ha. produces about 7,000 bottles on average.
The varieties planted are 95 per cent Sémillon, 3 per cent Sauvignon
and 2 per cent Muscadelle. The must is fermented in tank, and the
wine is aged in oak casks for between two and three years. The only
vintage I have tasted is the 1990, which was woody and rather
clumsy.

Mme Françoise Soizeau, Château Closiot, Barsac, 33720 Podensac,
telephone: 56 270592, fax: 56 271106

CHÂTEAU DUDON

Between Coutet and Broustet lie the 11 ha. of vineyards belonging
to Château Dudon. The house itself was built during the reign of
Louis XIII in the seventeenth century, but this imposing property
was badly neglected until the enthusiastic Mme Allien decided to
bring it back to life again. For fifty years, after the premature death
of her great-grandfather, its wine had been sold in bulk. The property had descended through the female side of the family and in the
1980s Mme Allien resolved to put Dudon back into production as
an estate-bottled wine. She restored the property, hired a cellarmaster who had worked at Coutet and issued her first wine from the
1988 vintage.

The soil is stony, but with plenty of sand and clay, and the subsoil
is typical Barsac limestone. No herbicides are used in the vineyard,
and yields are moderate at between 17 and 20 hl./ha. The *encépagement* is 80 per cent Sémillon, 15 per cent Sauvignon and 5 per cent
Muscadelle. Some of the vines are seventy years old, but their average age is about forty years. The grapes are pressed in a horizontal
press and fermentation begins in barrels. Rather oddly, the wine is
then transferred to tanks to continue its fermentation more rapidly,

then replaced in *barriques* for the final phase of the fermentation. After each racking the wine changes container, from barrel to tank and back again. In good years, one-third of the *barriques* are new. The wine is bottled about two and a half years after the harvest, but not all at once. At present, the production is 18,000 bottles.

The wine is good, but not outstanding. The 1989 has a waxy nose with little apparent botrytis and is peachy but dull on the palate. The 1990 is better, with typical Barsac *nervosité* and an attractive spiciness on the palate. The wine lacks concentration, although the average must weight was 21°. Much of the 1992 was sold off to wholesalers.

Mme Evelyne Allien, Château Dudon, Barsac, 33720 Podensac, telephone: 56 270737, fax: 56 272938

CHÂTEAU GRAVAS

This attractive estate, grouped around its charming ivy-covered house, has been in the Bernard family since 1850. Until recently, the wine was made by the sturdy Pierre, but he has now been succeeded by his son Patrick. The 12 ha. of vines are well situated on gravel and clay soil between Climens and Coutet, and close to the château. The varieties planted are 80 per cent Sémillon, and 10 per cent each of Sauvignon and Muscadelle. The average age of the vines is thirty years and yields are quite high, some 22 hl./ha.

The must is chaptalized by up to 2° when necessary. Pierre Bernard argues rather oddly that lots picked on different days with different must weights need to be levelled out by chaptalization to ensure consistency. After pressing in a horizontal press, the must is fermented in stainless-steel tanks at 22–23°C. After fermentation the wine is racked, filtered and then aged both in underground tanks and in *barriques*, of which one-third are new. Bernard doesn't want a wine that is tannic or woody, hence the rotation between barrel and tank. A light filtration precedes bottling, which takes place about two years after the harvest.

Bernard aims for a fairly hefty style, with between 14 and 15° of alcohol, and less rich in *liqueur* than most Sauternes. The fruit of Gravas is often excellent, but I find the style over-alcoholic and lacking in finesse, and exhibiting traces of oxidation, thus developing prematurely 'aged' flavours of caramel and tar.

The maximum production of Gravas is 30,000 bottles. In certain

years, such as 1983, 1986 and 1989, Bernard produces a special
cuvée of, as in 1983, 3,000 bottles. In certain markets he uses a
second label, Château Simon Carretey, though he insists that the
wine is identical to Gravas.

In 1983, the regular bottling was rather dull and lacked botrytis,
but the special *cuvée* was much more honeyed and rich. The 1985
is, however, one of the best wines of the vintage. Bernard attributes
its splendour to the fact that he sprayed his vines with nitrogen,
which provoked botrytis at a time when no neighbouring vineyards
had been attacked by it. This explanation seems baffling; but it is
possible, say his neighbours, that his soil retained more humidity in
1985, thus allowing botrytis to materialize. The wine is massive,
with 15.5° of alcohol and 5° of residual sugar, with smoky aromas
of stewed peaches, lush on the palate with rich toffee-apple and
barley-sugar flavours, and with just a hint of alcohol on the finish.
The 1988 has greater stylishness and balance than the 1990, which
is caramelly and stewed. The 1991 is rather peppery and coarse,
and, like the 1990, marked by that oxidative style that gives the
wine evolved flavours even in its youth.

Pierre Bernard, Château Gravas, Barsac, 33720 Podensac, phone:
56 271520, fax: 56 272983

CHÂTEAU GUITERONDE

This estate has a long history and was in the possession of a
member of the Bordeaux *parlement*, M. Journu, in 1810. The property is mentioned in various reference books, including Charles
Cocks's in 1850, by which time it was owned by Raymond Sarraute, in whose family it remained for over a century. The present
owner is André du Hayot, the co-proprietor of Château Romer du
Hayot, which is vinified and aged in the fine modern cellars that he
has constructed here at Guiteronde.

This is a large estate of some 45 ha., planted with 70 per cent
Sémillon, 20 per cent Sauvignon and 10 per cent Muscadelle. Guiteronde is an unashamedly commercial wine, produced from the
highest yields allowed. The must is fermented in stainless steel, then
aged primarily in tank, though the wine also spends six months in
barriques, of which one-third are new. Guiteronde is available
in generous quantities, up to 120,000 bottles. André du Hayot,
who is somewhat reticent in disclosing how he runs his many

estates, also produces Sauternes under the labels of Brassens-Guit-eronde, Camperos and Pebayle. It is not clear what differences, if any, there are between these labels.

I have not tasted this wine, but it is fair to say that it has rarely been met with acclaim, with the distant exception of the 1923 vintage.

André du Hayot, Château Guiteronde, Barsac, 33720 Podensac, telephone: 56 271537, fax: 56 270424

CHÂTEAU HAUT-MAYNE

See Château Caillou (p. 104).

CHÂTEAU LIOT

This estate was created in 1880 by Léon Cadillon, but has been in the possession of the David family for a number of generations. The present proprietor is the genial Jean Gérard David, who aims to make attractively priced wines that express the particular *terroir* of Barsac.

There are 20 ha. under vine, 19 ha. in production, all in Haut-Barsac. There are some parcels near the nineteenth-century château; others are located close to Climens. The *encépagement* is 85 per cent Sémillon, 10 per cent Sauvignon and 5 per cent Musca-delle. The average age of the vines is thirty-five years, as the majority were planted after the 1956 frost. Yields are quite high here, averaging 22 hl./ha., as David is open about producing a commercial wine, though one of good quality and reliability.

The grapes are pressed in a horizontal press and fermented mostly in tank but partly in *barriques*, except in weak vintages such as 1992 and 1993, when no wood was used. Few of the *barriques* are new, as David doesn't want to overpower the wine with oaky flavours. Ageing in barrel continues for up to eighteen months and the wine is then bottled. Declassified lots form the *deuxième vin*, Château du Levant. The maximum production of Liot is about 50,000 bottles.

The David family has long had strong connections with the Brit-ish market, as many years ago Harveys of Bristol bottled the wine. Bottles destined for British outlets are identified as Barsac, whereas other markets prefer the wine to be labelled as Sauternes. This surely tells us something about an ancient British preference for the elegance of Barsac.

Thanks to the Davids' hospitality, I have drunk the 1961, which had become bronze in colour; although dumb on the nose, on the palate there were rich caramel and candied-orange flavours – perhaps too much of a good thing, but a concentrated and sumptuous wine. More recent vintages have lacked personality. The 1975 had a good reputation, but I found it hard to get excited by the pallid 1983, with its marzipan nose and rather flabby texture. The 1986 is pleasant but dilute, agreeably fresh but with little botrytis. I haven't tasted the 1988, but the 1989 is very good, with racy acidity, plenty of botrytis and real Barsac typicity. It is not especially complex, but one must bear in mind that this is a fairly inexpensive wine. The 1990, which has 15° of alcohol and 5.2° of residual sugar, has been opening up slowly since it was bottled and improves with every encounter. Peachy and voluptuous for a Barsac, it is unusually well structured for Liot and there is no shortage of botrytis. The 1991 was blended with the 1992, at least for the British market. The 1993, tasted from tank in the spring of 1994, was distinctly nasty.

Jean Gérard David, Château Liot, Barsac, 33720 Podensac, telephone: 56 271531

CHÂTEAU DU MAYNE

This 8–ha. estate is owned by Jean Sanders, who is responsible for one of the most charming red Graves at Haut-Bailly. The varieties planted are 80 per cent Sémillon and 20 per cent Sauvignon, and the soil is unusually gravelly for Barsac. The vineyards lie between the railway line and Château Suau. The production, part of which is aged in barrels, is about 20,000 bottles. I have never seen the wine, but older vintages have a very good reputation.

Jean Sanders, Château Haut-Bailly, 33850 Léognan, telephone: 56 647511, fax: 56 645360

CHÂTEAU MÉNOTA

This splendid property is a fortified manor still partly surrounded by a crenellated wall that flanks the entrance gate. As the architecture suggests, it is an ancient property. One of the early owners was

François de Pignéguy, who in the sixteenth century was president of the Bordeaux *parlement*. From the mid-nineteenth century until well into the present century, the owner was the Teyssonneau family, also the owners of Château Doisy-Védrines. One of the Teyssonneau daughters married into the Castéja family, the present proprietors of Doisy-Védrines. The current owner of Ménota is Noël Labat, whom I have encountered only once, as he drove into the courtyard while I was talking to his wife. He did not take kindly to my presence and yelled at me while peeing against the wall of the *chais*. I took a hasty departure, so my researches are incomplete.

Ménota is run on very commercial lines. The 29 ha. of vines are equally divided between Sémillon and Sauvignon. The wine is fermented and aged only in steel tanks. Up to 100,000 bottles are produced and there is also a second wine, Château Menatte. The only vintage of Ménota I have tasted is the 1983, which did not incline me to taste any others.

Noël Labat, Château Ménota, Barsac, 33720 Podensac, telephone: 56 271580, fax: 56 270079

CHÂTEAU PASCAUD-VILLEFRANCHE

I encountered the 1989 vintage from this estate in London recently and was attracted by its simple charm, although it had little depth of flavour. Later, in Barsac, I learnt that the owner is none other than Pierre Pascaud, the long-serving *régisseur* at Suduiraut. Pascaud-Villefranche has been in his family for four generations, and is now run by his son Fabien. Its 8 ha. are planted with 75 per cent Sémillon, 20 per cent Sauvignon and 5 per cent Muscadelle. Some of the vines are one hundred years old. The must is fermented in temperature-controlled stainless-steel tanks and partly aged in *barriques*. The maximum production is 25,000 bottles. This is not a wine of any great pretensions, but it is well made and worth looking out for.

Pierre Pascaud, Château Pascaud-Villefranche, Barsac, 33720 Podensac, telephone: 56 271609

CHÂTEAU PETIT-MAYNE

See Château Caillou (p. 104).

CHÂTEAU PIADA

This is yet another estate that once belonged to the Lur-Saluces family. In 1809, they sold the estate to the Pinsan-Lataste family and it came into the hands of the Brunet family in the mid-nineteenth century. The estate was subsequently acquired by Jean Lalande's father in 1940. Lalande, now assisted by his son Frédéric, has consolidated this well-run estate into a reliable source of good Barsac. Lalande is sturdily built, bald, energetic, a *bon viveur*, fond of his food, his wine, his cigars. One hesitates to link personalities with their wines, but the vigour of Piada does seem a reflection of its owner's character, just as the drabness of other Sauternes seems mirrored by the dullness of their proprietors.

Close to Château Coutet, Piada's vineyards have the typically reddish soil of Barsac. Its 9 ha. are entirely planted with Sémillon. Yields vary widely, but the only time since 1962 that the maximum permitted yield was attained was in 1989; in 1990, the yield was 20 hl./ha. Lalande also owns the Clos du Roy, where a little Muscadelle is planted as well as Sémillon. Lalande is not keen on his Muscadelle, as the clones planted have proved over-productive. Clos du Roy is in effect the second wine of Piada. Only vines that are at least ten years old are used for Piada; must from younger vines is consigned to Clos du Roy. Piada is almost never chaptalized, so any lots that need to be sugared end up as Clos du Roy, or are declassified altogether. Piada is *barrique*-fermented and one-quarter of the oak is new, except in lesser vintages such as 1991. The wine remains in *barriques* for almost a year and is bottled about fifteen months after the harvest, as Lalande wants the wine to retain its freshness.

The maximum production of Piada is 30,000 bottles. No wine was bottled in 1992 or 1993, though there was a 1992 Clos du Roy. Piada is not cheap: the excellent 1990 was priced at 165 francs, considerably more than some *Crus Classés*, but the lighter 1991 was more sensibly priced at 105 francs.

Piada produced a fine, slightly citric wine in 1986, though it lacked some concentration. The 1988 is more elegant, with a lovely lemony freshness and the *nervosité* one looks for in a Barsac. The 1989 is more rich and plump, a simply delicious wine, though it doesn't have quite the length and stylishness of the more classic 1988. The sweetness of the 1990 is balanced by an almost peppery aftertaste and fine acidity. It will need more time to develop, I suspect, than the 1989. The 1991 is good for the vintage, a vigorous wine marked by botrytis and given a touch of structure by the oak. Clos du Roy is, predictably, of less interest, though the 1991 is quite good.

Jean Lalande, Château Piada, Barsac, 33720 Podensac, telephone: 56 271613, fax: 56 272630

CHÂTEAU PIOT-DAVID

This estate, close to the River Ciron in the eastern part of Barsac, was once part of a larger property known as Château Piot, and it was further diminished in size when 3 ha. were acquired by the Dufours of Château Simon. Since 1983, the estate has been owned by M. David, who is based on the other side of the Garonne in the Premières Côtes where, among other wines, he makes a Cadillac. The property now consists of a single walled parcel of 7 ha. planted with 80 per cent Sémillon and 20 per cent Sauvignon, which David says gives unsatisfactory results here. The soil is complex, composed of clay, gravel and sand, and the drainage is excellent. The vines are quite old and there is one parcel that is sixty years old, but yields are usually the maximum permitted. Until 1988, the wine was fermented in tanks, but in response to demands from private clients and his Italian customers, David began fermenting part of the wine in *barriques*. It is still aged in tanks, but David hopes to age a proportion of the wine in new oak in the future. Maximum production is 20,000 bottles and prices are moderate. The second wine is Château Bourdon.

Jean-Luc David, Domaine de Poncet, 33410 Omet, telephone: 56 629730, fax: 56 626676

CHÂTEAU PROST

This 15–ha. estate is named after the owner who acquired the property after the Revolution and the subsequent flight of its previous proprietor. Since 1966, it has been owned by Jean Perromat, the mayor of Cérons. The vines lie opposite Château Nairac on the river side of the *route nationale*. The *encépagement* is 65 per cent Sémillon, 20 per cent Sauvignon and 15 per cent Muscadelle. The wine is vinified in *barriques* and the maximum production is

30,000 bottles. Sold mostly in France and Luxembourg, it is rarely seen outside those countries. Judging by the 1979 and 1985 vintages, Prost is a light, lemony wine, fresh and simple, and not very exciting.

Jean Perromat, Château de Cérons, Cérons, 33720 Podensac, telephone: 56 270113, fax: 56 272217

CHÂTEAU ROLLAND

As you go towards Preignac from Barsac, on the right you pass the gateway and drive that lead to Château Rolland. The château is now detached from the vineyard and is operated as a hotel. The surrounding vineyards, close to the Ciron, are vinified in a large old building nearby. The property used to be owned by a gentleman called Combefréroux, who sold it in 1971 to Jean and Pierre Guignard. (Jean's sons have bought the *Deuxième Cru* now known as Château Lamothe-Guignard.) The estate used to be planted with red grapes, but was replanted with white varieties in 1942, at which time it was owned by Pierre Bert. Under M. Combefréroux the wine was mostly sold in bulk and had little reputation. The Guignards are actively involved in the winemaking and commercialization of this attractive wine.

The soil here is gravel and clay, well drained, over a limestone subsoil, located right at the end of the plateau of Barsac. There are 16 ha. under vine, but 3 ha. are not entitled to the Barsac appellation. The varieties planted are 80 per cent Sémillon, 15 per cent Sauvignon and 5 per cent Muscadelle. There are many old vines, and the average yield is 18 hl./ha.

The grapes are pressed in both horizontal and hydraulic presses. The must is fermented in small temperature-controlled tanks for about four weeks. No cultivated yeasts are added, but there is chaptalization in certain vintages. The wine is aged in *barriques*, of which 15 to 20 per cent are new. Rolland is bottled about twenty months after the harvest.

The Guignards are not looking to make an especially rich or unctuous wine. They want finesse above all, which is the contribution of the Sauvignon and Muscadelle in the vineyard. The maximum production is about 40,000 bottles and there is a second label, Château Arnaudas, used only in export markets. The Guignards used to operate a tasting and sales room in a cabin near the *route nationale*, but this was closed after repeated break-ins. But visitors are welcome to visit and taste at the winery. Prices are moderate.

The oldest Rolland I have tasted is the 1982, which I found fat but charmless, reasonably sweet but blowsy and lacking in acidity. The 1984 had a hard, rather Muscatty flavour which was not agreeable. The 1990 is very good, with botrytis apparent on the nose, and a palate that is rich and creamy yet fresh. This is not a top 1990 because it lacks concentration and persistence, but it is none the less a delicious wine. The 1991 has a strong apricot tone and slightly *rôti* flavours; a correct wine, well made, but rather lean. The 1992 is dilute and rather short, but pleasant for early drinking; very little was bottled.

Jean and Pierre Guignard, Château Rolland, Barsac, 33720 Podensac, telephone: 56 271502, fax: 56 272858

CHÂTEAU ROUMIEU

This 14–ha. estate adjoins Climens and Doisy-Védrines, and is located on typical Haut-Barsac soil. The varieties planted are 90 per cent Sémillon and 10 per cent Sauvignon. The wine is fermented and aged in *barriques* and the maximum production is 45,000 bottles. It is not a wine that has greatly impressed me: the 1976 was still marred by sulphur dioxide after fifteen years, and it had a waxy astringency that was far from pleasant, a blend of high alcohol and sulphur. The 1990 is far better, grapy and succulent, but with less botrytis than one would expect in so sumptuous a vintage. But it is certainly a good wine. It should not be confused, though it is easy to do so, with either Château Roumieu-Bernardet (now owned by Olivier Bernardet and rarely encountered) or Château Roumieu-Lacoste, also in Barsac.

Catherine Cravéla-Goyaud, Château Roumieu, Barsac, 33720 Podensac, telephone: 56 272101, fax: 56 270155

CHÂTEAU ROUMIEU-LACOSTE

Like Châteaux Roumieu and Roumieu-Bernardet, this once formed part of a single estate, which was split in three in about 1900. Dubourdieu's great-grandfather was a Lacoste, so the name was appended to their portion of the property. The youthful Hervé Dubourdieu has bought out his two brothers' share of the estate

SAUTERNES

and now runs it on his own. If he encounters problems, he can presumably consult his uncle Pierre at Château Doisy-Daëne just down the road. The 11 ha. of vineyards are located opposite Climens. In addition, Dubourdieu owns 8 ha. of white Graves, which has helped him through the difficult years of the early 1990s. The *encépagement* is 95 per cent Sémillon, 3 per cent Sauvignon Blanc and 2 per cent Muscadelle. There are many old vines and Dubourdieu estimates the average age at forty-five years. Average yields are about 20 hl./ha. He seeks to make a wine that is, in his words, rich, masculine and structured.

The winery is spotless and well equipped. The grapes are pressed in a pneumatic press and fermented in temperature-controlled tanks. Yeasts are added only when it is difficult to get the fermentation going. He chaptalizes as little as possible. The wine is aged in tanks and *barriques*, in which it stays up to twelve months. Most of the barrels are one or two years old. The maximum production is 35,000 bottles and there is a second label, Château Ducasse, for less satisfactory lots. Dubourdieu is keen to set high standards for himself and released no Roumieu-Lacoste in 1991, 1992, or 1993, and no Ducasse either in 1992 and 1993. His prices are fairly high and though I was unimpressed by the bland 1990, it is the only vintage I have encountered, so it would be rash to attempt an overall judgement on that basis.

Hervé Dubourdieu, Château Roumieu-Lacoste, Barsac, 33720 Podensac, telephone: 56 271629, fax: 56 270265

CHÂTEAU SAINT-MARC

Around a neat courtyard stand the linked buildings of the house, offices and large *chais* that form the core of this estate. From the courtyard gates there is an excellent view on to Château Broustet, which Didier Laulan bought in 1994, a rare example of a local *viticulteur* exercising upward mobility. The tall chatty Laulan is enjoyably indiscreet. He once allowed me to taste a tank full of rot-wrecked 1993 that, we both agreed, was so disgusting that it couldn't even be fobbed off on to wholesalers and would be destined for the drains of Saint-Marc. Indeed, no 1993 Saint-Marc at all will be bottled.

The 10 ha. of the estate are divided between 5 ha. on sandy soil near the house, 3 ha. near the church on clay soil, and 2 ha. on

158

classic Haut-Barsac soil near Château Caillou. The varieties planted
are 85 per cent Sémillon, 10 per cent Sauvignon and 5 per cent
Muscadelle. Their average age is thirty-five years. Yields are moderate at 17 hl./ha., though for the second wine, Château Bessan,
yields of 25 hl./ha. are routine. Bessan is sold primarily in supermarkets.

Saint-Marc is not a very complex wine. Laulan uses a horizontal
press, vinifies in tanks with natural yeasts and, until 1992, aged the
wine entirely in tank. Now each lot spends at least six months in
barriques. Laulan buys his own wood and has the barrels made
locally. There is a single bottling, some eighteen to twenty months
after the harvest, and the wine is not released until three months
later. In terms of style, Laulan wants Barsac *nervosité* and fairly
high alcohol, which is attained by means of more or less routine
chaptalization.

Laulan runs a commercial operation, has a well-organized net-
work of clients and keeps little stock. Yet the wines are quite good.
The 1989 was lemony and elegant on the nose, and on the palate it
was plump but not heavy, having exactly the racy *nervosité* one
looks for in Barsac, even from rich years such as this. In 1990, he
made 6,000 bottles of a very fine Cuvée Speciale from grapes picked
at 21° and unchaptalized. It has ample honeyed botrytis on the nose
and delicious unctuous fruit on the palate, yet without undue fat. If
only, I couldn't help wondering, such excellent fruit had had the
benefit of some oak-ageing. The 1991 tasted citric, and slightly flat
and sulphury, but I tasted it shortly after bottling. It will no doubt
settle down, but it will never be more than workmanlike.

Didier Laulan, Château Saint-Marc, Barsac, 33720 Podensac, telephone: 56 271687, fax: 56 271505

CHÂTEAU SIMON

This well cared-for estate of 17 ha. has been in the Dufour family
for five generations. The vineyards are in various parcels so the soil
varies from the clay and limestone of Barsac to the more gravelly
soil of Preignac. The grapes planted are 90 per cent Sémillon, 7 per
cent Sauvignon and 3 per cent Muscadelle. Their average age is
thirty years. Yields are fairly high, at 22 hl./ha.

A horizontal press was used until 1994, when it was replaced by
a pneumatic press. The must is chaptalized when necessary and

fermented without cultivated yeasts in temperature-controlled stainless-steel tanks. The wine is aged for one year in *barriques*, of which only 15 per cent are new, but in exceptional vintages, such as 1989 and 1990, a higher proportion of new oak was employed. Dufour also makes a dry white wine fermented in new oak, so he tends to use those barrels subsequently for his Sauternes. There are usually two bottlings: one in the spring following the second winter after the harvest and the second in the early autumn.

Dufour seeks to make a wine with good aromas and no excessive sweetness. Even he could not resist the sumptuousness of the 1989 and 1990 vintages, so he produced outstanding *cuvées* of 12,000 bottles which he aged for two years in new oak. Dufour admits that by producing this separate *cuvée* he probably lowered the overall quality of his standard wines, but he felt compelled to preserve the special character of the vintages. He considers 1990 the equal of the legendary 1929, 1947 and 1949 vintages.

The maximum production is about 30,000 bottles and there is also a second wine, Château Grand Mayne. Visitors are welcome and a good selection of older vintages, from 1970 onwards, is offered for sale. Prices are reasonable: in 1994, the 1990 was priced at 105 francs; the 1991 at 84 francs; the 1990 Cuvée Exceptionelle at 150 francs, which is moderate given its quality.

The oldest vintage of Château Simon I have tasted is the 1980, which after fourteen years was still lively and fresh, though not especially aromatic or complex. The 1989 was delicious and finely concentrated, the 1990 a touch lean and lemony, since the best grapes had been used for the magnificent Cuvée Exceptionelle, which is lushly botrytized and honeyed, yet without a trace of heaviness. This is a wine that I have heard even owners of *Crus Classés* refer to with awe. In 1991, only 12,000 bottles were produced; it had an odd lemon-curd and almonds nose, and was well balanced and stylish on the palate. Much of the 1992 and 1993 was sold to wholesalers; the 1993 that was bottled was light and charming, a good aperitif wine to be drunk young.

Jean Hugues Dufour, Château Simon, Barsac, 33720 Podensac, phone: 56 271535, fax: 56 272479

CHÂTEAU VILLEFRANCHE

It is a pleasure to be received at Villefranche by Henri Guinabert, who resembles in appearance the benign Spencer Tracy. He acquired the property by marrying the daughter of the proprietor; today his son Benoît is poised to take over the management of the estate, and his other son Pierre leases Château Cameron in Bommes. Forty years ago there were only 4 ha. under vine, producing a mere 2,000–3,000 bottles, as most of the wine was sold in bulk to the wine merchants Nicolas. Today there are 14 ha. under vine at Villefranche, all located in Haut-Barsac between the house and the *autoroute*; their average age is thirty years. The varieties planted are 85 per cent Sémillon, 10 per cent Sauvignon and 5 per cent Muscadelle. Yields are usually close to the permitted maximum.

The grapes are pressed in a horizontal press, fermented in tanks with the natural yeasts and then in the spring following the harvest the wine is transferred to *barriques* for twelve to twenty-four months. The barrels come from Yquem and are two to four years old. There are at least two bottlings, totalling 25,000–30,000 bottles.

I have not encountered any Villefranche older than the 1990, which was an excellent wine, quite rich and marked by botrytis and a certain spiciness, though it lacked concentration of flavour. The 1991 was waxy on the nose and light on the palate, and I was unimpressed by the 1992 and 1993, though I tasted them in their extreme youth.

Henri Guinabert, Château Villefranche, Barsac, 33720 Podensac, telephone: 56 271639

CLOS MERCIER

Both Château de la Bouade and Clos Mercier are the property of Mlle Violette Pauly, who lives at La Bouade. Her wine has been bottled since 1967 and in 1990 she leased her vineyards to the grizzled, reserved M. Le Roux. The two estates consist of 17 ha., with vines between the house at La Bouade and the railway lines, and a 3–ha. parcel near Château Simon. Clos Mercier is located in Haut-Barsac and its wines are slightly finer than those from La Bouade. The estates are planted with 90 per cent Sémillon and 10 per cent Sauvignon Blanc. The average age of the vines is thirty years, since there are some very old vines of eighty years as well as recent plantations. Yields are quite high.

The must is fermented in tank and then aged in *barriques* for between six and nine months, with a rotation between barrel and tank. Very little new oak is used and the oldest barrels are five years old. The wine is bottled about thirty months after the harvest in a single bottling. The average production is 10,000 bottles of Clos Mercier and 12,000 of Château de la Bouade. No La Bouade was produced in 1991. M. Le Roux seeks to make the two wines in a different style. La Bouade has higher alcohol and lower residual sugar; Clos Mercier, which is labelled as Sauternes, has a richer style with lower alcohol.

The wines of Clos Mercier are attractive, but tend to be undernourished and lacking in structure. They are correct but hardly exciting. Prices are low.

M. Le Roux, Château de la Bouade, Barsac, 33720 Podensac, telephone: 56 273053

12

Other Wines of Preignac

───────

CRU D'ARCHE-PUGNEAU

This 12–ha. estate has been owned by the Daney family since 1923 and the present owner is the exuberant Jean-Francis Daney. The estate is composed of many parcels: 70 per cent of the vines are planted on gravelly soil between Lafaurie-Peyraguey and Rayne-Vigneau; other lots are found near Rabaud-Promis. About half the vines are younger than twelve years old, but some parcels have octogenarian vines. The *encépagement* is 75 per cent Sémillon, 20 per cent Sauvignon and 5 per cent Muscadelle. In 1993, Daney experimented with cryo-extraction, but the results did not convince him that the process was worthwhile.

Daney uses a horizontal press, but the final pressing is usually made with a hydraulic press. After a *débourbage*, the must is mostly fermented in barrels after being chaptalized. There are no added yeasts. Some of the wine is fermented in tanks. The wine is aged in barrels for at least eighteen months and it is not unusual for some lots to remain in barrel for four years. Since the average age of these barrels is ten years and the proportion of new oak is very small, the casks serve essentially as neutral containers. However, there are a number of bottlings, so there are bound to be inconsistencies in certain vintages. Daney bottles the wine only in good years, and there is no second wine. Anything that he finds unsatisfactory, such as the entire 1992 crop and half that of 1993, is sold off to Bordeaux wholesalers. The style he favours is one of considerable power, but without heaviness. The maximum production is 25,000 bottles.

In 1987, he initiated a special *cuvée* called Trie Exceptionelle, and this was also produced from 1988 to 1991 inclusive. Visitors

SAUTERNES

are welcomed to this estate, which has an attractive *chai de barriques*. Some older vintages are for sale, such as 1979 and 1981,
and prices are fairly expensive for a non-classified growth.

Arche-Pugneau is a big peachy wine with immediate appeal. The
1982 was slightly blowsy, but very enjoyable, as was the sweeter,
more intense 1983. The 1985 was good for the vintage. The only
Trie Exceptionelle I have tasted is the 1990, which is thick with
confit botrytis flavours, a rich, sweet, orangey wine with little subtlety, but excellent length of flavour.

Jean-Francis Daney, Cru d'Arche-Pugneau, Preignac, 33210
Langon, telephone: 56 63 50 55, fax: 56 63 39 69

CHÂTEAU D'ARMAJAN-DES-ORMES

There has been a château on this site since the thirteenth century,
although it was rebuilt in the 1640s. Its greatest moment of glory
occurred in 1565 when Charles IX and his mother Catherine de
Médicis stayed here. At that time it belonged to the rich Pierre
Sauvage, whose fine tomb can be seen in the church at Preignac.
Before the rebuilding, this was a fortified farm and the medieval
chapel survives, cunningly incorporated into the present-day buildings. The Guichaner d'Armajan family owned the estate until the
Revolution, after which it was dismembered and sold off. M. Fiton
reassembled the estate in the early nineteenth century. It changed
hands in 1860 and was bought by the forebears of the present
owners in 1912. At that time, it was known simply as Château des
Ormes, consisted of only 6.5 ha. and had been grossly neglected.

The property descended through the female line to Michel Perromat's wife. They took possession of the estate in 1953. Recently
they acquired 4 ha. which had formerly belonged to the estate,
bringing the total area under vine to 15 ha. in a single parcel. The
varieties planted are 60 per cent Sémillon, 30 per cent Sauvignon
and 10 per cent Muscadelle. Yields are quite high at 20–25 hl./ha.
For the last ten years, no insecticides have been used and Perromat
is pleased with the results in terms of the health of his vines.

The grapes are pressed in a horizontal press, although in abundant vintages this is supplemented by the use of hydraulic presses.
The wine is always chaptalized, even in ripe vintages such as 1990,
as in good years Perromat wants a wine with up to 15° of alcohol.
The maximum production is 15,000 bottles. There is a second wine

called Château des Ormes. In 1988 and 1989, he produced a Crème de Tête, which after ageing in tanks for one year received a further year's ageing in new *barriques*.

I have been impressed by the 1986 vintage, which had plentiful botrytis on the nose, and was rich and soft on the palate, though it could have done with greater concentration. The 1990 had marked orangey flavours.

Mme Perromat-Machy, Château d'Armajan-des-Ormes, Preignac, 33210 Langon, telephone: 56 632217

CHÂTEAU BASTOR-LAMONTAGNE

This substantial estate was once the property of the kings of England, until by some misfortune ownership passed in 1453 to the kings of France. In 1711, it was purchased by a member of the Bordeaux *parlement*, Vincent de la Montágne, and it was he who planted vines here. One of his descendants took a M. Bastor into partnership later in the century. For many decades it remained a small estate, with no more than 10 ha. under vine. Subsequent owners included the Larrieu family and René Mileret. In 1936, the estate was acquired by the Crédit Foncier de France. Although acquisition by a financial house sounds like bad news, it is indisputable that Bastor-Lamontagne has gone from strength to strength under their ownership and now produces wine that is often superior to a number of *Deuxièmes Crus*, as was recognized by Cocks & Féret as long ago as 1949. Since 1987, the estate has been managed by the very professional Michel Garat.

By 1994, the property had expanded to 50 ha. in production. Most of the vineyards surround the modest château on flat land with sandy, stony soil just north of Château Suduiraut and other sectors adjoin Château de Malle. Not all the vineyards belong to the estate, as 7 ha. are leased. The *encépagement* is 78 per cent Sémillon, 17 per cent Sauvignon and 5 per cent Muscadelle. The average age of the vines is twenty-five years.

Bastor-Lamontagne is a frankly commercial wine, made from high yields. It is made in quite large quantities and Garat does not pretend that the selection during harvesting is as rigorous as it would be at some of his illustrious neighbours. Yet within those constraints the wine is very well made and sensibly priced, offering excellent value. The harvesters aim to pick grapes with a must weight of at least 18°, but tend to pick clusters rather than individual grapes, and overripe grapes with high must weights will be picked as well as botrytized fruit. Even so, the wine is not often chaptalized.

The grapes were pressed in horizontal presses until 1994, when a pneumatic press was acquired. After a light *débourbage*, the must is fermented in stainless steel at 20–22°C. The fermentation is stopped by the usual methods of chilling and adding sulphur dioxide. The *assemblage* is completed early and the blended wine is then aged in Allier and Limousin *barriques* for eighteen months. In good vintages, a quarter of these are barrels are new.

In 1992, Michel Garat introduced a second label, Les Remparts de Bastor, which is used for declassified wine. The advantage of having a *deuxième vin* is that he is no longer required to bottle not particularly good wines under the Bastor-Lamontagne label, such as the 1987 vintage. In good vintages, up to 120,000 bottles of Bastor-Lamontagne are produced. About half the wine is exported and in Britain it has long been recognized as exceptional value.

I have not encountered older vintages of the wine and the earliest I have tasted is the somewhat clumsy 1981, with its bitter finish; it was ready to drink by 1990. The 1982 was good for the vintage; it had botrytis character and high acidity that kept the wine vigorous. The 1983 is somewhat disappointing: quite attractive, but one-dimensional. The 1985 was lively, but had no botrytis that I could discern. In 1986, Bastor-Lamontagne produced a rounded, lush wine, but it is rather dull. The 1988 is considerably better; despite a neutral nose, it is sweet and silky and lively. Even better is the 1989, plump and honeyed on the nose, and very sweet and unctuous on the palate, with more concentration than usual. In this same year Garat produced 500 bottles of a Crème de Tête, a heavenly wine, similar in character to the regular bottling, but with even greater richness, power and concentration. It was made from the *trie* of 12–13 October, which had a must weight of 22°, and the wine received an additional six months of *barrique*-ageing. Sadly the wine is not commercially available, but it does show what Bastor-Lamontagne is capable of.

The 1990 is another splendid vintage here. There are ripe lemons on the nose and the lushness of the fruit on the palate is balanced by fine tangy acidity. The oak is more noticeable than usual, which is no bad thing in a wine with 14.5° of alcohol and 6.5° of residual sugar. No Bastor-Lamontagne was bottled in 1991–3, and much of the wine produced was sold to wholesalers; such wine as was bottled was released as Remparts. In 1993, for example, 70 per cent of the crop was rejected; what remained was aged in older barrels and will yield 20,000 bottles. I have tasted these wines only from cask, and could not work up much excitement.

Michel Garat, Château Bastor-Lamontagne, Preignac, 33210 Langon, telephone: 56 632766, fax: 56 768703

CHÂTEAU HAUT-BERGERON

This excellent estate of 22 ha. has been bottling its wines for half a century, and the unpretentious house and the unassuming character of Robert Lamothe and his sons Patrick and Hervé can give the misleading impression that Haut-Bergeron is a modest wine. In fact it is one of the best of the non-classified growths.

Although the house and winery are located in Preignac, the vineyards are scattered and more varied, with 5 ha. near the house, and other parcels in Barsac and Sauternes. They are planted with 90 per cent Sémillon, 7 per cent Sauvignon and 3 per cent Muscadelle. The vines are old, with one large ninety-year-old parcel, the average age being fifty years.

The Lamothes believe strongly in harvesting late, and average yields are about 18 hl./ha. In 1994, their horizontal press was replaced by a pneumatic press. In exceptional years, the second pressing takes place in a hydraulic press, which extracts more concentrated juice. After a *débourbage* at 8°C, the must is fermented in tanks at a relatively cool 18°C. There is chaptalization in poor years, but no addition of yeasts. The wine is aged for up to eighteen months in *barriques*, of which 20 per cent are new. The Lamothes are keen to adopt barrel-fermentation, but are waiting for another good vintage before making the investment.

The wine is not aged solely in barrels, but also spends time in tank. It is then chilled to precipitate tartrate crystals and after a bentonite fining, the wine is bottled about two and a half years after the harvest. In the past, bottling took place according to demand, so that there were up to five bottlings.

The style of Haut-Bergeron is deep-coloured, rich and luscious. Private clients account for 80 per cent of sales, which may explain why this fine Sauternes is not better known. In good years, the maximum production is 60,000 bottles. For the 1992 and 1993 vintages, some of the wine will be bottled under a second label. Visitors are welcome to taste and buy at the estate, and prices are moderate.

The oldest Haut-Bergeron I have tasted is the 1986, which did not show well when I encountered it soon after bottling, but by 1994 it had evolved into a sweet and silky mouthful, with ample botrytis aromas and marred only by a whack of alcohol on the finish. The 1987, most of which was picked after the rain and as late as 18 November, had vigour and acidity in its youth, but I have not tasted it recently. The 1988 has impeccable finesse, and the 1990 is superb: very sweet, as one would expect from a wine with 7.5° of residual sugar, but delicately oaky, plump and peachy, with an irresistible flamboyance of flavour and excellent length. The 1991 can't compete in terms of concentration and richness, but it is a good lean wine for early consumption. The 1992 is surprisingly sweet, the result of stern selection before bottling, but it too should be drunk fairly soon. In 1993, the Lamothes used cryo-extraction with, they report, good results, but even so, half the crop was rejected.

Robert Lamothe, Château Haut-Bergeron, Preignac, 33210 Langon, telephone: 56 632476, fax: 56 632331

CHÂTEAU L'HERMITAGE

This estate used to belong to the Tuytens-Laville family of Château Partarrieu in Barsac, but in 1991 it was bought by a small consortium comprising the cardiologist Professor Francis Fontan, his wife Maryse, her brother Jean Crampes (who makes the wine) and Mme Carol Pétrie. When it belonged to the Tuytens-Laville family, the wine was regarded as a second label and sold to wholesalers, but the new owners are more ambitious. They have begun by restoring the property and renovating the cellars.

The area under vine is 11 ha., including 4 ha. near the property and 3 ha. near Château de Malle on gravelly soil. The varieties planted are 80 per cent Sémillon, the rest being Sauvignon and a few vines of Muscadelle. The average age of the vines is about thirty years and yields are fairly high. The grapes are pressed in a horizontal press and fermented in tank, though the long-term intention is to ferment in *barriques*. The wine is aged for eighteen to twenty-four months in barrels purchased from Bastor-Lamontagne and La Tour-Blanche, where they had been used for one wine. In 1993, Crampes experimented with ageing the wine in new oak.

Given the middling quality of recent vintages, the production has been very limited: 6,000 bottles in 1991 and 7,500 in 1992. I have tasted the wines only from cask and they seemed promising examples of their vintages. It is too early to judge whether the quality of l'Hermitage matches the ambitions of its new owners, but this is clearly a property to watch.

Jean Crampes, Château l'Hermitage, Preignac, 33210 Langon, telephone: 56 762413, fax: 56 768325

CHÂTEAU GILETTE

This has to be the most bizarre Sauternes of them all. Gilette is a 5–ha. estate, which the Médeville family has owned since the eighteenth century. Its wines are produced only in outstanding years; they are aged not in wood but in large tanks, and not for two years but for up to twenty-five years. In 1993, the *current* vintage release was the 1971. This strange policy was established by René Médeville, the father of the very courteous Christian Médeville, who has left Gilette unchanged, though nowadays he is tending to bottle the wine after a slightly shorter period of incarceration. Of course, the reason why the wine was aged in large vats in the first place was as an economy measure, since *barriques* were too expensive in the depressed 1930s.

The soil at Gilette is of sandy gravel, with a subsoil of rock and clay. The soil is precocious so the wines tend to be picked relatively early, up to five days earlier than in other parts of the commune; of course *tries successifs*, up to ten of them, are employed to pick the grapes. The varieties planted are 94 per cent Sémillon, 4 per cent Sauvignon Blanc and 2 per cent Muscadelle. Yields can be as low as 9 hl./ha. Strict harvesting allows Médeville to produce Gilette without chaptalization.

The winery, attached to the ivy-covered Médeville house behind the church at Preignac, is far from romantic because of the absence of *barriques*. But it is spotlessly clean and very capacious, as it needs to be if your bottle stock alone amounts to 200,000 bottles. Médeville has acquired a cold chamber for cryo-extraction and made use of it in 1993 with, he says, satisfactory results.

Médeville also owns another estate nearby, Château les Justices, so any wine from Gilette that is not up its very high standards is either sold off or, if it's very good but not quite good enough, blended with Les Justices. After pressing in a horizontal press, the must rests for three days in underground tanks. It is then fermented in stainless steel at 20–22°C for up to fourteen days. When the wine reaches 14° of alcohol he chills it down to 10° so that the fermentation continues but much more slowly, for another two to three weeks. Médeville likes Gilette to have about 15° of alcohol by the time the fermentation is over and the final period allows the yeasts to coax another degree's worth from the remaining sugar. After fermentation, the wine is racked, often filtered, but then left untouched. Any wines that seem deficient at this stage are declassified. The wine is stored in epoxy resin-lined concrete vats of 2,000–4,000 litres, staying there until Médeville feels it is ready to be bottled. Because of the large volume in each tank, the wine ages very slowly.

There used to be a rather complicated hierarchy at Gilette. The very best years were released as Crème de Tête: these were made from the richest and most botrytized grapes so as to reward, as Médeville puts it, 'an extravagance of nature'. The next category is Doux, ripe and sweet but less concentrated and opulent than the Crème de Tête. This was last made in 1962. Finally there is the Demi-Doux, which, it has always seemed to me, defeats the purpose of Gilette, which is to age the best wines from the best vintages. By definition, the fruit used for a Demi-Doux cannot have been outstanding, at least not in terms of noble rot. This point has not escaped the Médevilles, who discontinued making such wines after 1958.

Some of the old Crème de Tête wines are marvellous, but I can't help wondering what the point of the exercise is. Médeville says that his ageing policy allows him to offer a large range of mature wines that are ready to drink, but can still be kept for decades. His best customers are allowed occasional access to the remaining reserves of 1937 and 1949 Gilette, which are no longer commercially available. However, the same goal could be achieved by making Sauternes in the usual way and then bottle-ageing the wines in the cellars. It would be considerably more expensive than ageing the wine in tank, but arguably the end result would be even better wine. And, of course, Gilette is not cheap. Although Médeville is maintaining the style of wine at Gilette, he is quietly compromising by bottling the wines sooner, which is probably a good idea. For instance, the 1955 and 1959 weren't bottled until 1982, but by 1993, the 1975 and 1976 were already bottled though not released. Since only Crème de Tête wines are now being released, the production is smaller than ever: a mere 6,000 bottles.

I have twice tasted the 1958 Demi-Doux, which I found rather peculiar, with a mango nose, butterscotch flavours and an unwelcome whack of alcohol on the finish. The 1950 Doux was also far too alcoholic, with about 16°, and the fruit itself was distinctly reticent. But the 1955 Doux was delicious, soft and honeyed on the nose, and surprisingly complex on the palate; it also had very good length.

But now for the *raison d'être* of Château Gilette: the Crème de Tête. The 1937 and 1949, which I have not tasted, had superb reputations and the 1950, which I have, is also typical of the Gilette style. It is opulent and almost syrupy; good acidity counters the richness of the wine, saving it from heaviness; both the nose and palate are dominated by marmalade flavours, which often develop in wines that are rich and botrytized but not oaked. The wine is sumptuous in the extreme, but I can't help wondering how much more complex it would have been with some oak-ageing. The 1953 is not as good; it is softer, but more alcoholic. The 1955, although alcoholic on the finish, is wonderfully honeyed and rich, with aromas of banana and caramel too; despite its power, it has elegance and excellent length. The 1959 has that typical Gilette nose of marmalade and caramelized orange; on the palate it is creamy and voluptuous, and has impeccable length. Although a perfectionist would remark on its lack of subtlety, the splendour of the fruit is irresistible.

The 1967 is quite different, with aromas of stewed peaches rather than oranges, and a more raisiny component on the palate; blessed with ample acidity, it still tasted very youthful in 1993. The 1970 is more closed up, but there is plenty of raisiny botrytis on the nose and intense fruitiness on the palate. I prefer it to the 1971, which is a lovely peachy wine, but doesn't have the power and unctuousness of Gilette at its most opulent. Between the 1975 and 1976 vintages, it is hard to choose. I marginally prefer the latter; it is more *rôti*, concentrated and raisiny, reeking of noble rot; perhaps the 1975 is more elegant and intense, but less complex. Both wines will still continue to evolve rewardingly in bottle for many years to come.

Christian and Andrée Médeville are happy to receive visitors here, but prefer appointments to be made in advance. Those daunted by the prices of Gilette should bear in mind that Médeville's other, more conventional Sauternes, Château les Justices, is good value.

Christian Médeville, Château Gilette, Preignac, 33210 Langon, telephone: 56 762844, fax: 56 762843

CHÂTEAU LES JUSTICES

Château Gilette is the wine that has made the Médevilles famous, but it is only one of their estates in Sauternes and the Graves. The other Sauternes property is the 9–ha. Château les Justices, which is divided between two parcels in Preignac just north of the village on the river side of the *route nationale*. The vineyard is planted with 88 per cent Sémillon, 10 per cent Sauvignon and 2 per cent Muscadelle. Christian Médeville likes to harvest the Muscadelle early, before it is attacked by noble rot. Yields are relatively high, up to 22 hl./ha.

Unlike Gilette, Les Justices is sometimes chaptalized. The must usually ferments without the addition of cultivated yeasts, but these are added if considered necessary. Fermentation takes place in temperature-controlled steel tanks and the wine is aged in *barriques*, of which one-third are new. Médeville first barrel-aged some of his wine in 1985 and now the wine stays in oak for twelve to eighteen months. The production of Les Justices is up to 22,000 bottles. About half the wine is exported.

The oldest Les Justices I have tasted is the 1976, which had rich botrytized Sémillon aromas and was rounded, but lively on the palate. Like some other wines in the Médeville collection, it is marred by high alcohol, which unbalances it. The same is true of the 1983, which in all other respects is a lively and elegant wine, with a flavour of apricots. The 1985 was very ripe and rounded, with the usual and welcome Les Justices acidity, but it was somewhat one-dimensional. The 1986 has a curious almondy nose and a disconcerting soupiness of texture; this medium-bodied wine is not as fine as I would have hoped for from this vintage.

The 1988 is much better, quite oaky on the nose, lean and stylish on the palate, well balanced and long in flavour. The 1989 is more sumptuous but does not have the length of the 1988, which I marginally prefer for its greater finesse and firmer structure. The 1990 is also excellent, perhaps a little lean for the vintage, but beautifully balanced. The peachy 1991 is light and rather short, but well made and will be enjoyable over the next few years; no new oak was used. Tasted from cask in 1994, the 1993 was showing much better than the dull, waxy 1992, which Médeville readily concedes is insufficiently ripe. Half the 1993 crop went through cryo-extraction.

Christian Médeville, Château Gilette, Preignac, 33210 Langon, telephone: 56 762844, fax: 56 762843

CHÂTEAU LARIBOTTE

The Lahiteau family have been farming this 15–ha. estate for two centuries. It can't have been easy, since it comprises thirty-two parcels in Preignac and Bommes. Not surprisingly the soil is very varied, with much clay and gravel over a rocky subsoil. The varieties planted are 90 per cent Sémillon, 8 per cent Sauvignon and 2 per cent Muscadelle. The average age of the vines is thirty-five years. Yields are close to the maximum permitted.

The grapes are pressed in a horizontal press, then fermented in temperature-controlled tanks. Yeasts are usually added and the must is often chaptalized. The wine is then aged in tank, except when a special *cuvée* is produced, as in 1990, in which case the wine spends twelve months in *barriques*. The wine is chilled to precipitate tartrate crystals and bottled three to four years after the harvest.

Lahiteau says he wants a lightish style of wine, which is just as well, since his harvesting and vinification are unlikely to result in much else. The maximum production is 40,000 bottles and prices are quite low. No Laribotte was bottled in 1991 and 1992, and in 1993 only the two-fifths of the crop picked before the rain proved usable. Lahiteau is particularly keen on his 1988, which I have not tasted, but the 1990 is distinctly dull, no doubt partly because the best lots were creamed off for the Cuvée Spéciale, which is more concentrated, fairly alcoholic, yet by no means exceptional.

Jean-Pierre Lahiteau, Château Laribotte, Preignac, 33210 Langon, telephone: 56 632788, fax: 56 622480

CHÂTEAU MONTALIER

The Seroin family own estates in Loupiac and at Illats in the Graves, as well as this 10–ha. property with vineyards in Preignac and Barsac. The former lie close to Château de Malle, the latter between Châteaux Nairac and de Myrat. Philippe Seroin is keen on Muscadelle and has recently increased its proportion in the vineyard to 20 per cent. Yields are high, usually 25 hl./ha., and the wine is fermented and aged solely in tanks. Up to 30,000 bottles are produced and the style is frankly commercial. The only vintage I have tasted is the 1991, which is lean, spicy, quite honeyed and does have botrytis aromas; a success for the vintage, though best drunk fairly young.

Philippe Seroin, Château le Moyne, 33410 Loupiac, telephone: 56 626461

CRU PEYRAGUEY

Parts of this small estate of only 6 ha. lie on clay and gravel over a subsoil of limestone; others on sandy gravel over a clay subsoil. The varieties planted are 80 per cent Sémillon and 20 per cent Sauvignon. The wine is fermented in tank and then aged for about six months in mostly new *barriques*. The production is 14,500 bottles. I have tasted Cru Peyraguey only twice, but was very pleasantly surprised. The 1990 was plump and peachy, an utterly delicious wine, but the greater surprise was from the unremarkable 1978 vintage, which showed rich Sémillon aromas and rounded apricot flavours.

Hubert Mussotte, Miselle, Preignac, 33210 Langon, telephone: 56 444348

CHÂTEAU SAINT-AMAND

This lovely château is the most northerly property in the commune and lies close to the River Ciron. Louis Ricard says it is one of the oldest properties in the Sauternais and in the grounds are vestiges of the ninth-century church or monastery that once stood here. The courtly white-haired Louis Ricard has now retired, though he still lives here, and the property is managed by his daughter Anne-Marie

Facchetti-Ricard. The vineyard is quite large, some 20 ha. divided into four parcels: 11 ha. around the château on pebbly soil, and two blocks two kilometres away on heavier clay soil. The *encépagement* is 85 per cent Sémillon, 14 per cent Sauvignon and 1 per cent Muscadelle. Ricard liked to keep old vines if at all possible and the average age of the vineyard is about forty years. The wine is made in a commercial style: average yields are quite high at 20 hl./ha., and there are rarely more than four *tries*. He doesn't want solely botrytized fruit, but a blend of nobly rotten and overripe grapes. None the less, he stresses that Sauternes is made in the vineyard rather than the winery.

The must is rarely chaptalized. It is fermented in cement or steel tanks, then the wine is racked and returned to tanks until March, when it is filtered. During its *élevage* it spends up to six months in *barriques*, more to round it out than to impart oaky vanilla flavours. The wine is bottled eighteen to twenty-four months after the harvest. There is no fining, but the wine is chilled to precipitate tartrate crystals.

Not surprisingly, Saint-Amand is a fairly light wine, often reminiscent of Barsac, which lies just across the Ciron from here. It is not especially unctuous, as Ricard wants to preserve the primary fruit in the wine, which is why he is opposed to longer barrel-ageing, which he fears could dry out the wine. The average production is 50,000 bottles. Somewhat confusingly, the wine is also bottled under the label of Château de la Chartreuse, which is used only for wine marketed by the wine merchants Sichel. Visitors can buy directly from the estate and prices are moderate.

The oldest Saint-Amand I have tasted is the 1981: lemony, lightly honeyed, fresh, but lacking in complexity and slightly alcoholic on the finish. The 1982 was rounded, a touch cloying, a pleasant, plump wine with little depth. In 1983, Saint-Amand produced a sweet, sappy wine with spicy acidity and reasonable concentration. Ricard considers his 1984 a great success for the vintage, but I have not tasted it. The 1986, at least in a bottling produced for Fortnum & Mason in London as their own-label Sauternes, was delicious, a plump, golden wine with fine botrytis character. The 1989 is lush, but does not have sufficient concentration for so broad and unfocused a style. More elegant are the beautifully balanced and persistent 1988 and the 1990, with its stylish peachy nose, and peach and marzipan flavours; it has good length and should evolve well. No wine was bottled from the 1992 or 1993 vintages.

Louis Ricard, Château Saint-Amand, Preignac, 33210 Langon, telephone: 56 632728

13

Other Wines of Bommes, Fargues and Sauternes

CHÂTEAU BÉCHEREAU

The owner of this estate was Franck Deloubes and after his death in 1989, his widow took over its management. When the Deloubes first came to Béchereau, all the wine was sold in bulk, but they expanded the property and began to bottle their wine. The well-maintained château, close to the banks of the Ciron, is famous for its underground cellars located in a former quarry, a rarity in the Sauternais. The cellars are well equipped and a new *chai de barriques* was built in 1989.

The vineyards, mostly located near the château, are 11 ha. in extent and Mme Deloubes also owns vineyards in the Graves from which dry wine is made. The varieties planted are 75 per cent Sémillon, 20 per cent Sauvignon and 5 per cent Muscadelle. The average age of the vines is thirty years and yields are fairly high.

The grapes are pressed in a horizontal press, fermented in stainless-steel tanks and then a preliminary selection is made. Wines not up to standard are sold in bulk and the remainder are aged in *barriques*, of which some are new, for eight to fifteen months and bottled about two years after the harvest. Mme Deloubes wants to produce a wine that is not too fat and opulent, but has good fruit and length. There is no *deuxième vin*.

The production is about 30,000 bottles and visitors are welcome to taste and buy at the château. Older vintages are still available. In 1994, the 1975 was priced at 220 francs, the 1982 at 150 francs and the 1990 at 100 francs.

The 1982, clearly picked before the rain, is a very good wine, with a nutty, *rôti* Sémillon nose; on the palate the wine is soft and creamy, with flavours of dried apricots and grilled nuts; not a wine with great flair, but undoubtedly charming and drinking well now. The 1990 is citric on the nose, creamy and quite sweet on the palate, but lacking richness and length; a disappointment for the vintage. The 1992 is lean and mean, with a nose of lemon curd and not especially sweet on the palate.

Mme Élianne Deloubes, Château Béchereau, Bommes, 33210 Langon, telephone: 56 766173, fax: 56 766784

CHÂTEAU BERGERON

This modest family estate is worlds away from the grand châteaux of the region. Bernard Laurans is a diligent *vigneron*, plying his trade, trying to produce an acceptable and saleable product for his principal market of retailers and restaurateurs. It is not a formula for great winemaking.

The 7.5–ha. estate is composed of many small parcels, mainly of red sand and gravel soils, and a parcel opposite La Tour-Blanche with a higher clay content. The average age of the vines is twenty-five years, and the varieties planted are 83 per cent Sémillon, 7 per cent Sauvignon and 10 per cent Muscadelle. Laurans is not very exacting in his harvesting. If botrytis comes reasonably early, well and good. If not, he is not disposed to wait indefinitely. Yields are nearly always close to the maximum allowed. He claims that his clientele does not want an especially *liquoreux* style.

The grapes are pressed in a horizontal press, then fermented in tanks without temperature control. No cultivated yeasts are used. After the fermentation, Laurans weeds out those wines which he will sell in bulk; they are aged in tank before being disposed of. Wines he plans to bottle himself are aged in *barriques* bought second-hand from Yquem and Clos Haut-Peyraguey. There is no new oak. Laurans recognizes that new oak is a tricky medium for those not accustomed to it, so he would rather stick with the older barrels he is used to. The wines stay in barrels quite a long time and are bottled only in their third year. The usual production under the château label is 8,000 bottles.

The 1990 was a good wine, with abundant botrytis on the nose and palate. It lacked depth and concentration, but was well made and will make an enjoyable bottle over the next decade. Frost reduced his yield in 1991 to 14 hl./ha. The wine is marked by

Sémillon aromas. There is some dilution on the palate and the wine lacks depth, but it is rounded and almost ready to drink. The 1992 is marred by a resiny lanolin nose and a bitter finish; not recommended. The 1993 is better, with considerable sweetness and high acidity.

Bernard Laurans, Château Bergeron, Bommes, 33210 Langon, telephone: 56 766071

CHÂTEAU CAMERON

Although the property of Paul Lanneluc, since 1981 the estate has been leased to Pierre Guinabert, the son of Henri Guinabert of Château Villefranche. The estate consists of 16 ha., of which only 13.5 ha. were producing Sauternes in 1994, but by 1996 the whole vineyard will be in production. Not all the vines are in Bommes; the property includes 5 ha. in Barsac between Climens and Caillou. The vines are all Sémillon and their average age is thirty-five years. Average yields are 22 hl./ha. Guinabert owns both a horizontal and a hydraulic press, and he prefers the latter in years when the grapes are particularly rich. After pressing, there is a *débourbage* before the must is fermented in tanks without temperature control. The must is chaptalized when necessary and the wine is aged alternately in subterranean vats and *barriques*. Guinabert buys one-year-old barrels from Yquem, but keeps them for up to five years. The wine is bottled after twenty months. About half the production is sold in bulk, leaving about 15,000 bottles with the estate label. I have tasted only recent vintages, but the 1991 was surprisingly rich and supple, with considerable finesse, though no complexity. The 1992, like so many wines from this vintage, was mean and lacking in richness.

Pierre Guinabert, Château Cameron, Bommes, 33210 Langon, telephone: 56 766714

DOMAINE DE CARBONNIEU

This estate has been in the possession of the Charrier family since 1947. Alain Charrier is a conscientious *vigneron*, trying to make good wine within the financial constraints that afflict most small growers. The 11 ha. of vineyards are planted on gravel and sandy soil quite close to the Ciron. The varieties planted are 90 per cent

Sémillon, 5 per cent Sauvignon and 5 per cent Muscadelle. There are old vines here, some of which are eighty years old, though Charrier estimates the average at forty-five years which, if accurate, makes this one of the most mature vineyards in the district. *Triage* is practised and even in 1990 there were four *tries*. Average yields, however, are high, often at the legal maximum.

The grapes are pressed in a horizontal press, and the must is fermented in tanks, without temperature control. Yeast is only added when it is difficult to get the fermentation going. Most of the wine is aged in tanks, though the wine that Charrier sells under the estate label is aged in fairly old *barriques* that began their life at Yquem and La Tour-Blanche. The wine is bottled after eighteen months. The estate-bottled wine is sold to private clients and a few retailers, and the quantities are small: 7,500 bottles in 1990; 4,000 in 1992. The 1991 vintage was sold off in bulk. In 1992 he made some satisfactory wine from the first *tries*, but in 1993 no harvesting was done before the rain. The 1989 tastes as if it had been picked early; it is fresh rather than rich. The 1990 shows more botrytis and is a wine of some intensity, though little structure.

Alain Charrier, Domaine de Carbonnieu, Bommes, 33210 Langon, telephone: 56 636448, fax: 56 766995

CHÂTEAU DE COMMARQUE

This secluded estate, in the south-west corner of Sauternes, was listed as a *Cru Bourgeois* by Edouard Féret in 1874. In this century it was the property of M. de Souza, who was not much interested in wine and stopped making it in 1972. In 1981, the estate was bought by Geoffrey Kenyon-May, who replanted the vineyard in 1984. He sold the estate to Dr Nigel Reay-Jones in 1987 and it was only the following spring that Dr Reay-Jones realized that one-fifth of the vines had been incorrectly planted and were not productive. So he had to replant some of these new vines. At the same time he was converting the château into a hotel and restaurant.

There are 3.5 ha. under vine, planted with 80 per cent Sémillon and 20 per cent Sauvignon and Muscadelle. The vineyards are surrounded by woods, which has the undesirable effect of turning the vineyard into a frost-prone pocket, so the vines are usually far behind those of other estates in terms of their development. The grapes are pressed in a horizontal press, chaptalized when necessary, fermented in reconditioned *barriques* and aged in them for about eighteen months. The estate produced two wines in 1990, a regular bottling and a Crème de Tête. But the following four vintages have broken the spirit of the British owners. They have no stock to sustain them through these difficult years and, rather than bleed their hotel business to subsidize the vineyard, they have sadly decided to sell their vines.

Dr Nigel Reay-Jones, Château de Commarque, Sauternes, 33210 Langon, telephone: 56 766594, fax: 56 766430

DOMAINE DU COY

See Château Suau (p. 126).

CHÂTEAU DE FARGUES

This is the ancestral home of the Lur-Saluces family, even though the castle itself is a ruin. It was built in the early fourteenth century for Cardinal Raymond Guilhem, a nephew of Pope Clement V. It was later owned by the de Foix and Monferrand families, all powerful players in the region. It came into the hands of the present family in 1472 when Isabeau de Monferrand married Pierre de Lur. In 1586, Jean de Lur, the Vicomte d'Uza, married the only daughter of the Marquis de Saluces and from that moment on the names of the families have been joined. The castle was gutted in 1687.

Curiously, Fargues was known not for its sweet wines but for its red. Today there are scarcely any red vines left, but the first vintage of the Sauternes from Fargues was 1942, from grapes planted on the instructions of Marquis Bertrand de Lur-Saluces in 1935. The estate as a whole is 175 ha. in extent, but only 12 ha. are under vine; the rest consists of trees and arable land and, of course, the dramatic ruined hilltop castle, with its gaping windows, which stands behind the *chais* and workshops. The *chais* have to share the courtyard with the cow shed, the chickens and the horses. By the late 1990s, the area under vine will have increased to 15 ha., as the remaining red vines are being dug up and replaced with white varieties. The viticulture is identical to that practised at Yquem and so is the *encépagement*: 80 per cent Sémillon and 20 per cent Sauvignon Blanc.

Those who work at Fargues are the first to admit that the soil – mostly sand, gravel and clay – is not exceptional here. Indeed, the view from the château is of wheatfields and woods, indicating that this is a marginal area for vines. The excellence of Fargues is a triumph of harvesting and winemaking over *terroir*. It is much colder here than in most other parts of the Sauternais and the grapes generally ripen a week later than they do at Yquem. Frost can also menace the Fargues vineyards. Because of this tendency for the harvest to continue well into the cold weather, the precocious vintages here are often the best. One positive factor in the microclimate is the strength of the wind, which can be beneficial after wet spells; in 1994, for instance, the grapes dried rapidly and gained in concentration, despite two weeks of rain.

Yields are even lower than at Yquem, averaging 7.5 hl./ha. Pierre Meslier used to say that because of the difference in soil, it was more of a challenge to make Fargues than Yquem. As at Yquem, only fruit with high must weights is harvested. The average must weight for 1984 was 19.2°; for 1985, 19.3°; for 1986, 19°; for 1987, 18.8°; and for 1988, 20.9°.

The vinification is similar to that at Yquem, except that a pneumatic press has replaced the old hydraulic presses. The must goes straight into *barriques* for the fermentation. They are not new barrels, but casks that have been used once at Yquem. Usually, but not always, the wine is aged for three and a half years and bottled without filtration. The maximum production is 22,000 bottles.

Since September 1993, Château de Fargues has been managed by François Amirault, formerly of Château Nairac. The only member of the Yquem team to be involved at Fargues, other than Alexandre de Lur-Saluces, is Francis Mayeur, the director of production. So Amirault enjoys considerable autonomy, partly because Alexandre de Lur-Saluces wants to dispel the widespread but false notion that Fargues is the second wine of Yquem. One of Amirault's innovations will be the vinification of some of the grapes from Fargues as a dry wine, especially from parcels not well suited to sweet-wine production. He can also benefit from the additional space that was created when in 1989 a barn was converted into a stone-walled *chai*.

Given its intense concentration and long oak-ageing, it is not surprising that Fargues is often compared with Yquem, though it has less complexity and less body. Occasionally, when the two wines are tasted side by side, Fargues seems the more impressive. This happened with the 1980 vintage, but Pierre Meslier, who made both wines, was convinced that in the long haul the Yquem would prove superior. He liked to say that the problem with Fargues is that it did not age as well as Yquem. When I asked how long it would age, he would reply with a shrug: 'Sixty years?' Time will tell.

Old vintages of Fargues have not come my way, alas, but other tasters' notes suggest that the 1947, 1949, 1967, 1971 and 1976 were all very fine. I found the 1980 splendid, very soft and rich, with lovely depth of flavour and elegance; it was perfectly balanced and the spiciness of the oak showed positively on the finish. I was slightly disappointed by the 1983 when I tasted it against other Sauternes of the vintage. It was certainly very good, though closed, but lacked some finesse and persistence of flavour. The 1984, harvested from 20 October to 12 November, is said to be good for the vintage; only 11,000 bottles were produced. In 1985, Fargues picked almost as late as Yquem, ending the final *trie* on 16 December. The estate produced a highly concentrated wine, oaky and finely structured, and botrytis character should emerge in time, as Fargues attracted botrytis more easily in this year than did Yquem.

The 1986 is marvellous and when young it showed better than Yquem. It is very marked by oak, but has abundant fruit and extract, and lingering apricot flavours. It should evolve magnificently. The 1987 vintage, aided by cryo-extraction, yielded 10,000 bottles of supple, oaky wine that had botrytis but insufficient concentration. In 1988, the best grapes were picked on 15 and 16 November, and 22 and 23 November. The wine was very closed when I tasted it in 1994. It will be superb; it has real concentration and superb length, and the dominant oakiness does not obscure the splendour of the fruit. As with Yquem, one waits impatiently for the release of the 1989 and 1990 vintages, which should be great.

In 1991, following the example of Guiraud and Sigalas-Rabaud, Fargues bottled all its wine, a mere 8,000 litres in any case, in 50–cl. bottles. There will be no Fargues in 1992, but Amirault believes the small quantity of 1993 that was made might yet make a good bottle. There is likely to be a small crop in 1994, no more than half the usual, but by 6 October, when the main *trie* began, whole bunches were botrytized and the must weight was the longed-for 20°.

Fargues follows the Lur-Saluces policy of no *en primeur* sales, no tastings until well after the wine has been bottled and no direct sales. Fargues is extremely expensive, the most costly Sauternes after Yquem. Because of the small production and the lustre of the Lur-Saluces pedigree, not to mention the first-rate quality of the wine, it sells with little difficulty, a remarkable achievement for a wine that didn't even exist at the time of the 1855 classification.

François Amirault, Château de Fargues, Fargues, 33210 Langon, telephone: 57 980420, fax: 57 980421

CHÂTEAU HAUT-BOMMES

See Château Clos Haut-Peyraguey (p. 69).

DOMAINE DU HAUT-CLAVERIE

The amiable Philippe Sendrey is the fourth generation of his family to make wine at this estate up on the plateau to the south of Fargues. Of the 15 ha. under vine, only 11 ha. are entitled to the Sauternes appellation. Six are in one parcel planted on gravelly sand and the remainder are scattered throughout the commune. Their average age is thirty years and average yields are quite high at 22 hl./ha. The *encépagement* is 80 per cent Sémillon, 17 per cent Sauvignon and 3 per cent Muscadelle.

After pressing in a horizontal press and a *débourbage* at low temperatures in an underground tank, the must is fermented in temperature-controlled stainless-steel tanks. Sometimes Sendrey adds yeasts, sometimes he chaptalizes; there is no formula followed each year. The fermentation is arrested with chilling, racking and a dose of sulphur dioxide, and the wine is then aged partly in tank and partly in barrels. Sendrey admits that he does not care for the taste of wood in his wine because it masks its natural fruitiness, but in vintages such as 1990, even he felt compelled to age part of the crop in barrels, rotating the wine between tank and barrel. The wine is bottled about two years after the harvest.

Haut-Claverie is not an estate of any pretensions. Sendrey is making wine for a clientele that likes its Sauternes young. He does not seek to give his wine any great structure or depth; he wants aromatic wines of a distinct finesse that are accessible soon after bottling. The production varies from 15,000 to 30,000 bottles and prices are low. In 1994, the 1990 was selling for 80 francs and the 1992 for a very reasonable 57 francs. The 1990 is a delicious wine;

what it lacks in complexity it makes up for with its wonderful ripeness of flavour. The 1991 has a lanolin Sémillon nose; medium-bodied and well balanced, it will be ready soon, as will the light and simple 1992.

There are many better wines among the non-classified growths of Sauternes, but Haut-Claverie, for all its limitations, is attractive, well-made, balanced and a sound choice for those who like their Sauternes as an aperitif.

Philippe Sendrey, Domaine du Haut-Claverie, Fargues, 33210 Langon, telephone: 56 631265, fax: 56 635116

CHÂTEAU LAFON

In the early nineteenth century, this small estate of 6 ha. was linked to what is now Château Raymond-Lafon. It came into the possession of the Dufour family in 1938 and the plump, jolly Jean-Pierre Dufour is the third generation to look after the property. Dufour also owns vineyards in Sainte-Croix-du-Mont and Loupiac. Since 1990 he has been helped at Lafon by his son-in-law Olivier Fauthoux. Much is made of Lafon's proximity to Yquem and indeed there are some vines on clay soil at the foot of one of the slopes of the Yquem hill. But other parcels are scattered, some on gravelly soil behind Raymond-Lafon. At least 90 per cent of the vines are Sémillon, the rest being Sauvignon. Their average age is thirty years.

Yields are high, close to the maximum, and unfortunately it shows in the wine, as does Dufour's reluctance to delay harvesting until the optimal moment. In 1993, for instance, there had been three *tries* before the rain even began. They produced aromatic wine, but it could hardly have shown much richness. Dufour grins, noting, '*Il faut sauver les meubles*' (when the house is on fire, you get the furniture out fast).

They use a horizontal press, and ferment the must in cement and stainless-steel tanks, using only natural yeasts. The must is chaptalized in most years. The Bordeaux *négociants* Dourthe take most of Lafon's production, leaving Dufour with about 2,000 bottles that he sells to regular clients in top years. Lots destined for Dourthe stay in tank until bottled; wine that will be estate-bottled is aged in old *barriques* for twelve months, and bottled eighteen to twenty-four months after the harvest. Dufour wants aroma and finesse, not lusciousness: 'If you want alcohol, drink Cognac,' he says, somewhat irrelevantly.

With its limited production, Lafon is rarely encountered. In 1991, 1992 and 1993, no estate-bottled wine was released. I have not encountered old vintages of the wine, but anyone with 3,000 francs to burn can find a bottle of the 1893 on the wine list at Les Berceaux in Épernay. The 1990, which Dufour considers the best Lafon since 1929, is a disappointment: there are aromas of boiled sweets that are not altogether agreeable, and on the palate a simplicity and dilution not really worthy of the vintage. Given the nobility of the wines produced by his neighbours Yquem and Raymond-Lafon, it is rather sad that the genial M. Dufour should be so very pleased with his undistinguished wine.

Jean-Pierre Dufour, Château Lafon, Sauternes, 33210 Langon, telephone: 56 633082

CHÂTEAU LAMARINGUE

The Sessacq family are proprietors of estates in Sainte-Croix-du-Mont and the Graves, and also own 4 ha. scattered about the Sauternes appellation. The main portion of Lamaringue is at Boutoc, and there are other parcels near Châteaux La Tour-Blanche and d'Arche. The *encépagement* is 80 per cent Sémillon, 15 per cent Sauvignon and 5 per cent Muscadelle. Some parcels of vines are eighty years old. Yields are high, at 22 hl./ha. The must is tank-fermented, then aged in old *barriques*. The maximum production is 10,000 bottles and the wine is over-priced in relation to its humdrum quality.

The 1981 was marked by a lanolin nose lacking in botrytis; on the palate, it was quite alcoholic and pineappley. The 1988 also had tropical-fruit flavours, including lemon and banana on the nose, aromas that I don't particularly want to find in Sauternes. The 1992 is mediocre.

Rémy Sessacq, Clos La Maurasse, 33211 Langon, telephone: 56 633927, fax: 56 631182

CHÂTEAU LAMOURETTE

This modest 8–ha. estate, not far from the River Ciron, has been in the hands of the Leglise family since 1860. Most of the vineyards lie in a single parcel on sandy soil around the house, but there are also vines near Filhot and Rabaud-Promis. The *encépagement* is 90 per cent Sémillon, 5 per cent Sauvignon and 5 per cent Muscadelle. However the Sauvignon has been planted recently, so hardly any of it appears in the blend as yet. Yields appear to be about 20 hl./ha.

The grapes are pressed in a horizontal press, fermented in stainless steel and then aged in cement tanks. There is no wood-ageing and the wine is bottled young, eighteen months after the harvest. The resulting wines are simple, clean, with fresh apricot flavours, but no great structure or persistence on the palate. The very sweet 1990 was better than the rather hard 1989.

Anne-Marie Leglise, Château Lamourette, Bommes, 33210 Langon, telephone: 56 766358, fax: 56 766085

DOMAINE MAGNI-THIBAUT

This is a family estate and for Claude Magni it seems an occupation much like any other. Of the 10 ha. under vine, 8 ha. are entitled to the Sauternes appellation. The soil is sand and gravel over a limestone and clay subsoil. The *encépagement* is 80 per cent Sémillon, 15 per cent Sauvignon and 5 per cent Muscadelle. Until 1994 there were some 100-year-old vines on the property, but their productivity had ground to a halt and they were grubbed up. Now the average age of the vines is about twenty years. Average yields are 20 hl./ha.

The grapes are pressed in a horizontal press and the must is fermented in stainless-steel tanks. Magni never uses cultivated yeasts, even when his consultant oenologist recommends it, but he chaptalizes when he considers it necessary. All the wine is aged in tank, though Magni would like to buy some *barriques* one of these days. He bottles the wine according to demand, but not until it has been aged for two years. His clients are mostly French and are looking for a fruity wine to drink young. The maximum production here is 22,000 bottles and prices are low. The 1991 and 1992 vintages are lacking in aroma, but simple and fresh on the palate, making them acceptable aperitif wines.

Claude Magni, Domaine Magni-Thibaut, Fargues, 33210 Langon, telephone: 56 631689, fax: 56 635116

CHÂTEAU RAYMOND-LAFON

Driving from the hamlet of Boutoc towards the village of Sauternes, with Château d'Yquem looming down on the left, you will pass a pretty double-gabled ivy-covered house and garden that would not look out of place in Norfolk. This is the home of the Meslier family, now extended to include the adjacent house, and the *chai* of Château Raymond-Lafon is located just behind the house. The origins of this estate are obscure and it is not entirely clear when it became detached from Château Lafon across the road. Pierre Meslier suggests it was in 1850 and that the estate failed to be classified in 1855 only because the vines were too young. The 1868 edition of Cocks & Féret was making a distinction between the two. Other contemporary accounts suggest that the vineyards were small (about 8 ha.) but well regarded, and that the estate included parcels that had once belonged to Châteaux d'Yquem and d'Arche. Château Lafon belonged to Désir Lafon; Raymond Lafon was his cousin and the mayor of Sauternes.

Raymond Lafon's son-in-law Louis Pontallier inherited the estate in 1904. In 1907, according to Cocks & Féret, Pontallier was one of the judges at the Bordeaux exhibition who awarded the Raymond-Lafon a gold medal, showing again how unwise it is to place too much reliance on medals and awards. I have seen a wine merchant's list from 1922 in which 1918 Yquem and 1916 Suduiraut are both priced at 15 francs; the next most expensive wine is 1917 Raymond-Lafon at 14 francs, followed by 1918 Lafaurie-Peyraguey and 1913 Coutet at 13 francs. So Raymond-Lafon clearly had a fine reputation during the Pontallier years.

In 1958, Pontallier's descendants sold the estate to Dr Bourdier. By the time the Mesliers bought Raymond-Lafon in 1972, the estate was in poor condition and the vineyards had declined from 8 ha. to a paltry 3.5 ha.

Pierre Meslier was, at the time he bought the property, the *régisseur* at Yquem, where he had arrived nine years earlier, having previously worked in the Médoc with Alexis Lichine. It is not unusual for an experienced and no doubt well-paid winemaker to acquire a small property of his own. But what was unusual was Meslier's determination to make his wine on the same epic scale as Yquem. Of course it makes sense. Entrusted with the vinification of Yquem and Fargues, why should he lower his standards in producing his own wine? None the less, his dual role would lead to conflict with his employers in the late 1980s. Meslier soon consolidated his vineyard holdings and today he owns 18 ha., 15 ha. of which are in production. The principal vineyards are adjacent to Yquem and Sigalas-Rabaud. The soil is a blend of clay, sand and gravel.

The *encépagement* is 80 per cent Sémillon and the remainder is Sauvignon Blanc. Many of the vines are old, and Meslier claims that their average age is over forty years. No herbicides are used. Meslier, who was born in 1930, is now retired, but still keeps a paternal eye on the affairs of his estate. The winemaking is entrusted to his son Charles-Henri. Another son, Jean-Pierre, used to handle the marketing of the wine, but left for California in 1991. Pierre Meslier's wife Francine is no longer in robust health, so her responsibilities – partly commercial, partly looking after visitors and potential customers – have been taken over by their daughter Marie-Françoise.

Pruning is very severe, no more than six eyes for each variety. Meslier is looking only for botrytized fruit with must weights of 19–21° and yields are said to be 8–9 hl./ha. There is no chaptalization. Grapes are pressed in a hydraulic press and the must is barrel-fermented for three to five weeks. Meslier has always insisted that no sulphur is added to stop fermentation, thanks to the action of the antibiotic botryticine, but this statement is controversial, as has been explained in Chapter 4. The wine is racked every three months and now stays in fine-grained new oak for three years. (Earlier vintages were aged in 15 per cent new oak and by 1986 the proportion had risen to 60 per cent.) Thus the vinification is virtually identical to that at Yquem. The wine is fined before bottling. Can Raymond-Lafon support such an intensive regime of new oak? I think the answer is yes, because the wine has sufficient richness and concentration, even in modest vintages. But there is no doubt that the lengthy sojourn in new wood gives the wine a tannic structure and an overt oakiness that keep it closed for many years, unless you particularly relish a mouthful of oak. But patience is rewarded and after ten years Raymond-Lafon can be one of the most sublime Sauternes you are likely to encounter. The maximum production is over 25,000 bottles.

The wine is very expensive. In the late 1980s it was the most highly priced Sauternes after Yquem and Fargues. Meslier has stopped selling his wines *en primeur*. There is no doubt that Raymond-Lafon has been shrewdly marketed, with an array of numbered imperials in fancy boxes and other stratagems designed to appeal to collectors and thus to enhance the prestige of the wine. Such razzmatazz goes against the grain in this very conservative wine region, but there is no disputing that Raymond-Lafon is an excellent wine. It can be bought directly from the property, but the Mesliers prefer appointments to be made.

In 1990, the Mesliers produced a *deuxième vin* for the first time. It is called Lafon-Laroze after the adjoining property which they also own. There is no 1991, but there will be a little 1992. Lafon-Laroze has the same vinification and barrel-ageing as the *grand vin*, but spends only eighteen months in *barriques*.

Old vintages of the wine are rarely encountered. The only one I have seen is the 1933, which was dried out in 1984 and barely drinkable. The 1971, made just before Pierre Meslier bought the property, is a pleasant wine, slightly raisiny, but with no evident botrytis. No wine was bottled in 1974. The 1975 is spicy and very lively, with orangey flavours and good length. I have not tasted the 1976. The 1978 is reputed to be one of the top wines of that none-too-distinguished vintage, but I must have been unlucky in tasting an oxidizing bottle. Only 5,000 bottles were made.

The 1979, however, is a triumph for a vintage that produced good but modest wines on the whole. It has ample botrytis, a lovely golden colour and there is no sign of ageing. It is drinking perfectly now, but will hold for a decade or more. It is a classic Sauternes of great breed and distinction. Sixty per cent of the crop was rejected. In 1980, only 20 per cent had to be declassified. It is voluptuous and intense, oaky on the nose and very long. I was very impressed by the highly concentrated 1981 in its rather sulphury youth, but have not tasted the wine since. The 1982 has become a sumptuous oaky mouthful, very concentrated, viscous and with excellent length.

The 1983 had tremendous potential in its youth, as one would expect from this outstanding vintage, when the yield at Raymond-Lafon was a mere 11 hl./ha. However, the wine has been going through a process you do not want to find in an expensive bottle: secondary fermentation. Pierre Meslier admits that some shipments did suffer from this problem because he did not use enough sulphur at bottling. The problem has only cropped up, to the best of my knowledge, in some of the wines sent to Britain.

Raymond-Lafon produced a small quantity of good, sweet, relatively light 1984, when picking continued until late November, and a rich, fat 1985, when picking continued well into December. The golden 1986 is lush, creamy and concentrated, with plenty of botrytis. I find it slightly disappointing, but it may become more harmonious with time. The delicious 1987 is excellent for the vintage, though it lacks persistence of flavour and is very marked by new oak. Yields were very low, only 5 hl./ha., and half the wine was declassified. Unlike most Meslier wines, it will be accessible soon. The 1988 is impeccable: racy, intense, with high acidity, great concentration and length. The 1989 is equally magnificent, but in an entirely different style; this is fatter, richer, more unctuous. The 1988 is more classic; the 1989 a wine for sybarites. Both need ten more years in bottle. I have not tasted the 1990. Tasted from cask, the 1991 was good in an oaky citric style.

Pierre Meslier, Château Raymond-Lafon, Sauternes, 33210 Langon, telephone: 56 632102, fax: 56 631958

CHÂTEAU TRILLON

The modern Italianate tower looms over the horizon as one approaches Sauternes, and it dominates the courtyard of Château Trillon and its agricultural buildings. The varieties planted on this substantial 20–ha. estate are 80 per cent Sémillon and 10 per cent each of Sauvignon and Muscadelle. Average production consists of 25,000 bottles, but a portion of the crop is always sold off to wholesalers. I have not tasted the wine, but the 1986 and 1988 had a good reputation, although the 1990 was considered disappointing for the vintage.

Jean-Claude Guicheney, Château Trillon, Sauternes, 33210 Langon, telephone: 56 636021

THE OTHER SWEET WINES
OF BORDEAUX

14

Sainte-Croix-du-Mont

If any appellation can be seen as a potential rival to Sauternes and Barsac, it is probably Sainte-Croix-du-Mont. It is not the excellence of its *terroir* that makes it a serious rival, but the commitment of a handful of top growers to produce the finest wines possible. These growers have made precisely the same kind of investments as their counterparts in Sauternes and have reduced their yields in order to produce wines of concentration and longevity.

Sainte-Croix is easily visible from the other side of the Garonne, especially from Preignac. Cliffs composed of fossil deposits that continue for almost a kilometre rise up behind the narrow coastal plain beyond the riverbank. On top of the cliffs you can plainly see the fifteenth-century Château de Tastes, which since 1928 has served as the town hall of the commune, and the tall spire of the neo-Romanesque church. From the church, steps descend to cliff-side terraces, from where you can inspect closely the extraordinary layers of fossilized oysters that make up the cliff itself. Burrowed into the cliff are a number of grottoes, some of which served as cellars, and one is open to visitors as the tasting room of the appel-lation. For a price you can taste vintages of Sainte-Croix going back to 1967 and buy the wines by the bottle. No individual producers are cited on the labels; instead each wine is a single *cuvée*, said to represent the best wine of each vintage.

About 450 ha. of vines are entitled to the Sainte-Croix-du-Mont appellation; any dry wines, red or white, produced in the commune must be sold as Bordeaux. There are about one hundred growers, of whom no more than thirty earn their living solely from the vine. About twenty-five are absentee proprietors, though many of these are based in Loupiac or elsewhere in the Bordeaux region. The annual production has held steady over the past decade at about

16,000 hl., from a maximum yield of 40 hl./ha., in contrast to the 25 hl./ha. imposed on Sauternes and Barsac.

The greater permitted yield is a major difference between these 'satellite' appellations and those of Sauternes and Barsac. The vines are also planted to a lower density than in Sauternes. There the density is usually 6,500–7,000 vines per ha.; here it tends to be 3,000–3,500, though some estates such as Château La Grave plant vines at 5,000 per ha. For producers such as Yves Armand at Château La Rame, the primary question is not the density of plantation but the yields cropped from the vines.

Another differentiating factor is the soil, which is exceedingly varied here. On its slopes and plateau the soil is clay, the subsoil limestone. Some areas near the centre of the commune and to the east are stony, and have very little clay and limestone. Vines planted on these stony soils tend to be more precocious than those planted on limestone, and the wines tend to be floral and charming but less long-lived. Further away from the cliffs and the river are less stony soils with much clay and little limestone. In general, the soil is richer than on the other side of the Garonne, which is one reason why it is so difficult for even the best wines to match the best that Sauternes and Barsac can offer.

Sainte-Croix-du-Mont enjoys a similar climate to Sauternes, and although there are autumnal mists, they are less frequent than in Sauternes and Barsac since there is no cold-river equivalent to the Ciron on this side of the Garonne. On the other hand, the greater height of the vineyards means that frost is rare and thus the crop is more regular than in Barsac. Up on the plateau it can be quite windy, so in wet autumns, such as 1993 and 1994, the grapes dried more rapidly than across the river. All harvesting is manual. Pruning *à cot*, widely adopted for Sémillon in Sauternes and Barsac, is not in fact permitted in Sainte-Croix-du-Mont; instead *Guyot* pruning, either *simple* or *double*, is ubiquitous. Winemaking regulations are much the same. Chaptalization by up to 2° is authorized. Sulphur-dioxide levels are a maximum of 400 milligrams per litre, as in Sauternes.

One difference I do discern is that the winemaking here tends to be more technological. Since there is little barrel-fermentation or barrel-ageing in Sainte-Croix-du-Mont, there is a tendency to intervene a good deal in the winemaking process. There is nothing necessarily wrong with that, as long as it is done with sensitivity and is more than the formulaic application of an oenologist's recipe. In addition to cold chambers for cryo-extraction (which are installed at Châteaux Loubens, La Grave and La Rame), another piece of equipment is becoming more common here.

This is the *filtre à bourbes*, also known as the *filtre presse*; its use has been authorized since 1987. After a *débourbage*, a considerable amount of juice is left in the lees-thick solution that is often discarded. This new filter is able to recover the juice. The machine sounds comparable to the centrifuge, but the *filtre à bourbes* is able to handle liquids with much heavier deposits. Not everyone who favours the use of this filter employs it for this purpose. Some growers in Cérons approve of it because it can be used to clean the wine and protect it from oxidation, or because juice extracted from the lees will give richer aromas. Lionel Bord of Loupiac is very keen on the filter, reporting that he can save about 20 per cent of the must after an overnight *débourbage*. He then ferments this portion of the must separately and blends it in later with the rest of the wine. He considers it a thoroughly worthwhile investment.

I have heard little talk of the *filtre à bourbes* in Sauternes, although I have heard that Suduiraut has acquired one. Nicolas Tari of Château Nairac points out that many Sauternes estates use hydraulic presses which give such clear juice that there are hardly any lees to speak of. In such circumstances, of course, it makes no sense to spend a lot of money on machinery that will recover only 2 or 3 per cent of the must.

Like the other 'satellite' appellations, Sainte-Croix is trapped in a vicious circle in relation to its illustrious neighbours across the river. Because its yields are higher and because the reputation of the appellation lacks lustre, prices are relatively low. In 1986, prices per *tonneau* of 900 litres were just over 6,000 francs (compared to 18,000–20,000 francs for Sauternes); by 1991, just after the outstanding 1990 vintage, the price had risen to 19,000 francs (but 45,000 francs for Sauternes). Thereafter, the differential diminished slightly and in 1994, the price for Sainte-Croix was 17,500 francs, in contrast to 25,000–30,000 francs for Sauternes. With prices at these levels, growers are reluctant to exercise ambition. New oak costs as much in Sainte-Croix-du-Mont as it does in Sauternes or Pauillac, and rigorous reduction of yields is also costly. There are some growers here who have made those choices, but it is difficult for them to demand prices that reflect those costs. The enterprising growers, however, console themselves that the climate here is marginally better than in Sauternes and thus in a vintage such as 1993, when Sauternes and Barsac had little to offer, the 'satellite' appellations had a reasonable quantity of acceptable wine. Most growers also protect themselves by making dry wines as well as a *liquoreux*; prices for such wines are low, but at least the growers can be sure of having something to sell each vintage. With higher yields and a less diligent practice of harvesting by *tries successifs*, it is hardly surprising that the wines of Sainte-Croix-du-Mont are less rich than those of Sauternes. The average must weights are about 17° and chaptalization is frequent. It is evident that many producers content themselves with merely overripe grapes, which they pick early to minimize risk and then chaptalize to 17°, if they can, to give an approximate balance of 13.5° of alcohol and 3.5° of residual sugar.

Many decades ago, the region had a much higher reputation than it enjoys today. Here, as in the other satellite sweet-wine regions, the rot set in after the Second World War when there was a great demand for sweet wines. What the consumers were looking for, however, was not a lush dessert wine, but basic nutrition. Sugar was expensive, but could be enjoyed in liquid form instead. The market was flooded with cheap and usually nasty sweet white wines, chaptalized to the limit and loaded with sulphur dioxide. It may have satisfied urgent dietary needs, but it wrecked the reputation of these regions as producers of great wine. Sauternes, as we have seen, made a strong recovery in the 1980s and the satellite appellations have trotted behind.

Some leading producers, not only here but also in Loupiac and Cérons, are keen to see an enforced reduction in yields, ideally to the same level as those imposed on Sauternes. There is resistance to this idea in Sainte-Croix-du-Mont. The president of the Syndicat Viticole, Arnaud de Sèze, the proprietor of Château Loubens, is less keen than his counterparts in other appellations. He points out that many producers have established a regular clientele for simple, well-made sweet wines, admittedly produced from maximum yields but sold at correspondingly low prices. If yields were halved, growers would be compelled to double their prices, thereby losing much of their market. He himself practises low yields and charges the highest prices in the appellation for his wines, but he is unwilling to enforce those standards on his neighbours. He wants to retain what he calls *une palette de produits*, so that all levels of the market can be satisfied. Jean Queyrens of Château des Graves du Tich adds that, having made considerable investments in the late 1980s, some producers did increase prices which their customers did not accept, so they were forced to bring prices down again.

It's a strong argument, but it also means that a large number of producers can continue to practise mediocre viticulture and wine-making. The future for all these sweet-wine appellations has to lie in an improvement in quality; anything that encourages the considerable complacency and cynicism that flourish here should be resisted. It is all too easy to justify lamentable standards in terms of offering good value to the consumer – far too many producers have offered this excuse to me. No doubt Arnaud de Sèze is right in saying that it is a bad idea for Sainte-Croix-du-Mont to try to compete with Sauternes, which it can never replicate, but surely it cannot hurt to encourage his fellow growers to make the same commitment to improving quality that he and other leading producers have been making for many years?

I often ask producers of Sainte-Croix, Loupiac and Cadillac whether they can tell their wines apart at blind tastings. It is an important question, as the basis of the appellation system is the assertion that different *terroirs* and microclimates deserve recognition as separate products. Marc Ducau, a leading producer of Loupiac, believes that Sainte-Croix is a touch more powerful and heavier in flavour than Loupiac, which has greater delicacy. Many growers would agree with him. Yves Armand, however, doubts that he could identify the different appellations in a blind tasting. Speaking for myself, I might be able to recognize the style of an individual producer, but not necessarily the character of the appellation in a blind tasting.

There are some who argue that the undisputed similarity of these wines is an excellent reason to regroup under a single appellation, just as the Sauternais have done. You may have a personal preference for Bommes or Preignac over Sauternes or Fargues and this can easily be satisfied, but no one argues that each commune entitled to the Sauternes appellation should have its own appellation (with the one exception of Barsac). Camille Brun, the mayor of Sainte-Croix, believes that having three appellations on this bank of the Garonne is a waste of resources. Each appellation by itself is too small in production terms to justify the efforts required to promote their wines. By consolidating under one appellation, they would have a substantial volume of wine to market and could pool their resources to publicize their wines more effectively.

Since appellations in France are multiplying rather than consolidating, I doubt that M. Brun's argument will win great support, but he does seem to me to have logic and common sense on his side.

Vintages are of much the same character as they are in Sauternes, although, as mentioned earlier, the rarity of frost and the drying effect of strong autumnal winds means that dire vintages in Sauternes are sometimes slightly less dire on this side of the river.

DOMAINE DES ARROUCATS

Mme Labat-Lapouge is the somewhat complacent proprietor of this 17-ha. estate. Since, by her own admission, she does not need to earn her living from making wine, she feels free to do much as she pleases. Unfortunately, this attitude does not lead to wines of exemplary quality, though she seems to have a loyal private clientele in Belgium and France. The vineyards are planted on clay and limestone soils with 79 per cent Sémillon, 20 per cent Sauvignon and 1 per cent Muscadelle. Yields are close to the maximum. The grapes are pressed in a horizontal press and fermented in large tanks; the wine spends most of its ageing process in tank, but is released for a spell of up to six months in barrels. Wines destined for sale to wholesalers are aged in tank only. The maximum estate-bottled production is 35,000 bottles.

I was unimpressed by the 1988, which was sticky and sulphury, but Mme Labat-Lapouge says the 1989 is better. It had must weights of 18°, which is satisfactory though hardly remarkable for the vintage. In 1991, she bottled no wine. She prefers her 1994 to 1993, though she harvested rapidly and admits that there was hardly any selection.

Mme Labat-Lapouge, Domaine des Arroucats, 33410 Cadillac, telephone: 56 601737, fax: 56 621314

CHÂTEAU DE COULINATS

M. Brun, an avuncular retired teacher, is the mayor of Sainte-Croix and most of his estates lie in the Premières Côtes de Bordeaux, where he makes one of the better examples, Château de Berbec. In Sainte-Croix he has only 4 ha. of vines, planted with 95 per cent

Sémillon and 5 per cent Sauvignon and Muscadelle. There is no fermentation or ageing in barrels because, he claims, the use of wood would add 10–12 francs to the price of a bottle and his clients would not accept this. He leaves the wine on the lees during its *élevage* and there is neither fining nor filtration until shortly before bottling. There are various bottlings of the wine, presumably according to demand, except for the Cuvée Reservée. The average production is 20,000 bottles.

Given that Camille Brun is trying to produce an inexpensive sweet wine, Coulinats is remarkably successful. Big vintages such as 1970, 1975 and 1976 have been marred by high alcohol and sulphur levels, but there is no disputing the powerful fruitiness of these wines, with their aromas of orange, pineapple and stewed peaches. I find the style somewhat overpowering, often blowsy and cloying on the finish. The 1989 is sumptuous, but soon betrays its lack of structure with a short finish. The 1990 Cuvée Reservée (with 15° of alcohol and 7° of *liqueur*) is a delicious mouthful of orangey fruit, though it does lack acidity.

Camille Brun, Château de Coulinats, 33410 Cadillac

CHÂTEAU CRABITAN-BELLEVUE

Since 1870, this estate has been in the possession of the Solane family, formerly coopers in the region, and the present occupant is the pugnacious Bernard Solane, assisted by his son Nicolas. It is quite a large property, with 33 ha. under vine, of which 20 ha. are in Sainte-Croix-du-Mont, divided among some sixty parcels. They are planted with 85 per cent Sémillon, 8 per cent Sauvignon and 7 per cent Muscadelle. Some of the vines are a century old. Yields are fairly high, but Solane does practise up to five *tries* when required.

The grapes are pressed in a horizontal press and after a twenty-four-hour *débourbage*, the must is fermented in temperature-controlled stainless steel. Fermentation is arrested by chilling and the addition of sulphur dioxide. There is no cold treatment to get rid of tartrate crystals. Solane stopped ageing the wine in wood in 1973, but has revived the use of *barriques* for his Cuvée Spéciale. He first made this *cuvée* in 1985, and again in 1988 and 1990. In 1988, he used a good deal of new oak, but slightly less in 1990. Rather confusingly, he made two Cuvées Spéciales in 1990, one from very rich musts that he aged for eight months in *barriques*; the other was made from must similar in richness to that used for the regular 1990, but was kept for a longer period in oak.

Solane also produces a Premières Côtes de Bordeaux using the same methods of harvesting and vinification. His prices are reasonable. In 1994, the regular bottling of 1990 was 42 francs, the Cuvée Spéciale 60 francs and the 1992 a modest 31 francs.

Bernard Solane was kind enough to extract some older vintages from his cellar for me to taste. The 1955 was drying out and showing slight maderization, but still had delicious orangey fruit and good length. The 1962 was slightly herbaceous and undernourished, well preserved but unexciting. The 1981 had flavours of ripe grapefruit; a simple medium-bodied wine with no great length. The 1988 Cuvée Spéciale is delicious, with apricot and lemon on the palate, and a hint of tropical fruit, not especially rich but attractive and well balanced. The regular 1990 is stylish but light, since the best lots were bottled separately. The first of the 1990 Cuvées Spéciales is very impressive: a huge wine, sweet and rich and smoky, with a superb attack; not much finesse here, but a mighty wine none the less. The second is very oaky and consequently rather dry on the palate; it has promising persistence of flavour, so I expect it will develop well. The 1991 is good for the vintage, fresh and light, and the 1992 is sweet and lean and fades fast, so it should be drunk young.

Bernard Solane, Château Crabitan-Bellevue, 33410 Cadillac, telephone: 56 620153, fax: 56 767209

CHÂTEAU DE L'ESCALEY

Saint-Marc is a winemaker of the old school, a farmer for whom wine is one product in a larger range. There are 8 ha. of vines here, mostly Sémillon, and some of them are seventy years old. He harvests late when he can, but yields are high. The grapes are pressed in a horizontal press, then fermented either in old casks or in small stainless-steel tanks. When I first visited the property many years ago, I was appalled by the state of the cellars and casks. Since then, matters have improved. There are still old casks here, but also newer *barriques* purchased from Yquem. Saint-Marc sells much of his wine to wholesalers and retains about 12,000 bottles with his own label. The wines are simple and without pretension. It is hard to be specific about individual vintages because Saint-Marc has the old-school habit of keeping his wines in cask for varying periods. Thus in 1994 I was still able to taste his 1989 and 1990 from cask, though the major part of those vintages had already been bottled and sold. The wines are light, sweet and simple, with neither depth nor complexity. At 36 francs they are inexpensive, but no bargain.

Roger Saint-Marc, Château de l'Escaley, 33410 Cadillac

CHÂTEAU GOUTEY-LAGRAVIÈRE

Most of the estate's production consists of Premières Côtes de Bordeaux, sold under the label of Château Haut-Goutey, but 2.5 ha. are in Sainte-Croix-du-Mont. The vines are in a number of parcels and many of them are very old. The *encépagement* is 85 per cent Sémillon, 12 per cent Sauvignon and 3 per cent Muscadelle. The average yields are 33 hl./ha.; the wines are vinified entirely in tanks and bottled eighteen months after the harvest. The maximum production is 12,500 bottles. The wines are very sweet and very simple, and even in great vintages such as 1989 and 1990 they lack richness and concentration and length.

Françoise Duperrieux, Château Goutey-Lagravière, 33410 Cadillac, telephone: 56 620885

CHÂTEAU GRAND PEYROT

See Château La Grave (below).

CHÂTEAU LA GRAVE

M. Tinon has owned La Grave since 1966 and since 1978 has also leased Château Grand Peyrot, which is vinified at La Grave. Château La Grave has been in existence for 250 years. In the early nineteenth century, it belonged to a M. Lujol and was purchased in the 1870s by the Andrieu family, who built many of the surviving outbuildings. In 1930, the estate was bought by the Bridet family, from whom the Tinons are descended. At La Grave there are 9 ha. of vines and 5 ha. at Grand Peyrot. Both estates are considerably larger, but not all the vines are entitled to the Sainte-Croix appellation. The difference between the two estates is in location and exposition. Grand Peyrot is on limestone soil, whereas La Grave is on clay and gravel, and has younger vines. At Grand Peyrot, some of the Sémillon vines are eighty-five years old. Although the estates are planted with Sauvignon Blanc as well as Sémillon, most of the Sauvignon is used for dry wines, so the Sainte-Croix is made almost entirely from Sémillon. The other difference between the estates is the average age of the vines, which at La Grave is thirty years and at Grand Peyrot fifty years. Yields are about 35 hl./ha.

Most of the grapes are pressed in a pneumatic press, especially bunches frozen in the cold chamber. The must is fermented in temperature-controlled vats at about 24°C, filtered the following spring and left in tank for eighteen months. The maximum production of Sainte-Croix is 25,000 bottles of Grand Peyrot and 55,000 of La Grave. However, since 1986 Tinon has been producing 4,500 bottles of a *barrique*-aged La Grave. This *cuvée* is aged for about twelve months in barrels, some of which are new and none of which is more than five years old. Tinon has the admirable habit of giving his wines considerable bottle age before release. Thus the 1990 *barrique*-aged La Grave was not put on sale until the summer of 1994. There was no special *cuvée* in 1991 or 1992.

Jean-Marie Tinon is keen on cryo-extraction, but believes it should be used in good years, rather than in poor vintages such as 1992. He used it from 1988 to 1991 and believes that his best lots in 1990 were those which had been frozen. Tinon is not alone in this strategy. Pierre Dubourdieu of Château Doisy-Daëne in Barsac holds similar views. For Tinon, cryo-extraction is a preferable alternative to chaptalization. He says he had good results from cryo-extraction in 1993, but did not use it in 1994.

I find these estates an excellent source of wine at very fair prices. The 1990 was quite sensational here – some of the lots had a potential alcohol of 29°, though of course they were blended with less vertiginously rich wines – in both the unoaked Grand Peyrot bottling and the unctuous, smoky oaked La Grave. The wines age beautifully too. I have often tasted the 1975 La Grave, which even now shows no sign of tiredness and has retained its tangy acidity. The same is true of the 1983 Grand Peyrot. In 1985, Grand Peyrot is superior to La Grave. The first *barrique*-aged La Grave in 1986 was not a success, but by 1988 Tinon had got it right, producing a rich, spicy wine in which the oak component was well integrated. The 1989 is excellent too, though closed at present, but 1990 is the triumphant vintage here. The delicious pineappley Grand Peyrot was priced at 40 francs on release, the oaked La Grave at 50 francs. It is no surprise that the wines sell fast.

Jean-Marie Tinon, Château La Grave, 33410 Cadillac, telephone: 56 620165, fax: 56 620004

CHÂTEAU DES GRAVES DU TICH

Although this large estate of 60 ha. mainly produces red and white wines, a relatively small quantity of Sainte-Croix-du-Mont is produced, some 14,000 bottles, all of which is sold in bottle. Queyrens also makes a rather dull Premières Côtes called Château de Pin-Franc. At present, the *encépagement* is 80 per cent Sémillon and 20 per cent Sauvignon, though as replanting takes place the balance is shifting more towards Sémillon. The grapes are pressed in a horizontal press; yeasts are added and fermentation takes place in tanks, but for the *élevage* there is a rotation between tanks and *barriques*. Queyrens doesn't want to waste a lot of money on costly *barriques* to make a wine that the majority of purchasers will drink young. Queyrens is one of the winemakers who employs a *filtre à bourbes* to recover the juice mixed with the lees. There are various bottlings, according to demand. My experience of this wine is limited and has not prompted any *frisson* of excitement.

Jean Queyrens, Château des Graves du Tich, Donzac, 33410 Cadillac, telephone: 56 629742

CHÂTEAU LOUBENS

Loubens occupies one of the finest sites in Sainte-Croix-du-Mont, its seventeenth-century mansion perched close to the cliff-face. From here there are clear views across the river to Rayne-Vigneau and Yquem. Tunnelled into the cliffs are seven nineteenth-century galleries, originally used as cellars, since the constant temperature and humidity were ideal for the *élevage* of wine. Since Loubens no longer practises barrel-ageing, the galleries are now empty of wine, which is to be regretted, since these are probably the finest cellars in the entire commune.

The de Sèze family acquired Loubens in 1927 and the present owner is Arnaud de Sèze, who is shy, slow-spoken and thoughtful. He is also the president of the Syndicat Viticole, which is appropriate as Loubens is the best-known estate in Sainte-Croix-du-Mont.

The 16 ha. of vineyards are all located on slopes composed of clay and limestone. De Sèze recalls that some of the Loubens vineyards were so steep that they had to be worked by pulley. He would dearly love to bring these superb sites back into production, but they would be dangerous to work and authorization is unlikely to be granted. (He also has no *droit de plantation*, so the question is academic.) The varieties planted include 5 per cent Sauvignon; this is rarely included in the blend for Sainte-Croix-du-Mont, which here is mostly made from Sémillon. The average age of the vines is forty years. The average yield is usually below 30 hl./ha. This was the figure in 1985, but in 1988 it was 26.5 hl./ha. and in 1989, 26 hl./ha. The maximum production is 40,000 bottles, though de Sèze will declassify unsatisfactory lots into his second wine, Château des Tours. Thus in 1981, there were only 20,000 bottles of Loubens; in 1982, only 30,000.

The grapes are pressed in a hydraulic press, but there is also a pneumatic press, which is better suited to cryo-extracted fruit. De Sèze chaptalizes on occasion and fermentation takes place in small tanks for a month or so. After fermentation is arrested with sulphur dioxide and chilling, the wine is racked, then racked again in March and filtered. The wine is blended, fined with bentonite and filtered again before bottling about three years after the harvest. The wine is given a year's bottle age before release.

I find Loubens a splendid wine, but can't help reflecting how much more complex it would be if it spent time in wood. Barrels were used when de Sèze's father was running the estate, but at that time he could not afford to renew them. There is no doubt that the Loubens vineyards are of superb quality. Noble rot is common and de Sèze practises harvesting by *tries successifs*. In 1983, for instance, there were eight *tries* over a period of two months. He does not succumb to the temptation to pick early to ensure a cellar full of wine each vintage. In 1985, which was as dry here as in Sauternes, he did not begin picking until 23 October and even then the grapes were shrivelled rather than botrytized. He continued picking until late November, when botrytis had at last attacked the fruit. In 1989, there was a great deal of botrytis and the must weights ranged from 21 to 23°, and for the first time de Sèze had to employ cultivated yeasts to ensure the fermentation did not stick. In 1990, the grapes were even richer, with the first *tries* bringing in lots with 28°, so they had to be blended with unbotrytized lots of 17°. No Loubens has been bottled in 1991, 1992 and 1993.

Prices are quite high, at about 80 francs. Curiously, the label states that the wine is *Grand Cru*, a term with no legal force in

Sainte-Croix. De Sèze says that for decades the words '*Premier Cru*' appeared on the label and when his father asked to be upgraded to *Grand Cru*, the authorities raised no objection.

Arnaud de Sèze says that he wants wines with finesse rather than fatness and power. But my frequent tastings of the wine suggest that the reverse is true and that the wines are very rich, sometimes at the expense of elegance. In general, these are heavy, lush, golden wines with strong orangey botrytis flavours. I keep noting tangerine, mango and peach aromas and flavours, a sumptuous palate and dense texture that sometimes comes close to soupiness. The 1990 is a great wine, in which the lushness is tempered by a fine acidity and immense concentration. It has 15° of alcohol and 7° of *liqueur*. The 1989 is superb too, with exemplary extract, and the 1988 has an attractive pepperiness that enlivens the creamy texture. The 1986 is very good but lacks structure, and the very sweet 1985 tastes of tropical fruit, but lacks complexity and length. The 1983 is excellent and the 1981 has exotic fruits on nose and palate, but a slight stickiness on the finish. De Sèze says that top vintages of Loubens can age for up to fifty years and I have no difficulty in accepting this.

Arnaud de Sèze, Château Loubens, 33410 Cadillac, telephone: 56 620125, fax: 56 767165

CHÂTEAU LOUSTEAU-VIEIL

The Sessacq family has owned Lousteau-Vieil since 1843 and their portfolio of vineyards also includes parcels in the Graves and Sauternes. In Sainte-Croix-du-Mont, the 17 ha. of vines are distributed among twenty-five parcels, mostly on clay and limestone, and planted with 80 per cent Sémillon, 15 per cent Sauvignon and 5 per cent Muscadelle. These vineyards are among the highest in the commune and their average age is twenty-five years, though there are pockets of ninety-year-old vines. Average yields are about 30 hl./ha., but the estate's second wine, Cap des Vignots, is made from maximum yields. The estate practises *triage* and tries to be selective in wet vintages such as 1987 and 1992. In 1991, when few vines escaped the spring frost, Sessacq felt compelled to vinify the lot. A peculiarity of the 1989 is the high proportion of Muscadelle in the blend.

The grapes are pressed in a horizontal press, chaptalized when considered necessary, and fermented in tanks that since 1984 have been temperature-controlled. In the spring the wine is racked, filtered, fined and then aged for about eighteen months in *barriques*, of which 15 per cent are new. Cap des Vignots is aged only in tank. The maximum production of Lousteau-Vieil is 50,000 bottles. The wines are quite expensive for the appellation. In late 1994, the 1991 was being sold for 50 francs, the 1988 for 56 francs. They are available from the estate in Sainte-Croix and from the roadside stand operated by the Sessacq family along the road from Langon to Bazas.

The quality of the wines is uneven. Certain vintages were marred by mustiness and excessive sulphur. Flavours of tropical fruit often dominate the wine – banana, mango, pineapple – giving it a one-dimensional tone that can be wearying. Often the alcohol levels seem excessive for the fruit. On the other hand, the Crème de Tête produced in 1970 was delicious twenty years later, still retaining a lively acidity and quite good length. The lean, elegant, lemony 1975 lasted better than the 1976, which was showing some oxidation after ten years. The 1978 and 1979 were mediocre, the 1981 rather cloying and the 1982 more satisfactory, a rounded, well-balanced wine of medium length. The fine 1983 was agreeably rich, while retaining an acidic bite. The 1984 was mediocre, the 1985 pretty and pineappley, the 1986 dull, the 1987 hard and simple, the 1988 bright and stylish, but with an odd lemon-curd nose. In 1990, a special *cuvée* was made, but I have not tasted it. The 1991 was light but attractive, the 1992 more lush but also slightly bitter.

Rémy Sessacq, Clos La Mourasse, BP 78, 33211 Langon, telephone: 56 633927, fax: 56 631182

CHÂTEAU DES MAILLES

This 14–ha. estate has been owned by the Derrieu family for two centuries. Some of the vines are red, but 12.5 ha. are used for Sainte-Croix-du-Mont. The vines have an average age of forty years, and some hundred-year-old vines still survive. The *encépagement* is 95 per cent Sémillon, the remainder Sauvignon and Muscadelle. The vineyards are south-facing on clay and limestone soils. Average yields are 35 hl./ha.

The grapes are pressed in a horizontal press; yeasts are added and then the must is fermented in temperature-controlled tanks. As it ages, the wine is rotated between tanks and *barriques*, where the wine stays for about nine months. In 1990, when some of the must was exceedingly rich, Derrieu barrel-fermented part of the crop, which ended up as 3,000 bottles of Réserve Personelle. The average production of Sainte-Croix is 45,000 bottles. Prices are moderate.

The only vintages I have encountered are recent ones. The 1989 is rich and rounded, with fine apricot flavours and quite good length. The 1990 is very good, but not outstanding; not surprisingly, the Réserve Personelle is far superior, a very sweet, intense wine with immense extract and powerful fruit; its excellent length promises a fine future. The 1992 is good for the vintage.

Daniel Derrieu, Château des Mailles, 33410 Cadillac, telephone: 56 620120

CHÂTEAU LES MARCOTTES

This family property with its large, well-equipped winery has been run since 1979 by the fifth generation in the form of the energetic Gérard Cigana, who has expanded the estate to about 100 ha. in all. Only about 20 ha., planted on the slopes behind the winery, are dedicated to Sainte-Croix-du-Mont. The varieties planted are 90 per cent Sémillon and 10 per cent Sauvignon. The average age of the vines is thirty years and average yields are 35 hl./ha.

The Sainte-Croix is vinified in tanks, except for the Prestige *cuvée*, which is made from old vines and fermented in barrels that are either new or acquired after one year from Yquem. The wine was first produced in 1990 (20,000 bottles) and again in 1993 (about 8,000 bottles). Declassified lots are sold as Bordeaux Supérieurs Moelleux, which is cheap but mediocre. The wines are inexpensive.

One has to admire M. Cigana's energy and enterprise, but I suspect he is more engaged in producing dry wines than sweet ones. In my admittedly limited experience, I have found his Sainte-Croix-du-Mont, even from the 1990 vintage, coarse and flat.

Gérard Cigana, Château Les Marcottes, 33410 Cadillac, telephone: 56 620544, fax: 56 620670

CHÂTEAU LA PEYRERE

Although this estate was founded by M. Dupuy's parents, estate-bottling began as recently as the 1980s. Dupuy owns 10 ha. of white vines, of which 80 per cent are Sémillon, 15 per cent Sauvignon and 5 per cent Muscadelle. The Sauvignon vines are young, but there are some Sémillon vines that are about ninety years old. Yields are high. Average production of Sainte-Croix is about 25,000 bottles, though he also sells wine in bulk.

The grapes are pressed in a horizontal press and the must fermented in cement vats. Half the wine is aged in old barrels. Dupuy favours a wine with high alcohol. Unfortunately this results in hot, sulphury wines with insufficient fruit and concentration of flavour.

J. P. Dupuy, Château La Peyrere, 33410 Cadillac

CHÂTEAU LA RAME

This fine 37–ha. estate was bought from Raoul Arbez by Armand's father in 1956. The 25 ha. of white vines are planted with 75 per cent Sémillon and 25 per cent Sauvignon Blanc. At present there is no Muscadelle, but Armand is toying with the idea of planting some. The vines have an average age of forty years and are located in six parcels around the house, mostly on clay and limestone soils. Armand is deeply interested in viticulture and has been collaborating with the local Chambre d'Agriculture in experiments with what antipodeans call canopy management; this involves training the vines with a split canopy above, which is supposed to give higher must weights as well as higher yields. At first Armand was quite impressed with the preliminary results, although he says that the cost of maintenance is one factor that weighs against adopting the system; more recently he said split canopy training does not seem to make a significant difference.

The grapes are pressed in a horizontal press and decanted by gravity into tanks where the must settles overnight. Fermentation takes place in temperature-controlled vats. Armand says he would ideally like to ferment his wines in *barriques*, but at present lacks the space to do so. As one who has clambered over and around pallets of wine in his cellars, I can vouch for the cramped conditions. He does not normally use cultivated yeasts but, like some other growers in this vintage, had to do so in 1989 because the must was unusually rich and thus reluctant to ferment. In March the wine is filtered, chilled to 4° to get rid of tartrate crystals and then the blending process begins. The wine is then filtered again and the best lots are aged in *barriques*, of which one-third are new. Until 1986, all the wine was aged in a blend of tanks and older barrels. The wine remains in *barriques* for twelve months. Armand looks for potential alcohol of at least 18° for his Sainte-Croix; less rich lots are usually consigned to his second label, Château La Caussade. He also produces a Premières Côtes de Bordeaux called Domaine du Barrail, which I have never tasted.

Armand is an enthusiast for cryo-extraction, which he finds indispensable in damp vintages. He also uses it to make dry white wines, as he believes the process makes them fatter and more perfumed. In 1993, he picked wet grapes with a must weight of 15.5–16° which after cryo-extraction had increased by 3°. The drawback was that he lost almost 40 per cent of volume in 1993, but at least he had must of excellent quality.

His total production of Sainte-Croix is about 65,000 bottles. The oaked wine is labelled Réserve du Château and has met, deservedly, with great acclaim. There is no fixed rule as to the quantity which is aged in barrels; in 1986 and 1988 it was no more than 20 per cent of the crop, but in 1990 it was 45 per cent. The wines are the most expensive in Sainte-Croix, about 100 francs for the Réserve, but demand is strong.

The first Réserve was produced in 1985, but Armand was unhappy with it and I have never tasted this wine. In 1989, he had must weights of 21–22° despite yields of 35 hl./ha. This wine spent twelve months in oak, but the 1990 Réserve was aged in *barriques* for twenty-five months. There was no La Rame in 1991 and very little in 1992, none of which was Réserve. In 1993, when the entire crop was subjected to cryo-extraction, he had fruit that was ripe though wet and was pleased with the eventual quality. Much the same was true in 1994.

The 1973 and 1975 La Rame were delicate elegant wines with good length. The 1982 was bigger and rounder, but rather cloying on the finish and lacking in elegance. The 1984 was a disappointment, but the 1983 and 1985 were fine stylish wines with very good length. I found the 1986 Réserve over-oaked and a touch dry on the finish, but the 1988 Réserve is a great improvement, although the oak is quite marked on both nose and palate. The unoaked

1988 is also very good. The 1989 is very impressive, but over-shadowed by the dense and concentrated 1990, which despite lash-ings of oak on the nose, has a spicy lemon-zest palate with liquorice undertones and good length.

There are many who would argue that La Rame Réserve is the finest wine of Sainte-Croix-du-Mont and I would not be disposed to disagree. However, Château La Grave is a strong rival, and wine lovers with a taste for lush, syrupy dessert wine will save their greatest affection for Loubens. These estates, despite their different styles of winemaking, provide exactly the kind of lead and inspir-ation that the more mundane properties need and demonstrate the fine quality of which, in good vintages, this underrated appellation is capable.

Yves Armand, Château La Rame, 33410 Cadillac, telephone: 56 620150, fax: 56 620194

15

Loupiac

Loupiac lies to the north-west of Sainte-Croix-du-Mont and borders the Garonne. There were vineyards here in the thirteenth century and possibly earlier. The presence of Roman remains – fragments of columns, mosaics and tiles – testify to early habitation, and local legend maintains that they are the remains of Ausonius's villa. Ausonius was a Roman poet and governor of Gaul. He was born in Bordeaux *circa* AD 320 and was known to have owned vineyards in the region. His name was borrowed by Château Ausone in Saint-Émilion and it is not surprising that other Bordeaux proprietors have tried to associate their estates with this wine lover of antiquity. However, there is little to suggest that there was any connection between the governor and the site of Ausone, let alone Loupiac.

The village of Loupiac is grouped around its fine Romanesque church and the vineyards creep up the slopes behind it on to the plateau where most of the vines are planted, enjoying a south and south-easterly exposition. The Syndicat Viticole was founded in 1900 and in 1936 the appellation was created, specifying a minimum potential alcohol of 13°, of which 12.5° must be actual alcoholic degree. Maximum yields are set at 40 hl./ha. Chaptalization is permitted up to 2°. As in Sainte-Croix-du-Mont, pruning *à cot* is not allowed and all pruning is *Guyot simple* or *double*. All harvesting is manual. There is no co-operative.

By 1874, there were 520 ha. under vine and the figures changed little over the following century. Today there are about 570 ha. in production, though only about 370 ha. produce sweet wine. As in Sainte-Croix-du-Mont, there is also a proportion of dry red and white wines. About seventy properties produce Loupiac, though only about fifty bottle their own wine. The annual production fluctuates: in 1981 it was 10,000 hl., by 1985 it had declined to 6,000 hl., in 1993 it rose again to 13,000 hl. In the past decade, average yields have ranged from 29.4 hl./ha. in 1985 to 38 hl./ha. in 1990.

The soil is varied. To the west, closer to the Garonne, the soil is alluvial. Moving eastwards the slopes are on clay and limestone soils, with limestone subsoil on the lower slopes, and a subsoil of clay and gravel up on the plateau.

It is not easy to distinguish what makes Loupiac different in character from Sainte-Croix-du-Mont. Jean Perromat of Cérons, whose wife owns an estate in Loupiac, points out that the south-facing vineyards of Loupiac often enable the grapes to dry out and become raisiny, giving the wines a more *rôti* quality than those from Sainte-Croix. Patrick Dejean, the president of the Syndicat Viticole, believes Loupiac has more *nervosité*. He also points out that there is relatively little selling off of wine to wholesalers. There is plenty of generic Sauternes and Sainte-Croix on the market, but much less Loupiac. This has given a stability to the market with fewer fluctuations in price from year to year than is the case with other sweet wines. (The wife of one grower added a malicious footnote to this statement by claiming that much of the wine sold as 1991 generic Sauternes was in fact Loupiac.) Prices peaked in 1991, when Loupiac fetched 18,500 francs per *tonneau*. In 1993 and 1994 they slipped, but not by much and they now stand at 16,000–17,000 francs. Even so, this is a significant advance on the prices obtained in the mid-1980s, when they stood at 5,000–7,000 francs. These prices are just a fraction less than those obtained for Sainte-Croix-du-Mont.

Many estates here are technically well equipped and there is little bad wine to be found in Loupiac. No estates are equipped with cryo-extraction facilities, though a few have made use of cold chambers elsewhere. Many decades ago, before temperature-controlled fermentation became common, wines were left to their own devices far more than is the case today. In the best vintages this didn't matter, as fermentation slowed down by itself when the wine had reached about 14°. But in poor years there was a tendency for the wine to ferment to near dryness, with unpalatable results. The wines used to be aged in old barrels, but with the slump in the market in the 1950s and 1960s, most estates switched to cement vats or steel tanks. In the mid-1980s, many estates followed the example of the Sauternais and reverted to a greater use of oak for the *élevage*.

If the majority of wines are correctly made today, that does not necessarily mean that they are of good quality. The commonly heard refrain that Loupiac is a light wine often serves as an excuse for dilution, as Patrick Dejean is the first to admit. Lionel Bord of Clos Jean insists that Loupiac must preserve its identity, which he defines as delicate and crystalline, without excessive richness. He argues that it is hard to obtain structure and power in a Loupiac and that it is a mistake to try. Moreover, the employment of *barrique*-ageing, which would give the wine greater structure in suitable vintages, means that prices would have to be greatly increased, which would in turn lead to a loss of clients. This is an understandable argument from a short-term commercial point of view, but it is a recipe for mediocrity in the long term. It also gives growers an excuse to skip harvesting by *tries successifs* or to practise it in a perfunctory way. Some wines taste as though everything had been thrown into the press without selection. If proprietors are practising *triage*, as they all declare, they are clearly not doing so very effectively.

Patrick Dejean admits with some shame that there are some growers who, in fine vintages such as 1989 and 1990, do not go out of their way to produce the outstanding wines which their vineyards and cellars are perfectly capable of, for fear that it would open too wide a gap between such top vintages and the run-of-the-mill wines they make in ordinary years. This is a profoundly foolish approach and one can only hope that it is not too widespread. The Syndicat is trying to stimulate an improvement in overall quality by making its members aware of the competition both from within the appellation and from neighbouring communes. Blind tastings are organized at which, one hopes, the weaker brethren can appreciate how far their wines lag behind the best of Loupiac.

Dejean is particularly keen to see the maximum yield lowered from 40 hl./ha. He has not yet succeeded, but has made greater progress than his counterpart in Sainte-Croix-du-Mont in persuading some of his fellow growers that the only path to greater commercial viability in the long term is an amelioration in quality, by means of lower yields.

Vintages are similar to those in Sauternes and Barsac. The 1990 vintage was outstanding, although some growers experienced problems in controlling volatile acidity during fermentation. In 1991, production was greatly diminished by the spring frost. In 1992 results were fairly disastrous; *pourriture grise* flourished in the wet, cool conditions that prevailed and many of the wines have a ciderish taste that is not entirely pleasant. In 1993, Loupiac fared better than Sauternes; many growers picked before the rain, while others waited until later in the autumn when drier weather continued into early November. There was some frost damage in 1994 and a wet September obliged many growers to begin *tries de nettoyage*. By late September the rain had stopped, wind dried the fruit and by 8 October botrytis was widespread and must weights, at the better-managed properties, were higher than originally expected.

CHÂTEAU DU CROS

Little is left of the fourteenth-century château built for the Ségur family that stood on the slopes overlooking the Garonne. The current proprietor is Michel Boyer, who despite his schoolmasterly manner is a tireless advocate for the wines of Loupiac. The estate is large, with 45 ha. under vine, of which about 20 ha. are used to produce Loupiac. The vines are on average forty years old, and are planted on clay and limestone slopes; some vines survive from 1903. The *encépagement* is 70 per cent Sémillon, 20 per cent Sauvignon and 10 per cent Muscadelle. Average yields are 35 hl./ha. Boyer has experimented with cryo-extraction, using rented facilities at Beautiran.

No yeasts are added before fermentation, which takes place in tank. No oak was used here between 1968 and 1983; since 1985, a proportion of the crop has been aged in *barriques* which he buys from Yquem. In 1986, one-third of the oak was new, but by 1989 the wine was spending eighteen months in *barriques* of which half were new. The 1990, exceptionally, was aged entirely in new oak and even the middling 1992 vintage spent twelve months in *barriques*.

Production fluctuates considerably. No Château du Cros at all was bottled in 1984, 1987 and 1991. In 1990, there were 80,000 bottles; in 1992, 25,000 bottles; in 1993, 40,000 bottles. A second label, Fleur du Cros, is used for less satisfactory lots and is usually found only in supermarkets. Prices of Château du Cros are relatively high, but so is the quality.

The wine ages quite well and in 1994, the 1973 was still fresh and lively, though somewhat neutral in flavour. A half-bottle of 1981 was holding up well, with an almondy nose and good attack on the palate. The 1985 is limey and vigorous. The oak-ageing is evident on the nose of the 1989; on the palate, the rich, ripe fruit, judiciously oaked, comes shining through. The powerful 1990 is even better, with a smoky elegance and concentration of flavour, and good length. The 1992 is, predictably, light and simple, but soundly made.

Michel Boyer, Château du Cros, 33410 Cadillac, telephone: 56 629931, fax: 56 621259

CHÂTEAU GRAND PEYRUCHET

Queyrens is a serious winemaker with very precise ideas about how he wants to produce his Loupiac. Only Sémillon is used for the sweet wine and the 8 ha. of vines, with an average age of twenty-five years, are planted on clay and sand soils, with an easterly and south-easterly exposition. Average yields are 35 hl./ha. and even in superlative years such as 1990 they did not reach 40 hl./ha. Queyrens experimented with cryo-extraction in 1993, but is doubtful about the benefits.

The winery is equipped with a pneumatic press. The must is fermented in tanks; half is aged in *barriques* and then blended with the other half, which remains in tanks. Queyrens insists he does not want a flavour of new oak in his wine, so only 25 per cent of the barrels are new, 50 per cent are two years old and 25 per cent are four years old. Even in modest vintages such as 1992 and 1993, he aged part of the wine in barrels for six to nine months. In 1990, a special *cuvée* called Cuvée Marie-Charlotte was produced. In normal years the production of Loupiac is 30,000 bottles and prices are moderate.

The 1985 was an aromatic wine with attractive tangerine flavours and shows rather better than the 1988, which is slightly herbaceous on the nose. The 1992 is unpleasant. Unfortunately I have not tasted the 1989 or 1990, which probably give a better idea of what M. Queyrens is capable of.

Bernard Queyrens, Château Grand Peyruchet, 33410 Cadillac, telephone: 56 626271, fax: 56 769209

CHÂTEAU LA GRAVETTE

The young and amenable Didier Lejeune, now in charge of this family estate based in Cadillac, offers up to 25,000 bottles of Loupiac produced from his 5 ha. planted on clay and limestone slopes. The varieties planted are 85 per cent Sémillon, 10 per cent Sauvignon and 5 per cent Muscadelle. The average age of the vines is forty years. The wines are vinified entirely in tanks and are bottled about eighteen months after the harvest. Prices are fairly low.

Lejeune produced a most attractive 1990, marked by botrytis but not weighed down by it; it is a lively wine with delicious fruit, but lacks persistence. The 1991 is fresh, racy and clean, but there is a slight bitterness on the aftertaste and a citric finish. The 1992 is surprisingly similar and quite successful for the vintage.

Didier Lejeune, Château La Gravette, 33410 Cadillac, telephone: 56 626730

CHÂTEAU LOUPIAC-GAUDIET

The charming château is reached along a straight drive from the main road along the Garonne. Marc Ducau is as urbane as the house and there is always a gracious welcome here. The property has been in his family for four generations and is one of the most respected names in Loupiac. The vineyards now incorporate Château Pontac, which lies on more gravelly soil further up the slope behind the house. The two estates combined consist of 26 ha. The fruit from both properties is vinified identically and only in exceptional vintages, such as 1988–90, is Pontac released separately. The *encépagement* is 80 per cent Sémillon and 20 per cent Sauvignon at both estates, and the vines are on average thirty years old.

Fermentation takes place in stainless steel. Yeasts are added and the must is chaptalized in mediocre years; during the winter, the wine is filtered and then remains in tank for two to three years before being bottled. Ducau says his clientele values the freshness and youthfulness of Loupiac-Gaudiet, which is why he does not use any wood; in his view, barrels age the wine too rapidly, masking the fruit and often drying out the wine altogether. Three years in tank, he argues, is equivalent to one year in *barriques*. When inexpertly used, barrels can indeed have the effects Ducau attributes to them;

but it seems to me he is commenting on poor workmanship, not an unsatisfactory medium.

None the less, these wines are very good. They have a purity of style and although uncomplicated they are well balanced, clean and have very good fruit. The maximum production is 100,000 bottles, of which 23,000 may be released as Pontac. There is also a second label, Château Martillac, used primarily for wines sold in supermarkets.

The only Pontac I have tasted is the 1976, which in 1990 was lush and peachy on the nose, yet still fresh and lively on the palate. Although Ducau says that his vineyards are often infested by botrytis, I don't recall discerning any in vintages of Loupiac-Gaudiet such as 1979, 1983 or 1985. The 1979 and 1985 were rather simple citric wines; the 1983 was richer, but lacked vivacity. The apricotty 1986 is very good here, and the 1989 is lush, spicy and forward, though it does lack flair. I prefer the 1991 to the 1992, and a tank sample of the 1993 looked promising. The style of Loupiac-Gaudiet has remained constant, offering a soundly made, well-balanced, stylish wine; correct, but in my experience not particularly exciting.

Marc Ducau, Château Loupiac-Gaudiet, 33410 Cadillac, telephone: 56 629988, fax: 56 626013

CHÂTEAU MÉMOIRES

Once known as Château Roumaud and Cru Rondillon, this estate was acquired by Menard and his wife Danielle, who operate their winery along the road from Cadillac to Saint-Maixant. They own 30 ha. in all, including 8 ha. they lease in Loupiac. Almost all the vines are Sémillon and many of them are old; they are planted on gravelly clay soils facing south and south-east. Yields are quite high. The Menards are quite ambitious in their ideas, but as yet lack the means to put them all into practice. They respect the effect of new oak on a rich wine, but only once, in 1990, did they have the raw materials with which to produce a special *cuvée* (rather daringly called, Alsace-style, Sélection de Grains Nobles). Their wine is vinified in tanks and then aged both in tanks and in large old casks and a few *barriques*. Very little Loupiac was produced in 1991, but there were some good lots in 1992, and the Menards are reasonably happy with the 1993. Much of the wine is sold off to wholesalers. Prices are low.

The 1990 Sélection de Grains Nobles is certainly very good, with the oak showing through strongly on the nose; on the palate it is rich and stylish, by no means swamped by the wood, but it does have some rather odd flavours. No doubt it will settle down with more bottle age. The 1991 had lanolin aromas and was hard on the palate; the 1992 is better, but not much. Still, the Menards do at least aspire to make good wine, which is more than can be said for many other growers in the region. Given some good vintages, they will no doubt succeed.

Jean-François Menard, Château Mémoires, 33490 Saint-Maixant, telephone: 56 620643, fax: 56 620432

CHÂTEAU LE MOYNE

The Seroin family are better known as the proprietors of Château Lionne in the Graves, but in 1986 they bought this property of 16 ha. Ten of these are planted with white grapes and the vineyards are mostly around the house on the plateau. Their average age is thirty-five years and average yields are 37 hl./ha. The must is fermented in cement tanks and there is no wood ageing. The wine remains in tanks for up to two years. Only one-third of the production is estate-bottled, yielding about 12,000 bottles. Once the wine is better known, they hope to expand this proportion. No 1991 was bottled. Prices are moderate. The only vintage I have tasted is the 1990, which is very good, pineapply on the nose, and rich, plump and spicy on the palate. Seroin recalls an average must weight of 21° in 1990, so it is not surprising that the wine is rich; fortunately, it also has good balance and length.

Philippe Seroin, Château Le Moyne, 33410 Cadillac, telephone: 56 626461, fax: 56 271463

DOMAINE DU NOBLE

This leading estate has been in the Dejean family for five generations. The present proprietor is the open-minded, genially raffish Patrick Dejean, who is also the president of the Syndicat Viticole. He owns 15 ha. in Loupiac and also rents 3 ha. in Sainte-Croix-du-Mont. The vineyards contain 80 per cent Sémillon; the remainder is Sauvignon and vinified separately. There are many old vines of forty-five years or more.

Dejean tirelessly advocates *triage* and lower yields. Even in poor years, such as 1987, he believes it is essential to make repeated forays into the vineyards to select only the best grapes. He criticizes those in Loupiac who use chaptalization as a substitute for selective harvesting. At Domaine du Noble, his average yields are 30 hl./ha. and never exceed 35 hl./ha. In 1992, the yield was 18 hl./ha.; in 1993, 23 hl./ha.

The must is usually fermented in tanks and Dejean is not worried if the temperature sometimes rises to 24°C. In 1988, he began fermenting part of the crop in *barriques* and bottling it separately. In 1989, he divided the must; half was fermented in tank, the other in *barriques*. No distinction was made on the label, unfortunately, but Dejean insists there was no real confusion as the wines were sold in different markets. After 1990, oaked and unoaked wines were distinguished on the label. The *barrique*-fermented 1990 spent sixteen months in oak. The maximum production is 50,000 bottles.

In 1987, he used cryo-extraction for the first time. Although he has no cold chamber of his own, he borrowed his brother's at Château Rabaud-Promis in Bommes. Fine vintages occurred in 1988–90, of course, but no wine was bottled in 1991. In 1992, there are only 3,000 bottles of oaked wine. In 1993, Dejean again used cryo-extraction. In 1994, there were *tries de nettoyage* to rid the vines of rotten grapes after the rain, but by early October he was obtaining must weights of 18°.

The wines are expensive by Loupiac standards – in 1994, the unoaked 1990 was priced at 60 francs – but very fine indeed. Unlike many wines from this side of the Garonne, they are slow to open up and in their youth tend to be tight and closed. The 1986 is delicious, with flavours of apricot and tangerine, and quite good length. The oaked 1988 is excellent, with good concentration of flavour and lively apricot fruit. The 1989 is more succulent, a broad-shouldered wine with good extract, robust yet fruity and still very closed. In 1994, the unoaked 1990 was not showing well, despite ample extract and acidity.

Patrick Dejean, Domaine du Noble, 33410 Cadillac, telephone: 56 629936, fax: 56 769131

CHÂTEAU PONTAC

See Château Loupiac-Gaudiet (p. 218).

CHÂTEAU PORTAIL ROUGE

Jean-Pierre Bernède, in addition to being the proprietor of this 12–ha. estate, is also the custodian of Loupiac's Roman remains, which his father Christian acquired in 1971. The vineyards are planted with 80 per cent Sémillon and the wines are vinified only in tanks. In good years, a special *cuvée* is produced. From 1983 I recall wines labelled '*Vin de Tête*' and '*Vin de Tête Très Liquoreux*', neither of which impressed me. The 1985 was no better. I have not tasted the wines recently. They are inexpensive.

Jean-Pierre Bernède, Château Portail Rouge, 33410 Cadillac, telephone: 56 629382, fax: 56 629998

CHÂTEAU DE RICAUD

Up on the plateau of Loupiac is this very large estate, formerly regarded as the finest in Loupiac. In medieval times it was the property of Bernard de Lamensans and his descendants. In the mid-nineteenth century it was owned by Charles de Bignon and subsequently by the Wells family, which restored the property. The grandiose neo-Gothic château surrounded by woods was the work of the architect Viollet-le-Duc. In 1980, by which time the estate was badly run down, Ricaud was bought by Alain Thiénot, who owns a Champagne house and Château Rahoul in the Graves. Today, the area under vine at Ricaud is 70 ha., but only 14 ha. are used to produce Loupiac, and half the wine from Ricaud is red. Average yields are 32 hl./ha. The *encépagement* is somewhat mysterious; at certain times I have been informed that it is entirely Sémillon; at other times that the varieties are 70 per cent Sémillon, 25 per cent Sauvignon and 5 per cent Muscadelle. It is probable that the latter figures apply to the white vineyards as a whole and the former to the vines intended for Loupiac.

There are at least three *tries* at Ricaud and the must is fermented at cool temperatures in stainless-steel tanks. The wine remains in tanks until the early summer. It is then blended, filtered and put into *barriques*, of which, in good years, 60 per cent are new; in lesser vintages, such as 1992, this figure is reduced to 25 per cent. By 1990, the Loupiac was spending up to fifteen months in oak. In

1993, Ricaud used cryo-extraction for the first time, though they have no cold chamber of their own; they were quite pleased with the results, despite a substantial loss of volume. In good vintages, the production is 30,000 bottles, though in 1991 there were only 5,000 and in 1993, 7,000. The wines are fairly expensive, but of good quality. From 1992 onwards, declassified lots have been sold under the second label of Les Hauts de Ricaud.

Ricaud is not an especially unctuous wine. It is refined and stylish, and relatively low in alcohol. The 1981 was an attractive, marmalady wine, which I preferred to the harder 1982, which lacked fruit. The 1986 is quite rich, almost jammy, and has good acidity and length; it is probably the best Loupiac of the vintage. The 1987 had an orangey character and slight bitterness on the finish. I have not tasted the 1990, but the 1991 is very good for the year, with flavours of ripe apples as well as a powerful oaky presence on nose and palate.

Alain Thiénot, Château de Ricaud, 33410 Cadillac, telephone: 56 629757, fax: 56 769330

CHÂTEAU LE TAREY

The plump, friendly Robert Gillet, recently retired, owns 7.5 ha. in Loupiac as well as 3.5 ha. in Sainte-Croix-du-Mont. Here his vines are scattered in various parcels, all on limestone and clay soils. The varieties planted are 90 per cent Sémillon and 5 per cent each of Sauvignon and Muscadelle. The average age of the vines is thirty-five years and the average yields 35 hl./ha. The wine is vinified entirely in tanks. Gillet used to age the wine for about two years, but now bottles more rapidly. The maximum production is 38,000 bottles, mostly sold to private clients. Prices are low. The 1992 is fresh, but very simple; however, I was impressed by the 1985, still fresh in 1994, with exotic fruit flavours on the palate, especially banana, which may not be to everyone's taste.

Robert Gillet, Château Le Tarey, 33410 Cadillac, telephone: 56 629999

CHÂTEAU TERREFORT

This estate is situated on the Loupiac plateau and there are 8.5 ha. of white vines, divided between 80 per cent Sémillon and 10 per cent each of Sauvignon and Muscadelle. The average age of the vines is thirty-five years and the average yields 35 hl./ha. The grapes are pressed in a horizontal press, fermented in tanks and left on the lees before being filtered. The wine is aged in tank and, since 1988, in one-year-old barrels from Yquem. Peyrondet uses oak cautiously, for no more than six months and only in rich vintages. The wine is aged overall for two to three years before being filtered and bottled. A second label, Château Bois de Roche, is used for wines sold to supermarkets.

No Terrefort was bottled in 1991 and no oak was used in 1992. Much of the 1993 was picked before the rain and Peyrondet is satisfied with the quality. I tasted a 1966 in 1994 which was losing its fruit; the nose was dieselly and the palate dry, though the wine was still drinkable – just. In 1990, Terrefort produced a good rather than outstanding wine; there is botrytis here, and some intensity and richness, but it does not have much style or length of flavour.

François Peyrondet, Château Terrefort, 33410 Cadillac, telephone: 56 626128

CLOS JEAN

Clos Jean is one of the most attractive properties in Loupiac, a former *relais* of the Knights of Malta. The personable Lionel Bord is the sixth generation of his family to run the estate, which consists of not only Clos Jean but also Château Rondillon. Rondillon is a 9–ha. property, of which 7 ha. are planted with white grapes; Clos Jean is larger, with 17 ha. under vine (11 ha. white). Rondillon has a clay soil, and the *encépagement* is 80 per cent Sémillon, 15 per cent Sauvignon and 5 per cent Muscadelle. Clos Jean has a similar *encépagement*, but with no Muscadelle and 20 per cent Sauvignon. Two-thirds of Clos Jean is on clay and limestone slopes, the remainder on the gravelly plateau of Loupiac. The average age of the vines at both properties is thirty-five years. The vinification of both wines is identical.

Bord is unashamed about aiming for the highest yields permitted. 'We derive all our income from wine, so we make as much as we can,' he says, with greater frankness than many other growers with the same views. The first pressing is in a horizontal press, followed by a second in a hydraulic press. The lees are processed through a *filtre à bourbes*, and the salvaged must is fermented separately and later blended with the rest of the wine. Bord claims that he can recover up to 20 per cent of the must in this way. Yeasts are added before fermentation and the must is almost always chaptalized. Fermentation takes place in temperature-controlled tanks. Bord is not keen on barrel-ageing, largely on grounds of cost, but in 1990 even he was persuaded to age the wine for six months in wood, in rotation with the usual tank-ageing. As the former son-in-law of Claude Ricard of Domaine de Chevalier, he was able to obtain one and two-year-old *barriques* from that illustrious domaine. No wood has been used in subsequent vintages. There are different bottling dates and some lots of 1990 were still in cask four years after the vintage.

In 1990 he made a special *cuvée* of 3,000 bottles, entirely aged in *barriques* and sold only at the estate. It is known as Cuvée Vin Nu, as it has no label. Despite Bord's wish to bottle as much wine as he can, he could not bring himself to bottle any of the 1992 under the estate labels.

Each estate has a second wine: declassified Clos Jean is sold as Château Jean-Fonthenille and declassified Rondillon as Château Loustalot. The total production of Loupiac here is 100,000 bottles. Prices are quite high for the appellation. The wines are indisputably well made, but they lack concentration and structure. The very features that Lionel Bord regards as virtues in his wines are the ones I single out as their shortcomings.

The Clos Jean wines age well. The 1955 was still lively and elegant in 1990, but both the 1971 and 1983 retained an unappealing hardness on the finish that may have derived from high sulphur levels. The 1990 is delicious, with abundant botrytis. I prefer it to the Cuvée Vin Nu, which had a splendid vanilla nose, but tasted of ripe bananas and lacked concentration. The only wine I have tasted from Rondillon was the 1964, with its flavours of caramel and marmalade; a lush, complex wine then, just past its best.

Lionel Bord, 33410 Cadillac, telephone: 56 629983, fax: 56 629355

CLOS DE LA MIGNONETTE

This estate, based in the Premières Côtes, includes 3.5 ha. in Loupiac, planted, unusually, with half Sémillon and half Sauvignon. The estate has been bottling its wine only since 1988. Yields are usually

the maximum. Bord is typical of those who use sophisticated vinification without coming up with very exciting results. The grapes
are pressed in a horizontal press; after a twenty-four-hour *débourbage*, yeast is added, as he seeks a rapid fermentation. The must is
fermented in tanks at about 21°C. Fermentation is stopped with
sulphur dioxide and chilling; the wine is then racked, more sulphur
is added and the wine is left on its own for a month. Then it is fined
with bentonite, racked again and then filtered at least twice one
month later. The wine then remains in tank for a year, is filtered
again, then bottled. Perhaps it is not surprising that after all this,
there is not much fruit left. Bord is particularly proud of the exceedingly sweet 1989 Crème de Tête, but I have not tasted it. The 1992
was lean and acidic, and not very appetizing.

Christian Bord, Bord Frères, Mouchac, 33490 Verdelais, telephone:
56 620040

16

Cadillac and the Premières Côtes
de Bordeaux

The small town of Cadillac, a geometrically designed medieval *bastide*, is the heart of a large wine region and some of the best producers are located here. The seventeenth-century château of the Ducs d'Epernon looms over the town. It was from here, according to legend, that Antoine Launet de la Motte Cadillac set off for America and founded Detroit, subsequently achieving immortality by having his name appropriated by General Motors. Other distinguished residents of the region have included François Mauriac, who lived at Château Malagar in Verdelais. Toulouse-Lautrec is buried in the Verdelais cemetery.

Cadillac is the newest of the appellations on this side of the river and there are about eighty producers. It is, in effect, a sweet-wine appellation within the vast acreage of the Premières Côtes, which encompasses no fewer than thirty-seven communes and stretches for some 60 kilometres along the right bank of the Garonne. Curiously, dry white wines made in the Premières Côtes are obliged to use the simple Bordeaux appellation. The Cadillac appellation is granted to those communes, mostly in the southern part of the Premières Côtes, where supposedly superior sweet white wine is capable of being made. These communes are: Baurech, Beguey, Cadillac itself, Capian, Cardan, Donzac, Gabarnac, Haux, Langoiran, Laroque, Lesiac, Le Tourne, Monprimblanc, Omet, Paillet, Rions, Saint-Germain-de-Grave, Saint-Maixant, Semens, Tabanac, Verdelais and Villenave de Rions. This amounts to a potential zone of production of 1,200 ha., although in practice only about 150 ha. are cultivated with a view to making sweet wine. It is not always clear why some communes were chosen and others not. Donzac is too far inland to attract botrytis except on rare occasions, while the wines from Langoiran are reputed to be short-lived.

The Cadillac appellation was granted to only five communes until it was expanded in 1973. The rules are essentially the same as for Sainte-Croix-du-Mont and Loupiac. One difference is that all the wine must be bottled if it is to retain the appellation; thus bulk sales are not permitted. At first there was considerable enthusiasm for the new appellation and a sizeable harvest of over 15,000 hl. was declared in 1973. Unfortunately the market showed less enthusiasm than the legislators and growers, and by the end of the decade production had slumped to around 2,000 hl. By 1986, it had risen slightly to 3,000 hl. and, by 1993, to 4,894 hl.

For Premières Côtes, yields are higher than for the other appellations: 50 hl./ha. (plus an additional 20 per cent that can be authorized in abundant vintages). Moreover, machine-harvesting is permitted. In 1986, 25,000 hl. were declared; in 1993, 23,000 hl. from 638 ha. Most of this wine is insipid stuff. Machines are efficient, but cannot select or distinguish good rot from bad. So there is no point looking for botrytis in a Premières Côtes; the best you can hope for is a mildly sweet and inexpensive wine made from overripe grapes, *moelleux* rather than *liquoreux*. One peculiarity of the Premières Côtes appellation is that the maximum amount of sulphur dioxide that can be employed is 300 milligrams per litre, as opposed to 400 for the sweeter Cadillac (the same as Sauternes). So if you have made an indifferent Cadillac with just over 300 milligrams, you are forbidden to declassify it to Premières Côtes as the wine exceeds the maximum-permitted sulphur levels for that appellation.

Curiously, production has been rising in the 1990s, though opinion is divided as to whether this is a coat-tail effect, since many Cadillac producers also produce Premières Côtes, or whether it is the consequence of the collapse of the market for dry white wines. In 1991, the price per *tonneau* for the latter was 7,000 francs; by 1994, it had plummeted to 2,500 francs. In 1994, Premières Côtes was fetching 8,000 francs per *tonneau*. Dry white wines had been produced as a kind of insurance policy, but it did not take long for buyers to realize that most Bordeaux Sec is indistinguishable and rather dreary. Now, it seems, the growers are reverting to the production of sweet wines, where there is at least a chance that somebody will buy it at a fair price.

Official figures combine statistics for the two appellations, which makes it difficult to focus on Cadillac itself. In the years from 1988 to 1990, the crop from both appellations was almost 30,000 hl. obtained from just over 700 ha. The highest average yield recorded in the last decade was in 1986, when the figure stood at 44.7 hl./ha.; the 1987 was only a shade lower. In 1989 and 1990, the yields were also above 40 hl./ha.

It is hard to see the justification for the existence of Premières Côtes. The best examples, such as Château de Berbec, are made from hand-picked grapes anyway and would presumably be Cadillacs if only the vineyards had not been located in the wrong commune. Some growers in Sainte-Croix-du-Mont and Loupiac, who of course have an axe to grind, don't even see why the Cadillac appellation exists. Camille Brun, the mayor of Sainte-Croix, argues that Cadillac is a pointless fabrication, ill-conceived because nobody had given any consideration to whether there was a market for yet another sweet-wine appellation.

There are, of course, a handful of producers who conscientiously make good wine. But they appear to be in the minority. Machine-harvesting is routine in the region as a whole, and although it is not permitted for Cadillac, some growers will admit that it goes on, just as it does in Monbazillac. Most producers tell me with some pride that they make the wine every year, regardless of quality. The justi-fication for this indifference to quality is that they fear any break in supply will lose them clients, many of whom want the same quan-tity of wine each year. The few quality-conscious producers some-times complain that their efforts are rarely recognized. Danielle Menard of Château Mémoires recalls that many elderly clients keep asking for 'sweet wine as it used to be made', which she assumes means over-sulphured, and aged in chestnut and acacia casks for five years until it had lost all its fruit. It is also probable that the sweet wines were made only in outstanding vintages and there was no attempt to make the wine year in, year out, as is the case today.

Vintages are much the same as they are for Loupiac or Sainte-Croix-du-Mont, with, in recent years, 1989 and 1990 outstanding. There is only one co-operative that produces Cadillac: the Celliers de Gramont at Langoiran.

The following gazetteer deals only with Cadillac. The great majority of Premières Côtes are mediocre at best and not worth discussion at length. Good examples include Château de Berbec, made from hand-picked grapes; Château Haut-Goutey, also hand-picked; Domaine du Barrail, made by Yves Armand of Château La

Rame in Sainte-Croix; and Château La Prioulette in Saint-Maixant. Producers of Cadillac with a good reputation, but who are not included in the list that follows because I have not tasted their wines, include: Châteaux Martindroit, Lardiley and Cousteau.

CHÂTEAU LA BERTRANDE

Queyrens also makes Loupiac and his Cadillac vines are spread over 10 ha. of clay and gravel soil. The must is fermented in tanks and half the wine is aged in *barriques*, of which one-quarter are new. The maximum production is 15,000 bottles. Rather confusingly, from 1993 onwards the name of the Cadillac estate is being changed to Château Peyruchet. The wine is inexpensive. I was greatly impressed by the sweet, rich 1990, thoroughly *confit* in flavour, but with good acidity and concentration and length. The 1992 is mediocre.

Bernard Queyrens, Château Grand Peyruchet, 33410 Cadillac, telephone: 56 626271, fax: 56 769209

CHÂTEAU FAYAU

The Médeville family, long established here and in Barsac, are descended from coopers based in Cadillac. Now they control one of the largest estates in Bordeaux, 140 ha. in all, producing 500,000 bottles. Their sweet wines are derived from 10 ha. in Cadillac and a further 7 ha. in Haux. Only Sémillon is used. When I first visited Fayau, I was told by the elderly Jean Médeville that yields were close to the maximum of 40 hl./ha. and that there were usually only two *tries*. By 1994, Jean had retired and the estate was being run by his sons Jean and Marc and their cousin Jacques, and they insisted that yields are considerably lower, closer to 23 hl./ha. on average, and that there are usually four *tries*. In 1993, for example, the yield was 28 hl./ha.

They use a horizontal press, chaptalize when necessary, and ferment the must in outdoor temperature-controlled tanks. They usually allow the first lots to ferment to about 15° of alcohol, and then blend them with less powerful batches. The style is quite burly, with plenty of alcohol and a lesser amount of residual sugar. This is because the Médevilles want *nervosité* in their wines, though I often find them heavy-handed and slightly coarse. No wood is used. There are various bottlings, but no second label for declassified wines; in 1992, 70 per cent of the wine was rejected. Production varies: in 1985 it was 80,000 bottles, in 1990, 50,000. Prices are low and they keep stocks of older wines on offer, though they find that most purchasers want recent vintages rather than older wines with plenty of bottle age.

I spent a convivial evening with the younger Médevilles, who used my visit as an excuse to fish out some old bottles from outstanding vintages. The oldest was the 1929, now copper-bronze in colour and with an elderly bouquet of caramel and candied oranges; on the palate there was caramel and barley-sugar, but the wine was frail and showed less well than the 1937. This was deeper in colour than the 1929, positively brown, but livelier on the nose and palate. There were aromas of candied oranges and coffee, and spicy caramel flavours on the palate; the wine still had impeccable length and was mature, but by no means flagging. The 1961 was golden in colour, with a *confit* nose of peaches and oranges, and a rich, peppery palate. The 1967 was past its best; the nose was fine, with barley-sugar and mandarin aromas, but on the palate the fruit was drying out and the alcohol excessive.

More recent vintages seem to show a slackening of standards. The 1978 and 1980 are drab, and the 1981 is only marginally better. The 1982 is fruity, but also rather flabby. Excess sulphur seriously mars the 1984 and 1986; the latter has ripe fruit, but no concentration of flavour and finishes short. The 1988, though reasonably fresh, is disappointing for the vintage. The 1990 is powerful, with ample botrytis on the nose and fine ripe fruit on the palate, though too alcoholic for my taste. The 1992 is quite good, creamy and spicy, but with no persistence of flavour.

The splendour of the older vintages and the more pallid quality of the recent ones surely reflect changing standards of viticulture and vinification. I recall an astounding 1929 from Château de Mont Célestin in Verdelais that I tasted ten years ago; this showed that in certain rare vintages the sweet wines of what is now Cadillac can rise to great heights. But no doubt in those years yields were lower, whether by design or because of unhealthy vines, and harvesting was more selective.

Jacques and Jean Médeville, Château Fayau, 33410 Cadillac, telephone: 56 626580, fax: 56 621822

CHÂTEAU LABATUT-BOUCHARD

There are 48 ha. under vine at this substantial estate and 15 ha. of these are white, planted half with Sémillon and half with Sauvignon. However, the Cadillac is made solely from Sémillon. The vineyards lie some way inland on the plateau and although morning fogs do reach this far, they tend to burn off rapidly. Bouchard favours a rapid pressing of the grapes, a *débourbage* lasting several days, and then fermentation and *élevage* in tanks. About 40,000 bottles are produced and prices are moderate. An older vintage, the 1953, was drying out when I tasted it in 1990, but it had rich and still-attractive bitter-orange flavours and medium length. The 1986 had a Sémillon floor-wax nose and pleasant tangerine flavours on the palate, which was marred by sulphur. The 1988 was much better, similar in flavour but better balanced. I have not tasted recent vintages.

Michel Bouchard, Château Labatut-Bouchard, 33490 Haut-Saint-Maixant, telephone: 56 620244

CHÂTEAU MÉMOIRES

Of the 30 ha. owned by the Menard family, only 4 ha. are entitled to the Cadillac appellation. They began making the wine in 1985. The wine is vinified and aged solely in tanks. The maximum production is 15,000 bottles. The 1990 was an attractive lemony wine, well balanced and spicy, with good acidity. The 1992 is good for the vintage, with surprising elegance though little concentration of flavour. The wine is inexpensive.

Jean-François Menard, Château Mémoires, 33490 Saint-Maixant, telephone: 56 620643, fax: 56 620432

CHÂTEAU PEYRUCHET

See Château La Bertrande (p. 230).

CHÂTEAU PONCET

Jean-Luc David, who is also the proprietor of Château Piot-David in Barsac, presents himself as a gentleman farmer. His estate in the Premières Côtes is quite large, with 38 ha. under vine, of which two-thirds are planted with white grapes. Only Sémillon is used for

Cadillac. These grapes, which have an average age of sixty years, are planted on mostly gravelly soils. David is aiming to make a wine of good quality and keeps his average yields down to 25 hl./ha. He wants a wine with a balance of 14° of alcohol and 4° of residual sugar, which was easy to obtain in 1988, 1989 and 1990, but in the following three vintages he declassified all his Cadillac to Premières Côtes, since it was *moelleux* in style. In 1990, the first *trie* was barrel-fermented and aged in wood for up to eighteen months, then blended with the rest of the wine, which had been fermented and aged in tank. No wood was used in 1991, 1992 and 1993. The maximum production of Cadillac here is 12,000 bottles; he could make more, but there is no demand at present for a greater quantity. There is also a second label, Château de Vigneau. I have tasted only one vintage of Poncet, the rich and floral 1989, which was developing honeyed tones in 1994; it was very sweet on the palate, but seemed to lack structure. A good Cadillac, none the less.

Jean-Luc David, Château Poncet, 33410 Omet, telephone: 56 629730, fax: 56 626676

DOMAINE DU VIC

See Clos du Monastère du Broussey (below).

CLOS DU MONASTÈRE DU BROUSSEY

M. Marcuzzi, whose grandfather came here from Italy, seemed quite disconcerted to find a journalist in his office, even though an appointment had been made. I assume that journalists armed with questions are a rarity in these hamlets of the Premières Côtes. Marcuzzi has a small portfolio of properties. There is a second Cadillac estate, Domaine du Vic, and two properties where only dry wines are made: Domaine de la Fontanille and Château du Payre. The Clos du Monastère is a 4-ha. parcel on steep south-facing slopes which Marcuzzi rents from a monastery. The production is 12,000 bottles. The Domaine du Vic, producing up to 5,000 bottles, is smaller and the wines tend to be less rich. They are produced from half Sémillon and half Sauvignon vines. Technically, Domaine du Vic is a *liquoreux*; in structure, it is more like *moelleux*. At both estates yields are high and in most years the wines are made from overripe rather than botrytized fruit. The grapes are pressed in a pneumatic press and chaptalization is frequent. The two wines are fermented in underground tanks to minimize evaporation, then aged in a blend of tanks and *barriques* for about two years. Both wines are simple and show no depth or complexity, but the fruit in Clos du Monastère is richer.

G. Marcuzzi, 33410 Cardan, telephone: 56 626901, fax: 56 626705

17

Cérons and the Minor Appellations of Sweet Bordeaux

As you drive north up the *route nationale* from Barsac, you soon come to the riverside village of Cérons, which is separated from Barsac itself by the tiny Saint-Cricq river. The busy road intersects the village. Between the road and the Garonne lies the old part of the village, the Château de Cérons and other grand houses behind high walls, and the Romanesque church opposite the château. In addition to Cérons itself, two other communes are entitled to the Cérons appellation: Illats and Podensac. The soil here is typical of the Graves and Sauternes: gravelly outcrops, sandier to the west, more clay to the east. There is, however, none of the red soil found in Barsac. The authorized pruning is *Guyot simple* and the maximum yield is 40 hl./ha. The three communes have 789 ha. under vine, of which about 310 ha. are planted with red grapes. Before the devastating frost of 1956 there were only 20 ha. of red grapes, so the expansion has been recent.

One peculiarity of the appellation is that growers have the right to make dry white wines from the same vineyards under the Graves appellation. Should they exercise that option, they can double the yield, dispense with *triage* and limit the risk of harvesting during or after bad weather. Not surprisingly, production of Cérons has declined. In 1970, 15,000 hl. were declared; by 1978, it was down to 5,041 hl.; in 1981, it rose slightly to 6,000 hl.; but in 1985 and 1986, it plummeted to 2,600 hl. and remains at about that level. There are 120 *viticulteurs* with the right to produce Cérons, although in 1992, for example, only twenty-six actually did so. The area declaring Cérons in the late 1980s varied from 82 to 120 ha. Average yields in good vintages are approximately 32 hl./ha. In the past, the Sémillon vines were pruned *à cot*, as they still are in Sauternes and Barsac, but this practice has been abandoned, since there is no requirement to limit yields to the levels of Sauternes. In 1989 and 1990, the price per *tonneau* was just over 9,000 francs and rose as high as 14,000 francs the following year.

The village is an ancient one. Cérons can already be spotted on Roman road maps of the region dating from the third century, where the port is identified as Sirione. Cérons thrived in medieval times, shipping not only wine, but also oak barrels from the many coopers in the village and stone quarried near by. The nineteenth-century historian André Jullien placed the best *crus* of Cérons on the same quality level as the *Deuxièmes Crus* of Sauternes. In 1850, Charles Cocks made the same claim in *Bordeaux et Ses Vins*. For Cérons, the problem was that none of its wines was cited by the Bordeaux merchants who drew up the 1855 classification. Inevitably its reputation faded and in the 1868 edition of Cocks's book, he wrote: 'The region of Sauternes begins on the slopes on the right bank of the Ciron.' That excluded Cérons. Various court cases were initiated to establish which communes had the right to sell their wines as Sauternes. Eventually, in 1921, one year after Cérons had formed its own Syndicat Viticole, Cérons was forbidden to do so; the gap it left was filled by the commune of Fargues, no doubt under pressure from the Marquis de Lur-Saluces. So Cérons was obliged to strike out on its own and, Jean Perromat proudly recalls, received its own *appellation contrôlée* ten days before Sauternes.

Jean Perromat has been the mayor of Cérons for almost twenty years and owns the beautiful Château de Cérons, where he produces one of the leading wines of the appellation. He is very protective of the renown of Cérons and proud of its long and distinguished history, but despite his best efforts, that has not prevented the wine from coming close to extinction. Sainte-Croix-du-Mont and Loupiac, whatever one thinks of their overall quality, are distinct from Sauternes and Barsac, and have an identity of their own. Cérons, whether it likes it or not, will always be perceived as being overshadowed by Barsac. Since growers have the option of producing white Graves from the same vines, many of them can be persuaded to make Cérons instead only if they can be sure of getting three times the price for the sweet wine. A few years ago that was unthinkable, but in the 1990s the plummeting prices of dry white Bordeaux may persuade the growers to think again. Of course, higher prices for Cérons can be sustained only if the wines are of good quality. Despite the presence of a few outstanding estates, standards remain variable.

The top vintages of Cérons are, not surprisingly, very similar to those of Barsac and Sauternes. There was a great year in 1943, with must weights of 26° not uncommon; more recently, 1975, 1976, 1989 and 1990 have been outstanding. In 1993, fine weather permitted a good harvest after 25 October, but few estates had been prepared to wait that long. In 1994, the April frost that damaged corners of Barsac was severe in Cérons.

Producers dissatisfied with the quality of their Cérons have the right to declassify it to the lesser appellation of Graves Supérieures. Jean Lalande of Château Hauret-Lalande did this in 1991, 1992 and 1993. Wines bearing this appellation can be produced anywhere in the southern Graves and tend to be *moelleux* in style; there is no requirement for the vines to be picked by *tries successifs*. Château Ménota in Barsac produces Clos Saint-Georges, which is widely distributed in Britain. Rémy Sessacq of Château Lousteau-Vieil in Sainte-Croix-du-Mont makes Graves Supérieures at his estate south of Langon, Clos La Maurasse. In the late 1980s, the production from about 400 ha. was declared as Graves Supérieures; average yields are about 40 hl./ha. The annual volume of production is about 15,000 hl. and the price per *tonneau* rose to 12,000 francs in 1991. The vast majority of the wine is sold in bulk.

Other minor sweet-wine appellations are Côtes de Bordeaux Saint-Macaire, which comes from the area south of Sainte-Croix-du-Mont, and Sainte-Foy-Bordeaux, which lies east of Saint-Macaire. These are *moelleux* wines, not a single example of which has ever come my way. This is not altogether surprising. The area declaring its production as Sainte-Foy fluctuates from 48 to 96 ha., and yields are usually over 50 hl./ha. and can be as ludicrously high as 68 hl./ha., as was the case in 1982. Production is declining and is now about 2,000 hl. The declarations of Saint-Macaire are even more minuscule, varying from 30 ha. under vine in 1986 to 66 ha. in 1983; by 1990, the area declaring the wine was only 51 ha. Yields vary from 40 to 55 hl./ha. and the highest prices per *tonneau* were attained in 1990, at 6,000 francs.

Finally, Bordeaux Supérieurs Blancs Moelleux can be produced anywhere in the Bordeaux region and is defined rather lamely as *demi-liquoreux*. The only example I have encountered is produced by Gérard Cigana at Château Les Marcottes. The area declaring this appellation has been shrinking. In 1983 it was 410 ha., in 1985, 214 ha. and from 1988 to 1990, just over 100 ha. Average yields can be as high as 56 hl./ha, encountered in 1990, though the more usual average is 40 hl./ha. This is clearly an appellation in decline and about four times as much is sold in bulk as in bottle. At the peak of its value over the past decade, in 1989, it fetched 6,000 francs per *tonneau*.

CHÂTEAU DE CÉRONS

The tall, white-haired Perromat is a member of a family to which wine estates are attached like limpets. He also owns Château Prost in Barsac and makes red Graves called Château de Calvimont, as well as other wines. His wife Suzanne owns Château Terrefort and an estate in Loupiac. His brother Pierre leases Château d'Arche in Sauternes and his other brother Michel is the owner of Château d'Armajan-des-Ormes in Preignac. Jean Perromat has adopted the patriarchal role in Cérons; he is the mayor as well as its leading producer. Now his son Xavier assists him in the cellars. I once spent a morning here tasting from the barrels in the *chai*; as we progressed we were joined by more and more people, until by noon fourteen growers from Cérons and the Graves were sitting down to lunch at the château.

The fine seventeenth-century château was once the home of the Marquis de Calvimont and in his day the estate was much larger and included what is now a separate property, the Grand Enclos au Château de Cérons. Ten hectares of very gravelly soil are used to produce up to 35,000 bottles of Cérons. Sémillon accounts for 70 per cent. It is unusual for yields here to exceed 25 hl./ha. and Perromat urges his fellow growers in Cérons to follow his example voluntarily, though few seem to do so. In 1988, his yields were 21 hl./ha.; in 1989, 26 hl./ha.

The wines used to be aged in old barrels, often for as long as seven years. I recall tasting the 1979 from cask in 1986. I suspect this had nothing to do with winemaking theory, but reflected the difficulty of selling the wine. Rather than racking and sulphuring, Perromat claimed that he filtered the wine frequently to keep it clean and fresh. It doesn't sound a very good idea, but the wine here is always elegant and attractive.

Perromat is an ardent believer in *tries successifs*. In 1988, there were eight *tries* spread over two months and the harvest ended on

23 November. There were the same number in 1989, when the harvest ended twelve days earlier. With the 1988 vintage, Perromat reverted to barrel-fermentation for half the crop; the following year, one-third of the must was barrel-fermented. I recall tasting both 1989s; the tank sample was pure in flavour, but the *barrique*-aged version was richer and more complex. I thought there was a case for releasing two *cuvées* of 1989, but Perromat blended the two. He did retain four *barriques* from the third *trie* from mid-October; this had an astonishing 8° of *liqueur* and was exceedingly rich and concentrated. Perromat has rightly decided not to sell this wine, but to keep it for his eight children and innumerable grandchildren.

In 1990 there were seven *tries* and Perromat fermented the whole lot entirely in new oak. He still likes to keep his wines in barrels for three or four years. When they are eventually bottled, they are sold at quite high prices – the 1989 was priced at 75 francs in 1994 – which reflects the meticulous care taken in vineyard and cellar.

The oldest Château de Cérons I have tasted is the 1973, which had a curious but appealing nose of peaches and tobacco, and was intense and lively on the palate. The 1979 was very good, with plenty of botrytis on the nose and plump fruit on the palate. I found the 1983 rather dour and hard, and the 1985 had a similar character. The 1986 is delicious, with a lemon-zest nose, good extract and botrytis character, and quite good length. The 1989 was rich and apricotty on the nose, and concentrated and elegant on the palate, with a fine slick of glycerol. The 1990 will surely be magnificent and the 1991, still in cask in 1994, was very promising, with ripe, lemony flavours and good concentration. The 1993 seems more promising than the 1992, and Perromat is sure that the 1994 will be superior to both 1992 and 1993, but the crop will be small.

Jean Perromat, Château de Cérons, Cérons, 33720 Podensac, telephone: 56 270113, fax: 56 272217

CHÂTEAU DE CHANTEGRIVE

This huge estate of 92 ha. was started from scratch twenty-five years ago. Lévêque, the former president of the Bordeaux *courtiers*, or wine brokers, now has to create large quantities of the product he once dealt in simply as a middleman. He first made Cérons in 1990, after three *tries*, some of which yielded musts with 23°. The yield was about 25 hl./ha. The best lots were fermented entirely in new oak, though there was another *cuvée* aged only in tanks. The oaked version was a good wine, with aromas of pears as well as honey; the palate was rich and concentrated, but lacked some length of flavour. No Cérons was produced in 1991, 1992 or 1993, but some *barriques* were made in 1994, though it is too soon to say whether they will be of sufficient quality to be released as Cérons.

Henri Lévêque, Château de Chantegrive, 33720 Podensac, telephone: 56 271738, fax: 56 272942

CHÂTEAU DES DEUX MOULINS

The elegant, deferential M. Pastol is a chemical engineer who also runs this small estate in the Graves. He does not make Cérons every year. Eight of his 12 ha. are planted with white grapes and only the oldest vines are used to make the *liquoreux*. The *encépagement* is 90 per cent Sémillon, 8 per cent Sauvignon and 2 per cent Muscadelle. Yields are very low: 25 hl./ha. in 1989 and only 12 hl./ha. in 1990. In 1993, he declassified the wine and sold it as Graves Supérieures.

The grapes are pressed in a horizontal press and fermented in tanks; in January the wine is filtered, then given a further three years of ageing in tanks. The wine is filtered but not fined before bottling. Production is variable, but in a good vintage, such as 1989, only 5,500 bottles were made and moderately priced at 43 francs.

Deux Moulins is a full-bodied Cérons, a genuine *liquoreux*. The 1975, still on sale at the estate, was holding up well in 1994, an aromatic wine, juicy and medium-bodied on the palate, with good acidity and only a slight bitterness marring the finish. The 1989 was still rather sulphury in 1994, but sweet and supple and succulent, with good length. The 1990 was closed and sulphury, but is very sweet, with admirable extract and good length.

Bernard Pastol, Château des Deux Moulins, Illats, 33720 Podensac, telephone: 56 270243

CHÂTEAU GRAVAILLAS

There are 27 ha. under vine at Gravaillas, 19 of them planted with white grapes. The owners produce Cérons only in outstanding years and mostly use Sémillon. The grapes are pressed in a horizontal press, fermented in tanks and then aged in *barriques*. Unfortunately, very slow sales have deterred the owners from producing any Cérons since 1988. Even in the great 1990 vintage they decided they had too much stock remaining. The production varied from 10,000 to 15,000 bottles. Prices are modest.

In 1994, I tasted some older vintages at the château. The 1972, a weak year, was still showing well; though beginning to dry out, it retained good acidity and ample sweetness. The 1975 was better, with an apple-compote nose and pleasant, plump fruit on the palate, though no finesse. The 1986, which was vinified entirely in tanks, has a nose of mandarins and peaches, but seems over-alcoholic on the palate and is veering towards blowsiness. The 1988 is better: fresh, stylish, gently oaky, tasting of pears.

Marcel Roucel and Marcel Labarrière, Château Gravaillas, Caubillon, Cérons, 33720 Podensac, telephone: 56 270853

CHÂTEAU HAURA

When I last encountered Mme Leppert she was a lively ninety years old and had relinquished the winemaking to her granddaughter. The vineyards are planted with 60 per cent Sémillon, 30 per cent Sauvignon and 10 per cent Muscadelle, though I suspect the Sémillon forms the basis for the Cérons. The grapes are pressed in a horizontal press and vinified entirely in tanks. There used to be barrels in the *chai*, but Mme Leppert could never afford to replace them. The wine is bottled about thirty months after the harvest. She was not entirely pleased with the 1989, which she found excessively sweet, though she nevertheless compared the vintage to the great years such as 1928, 1929 and 1955, all of which she could clearly recall. I found the 1989 reasonably aromatic and agreeable on the palate, but by no means exciting.

Mme Leppert, Château Haura, Cérons, 33720 Podensac, telephone: 56 623338

CHÂTEAU HAURET-LALANDE

Lalande concentrates most of his efforts on his excellent estate in Barsac, but also produces some white Graves and, in exceptional years, Cérons from Château Hauret-Lalande. The last vintage in which it was produced was 1990. I have not tasted it, but given the fine and dependable quality of Lalande's Piada, I expect his Cérons is of good quality too.

Jean Lalande, Château Piada, Barsac, 33720 Podensac, telephone: 56 271613, fax: 56 272630

CHÂTEAU HURADIN

Yves Ricaud is now handing the reins over to his son-in-law Daniel Lafosse, the brother of Dominique Lafosse of Clos Bourgelat. The 15-ha. estate is planted with 9 ha. of white grapes: 80 per cent Sémillon, the rest Sauvignon and Muscadelle. The grapes are pressed in a horizontal press and vinified entirely in cement tanks. Production is limited to about 7,000 bottles, since there is not much demand for the wine, reports Ricaud. Prices are low. Both the 1989 and 1990 are pleasant wines, with little aroma, but rounded and sweet on the palate; perfectly agreeable, but hardly worthy of two such superlative vintages.

Yves Ricaud, Château Huradin, Cérons, 33720 Podensac, telephone: 56 270097

CHÂTEAU LARROUQUEY

In addition to his Loupiac and other wines, Lejeune makes up to 35,000 bottles of Cérons from this property. The must is fermented in tank, but aged in *barriques* for nine months, though no new oak is used. The wine is inexpensive, but Lejeune wishes he could charge more and thus invest in making even better wine, as he says the vineyard often succumbs to botrytis and is capable of producing excellent fruit. It tends to be more closed up than his Loupiac in its youth. I have tasted only the 1990, which was sulphury on the nose, but lush and almost earthy on the palate; a rather rustic wine with medium length.

Didier Lejeune, Château La Gravette, 33410 Cadillac, telephone: 56 626730

CHÂTEAU DE MADÈRE

This estate is located at the western end of the commune at its highest point, which is not saying much. A separate vineyard, the

Clos du Barrail, belonged to the Ducau family for two centuries, but was acquired and incorporated by Guy Uteau, the father of the present proprietor. Of the 32 ha. under vine, 30 ha. are planted with white grapes: 80 per cent Sémillon, 15 per cent Sauvignon and 5 per cent Muscadelle. Weather permitting, the yields are the maximum permitted. The grapes are pressed in a horizontal press, fermented in tanks, then filtered and fined. The *élevage* takes place in tanks and large old casks. Uteau is in no rush to bottle and some 1990 was still in tank four years later. He produces Cérons every year to maintain continuity of supply, as he sells much of his production to *négociants* who bottle the wine at Madère under their own labels.

The wine is acceptable but unexciting, but in 1990 he made a special *cuvée* he called Sélection. It has 16° of alcohol, suggesting that the fermentation went out of control, but it is balanced with 7° of residual sugar. In short, a monstrous wine, with a nose of botrytis and overripe melons; on the palate, very rich and concentrated and spicy, but with a discernible whack of alcohol on the finish. I can't help liking it. One doesn't often see wines as flamboyant as this from Cérons.

Claude Uteau, Clos du Barrail, Cérons, 33720 Podensac, telephone: 56 271438

CHÂTEAU DES MOULINS À VENT

Mlle Expert has entrusted the winemaking at her 14-ha. estate to her nephew Pierre Tourré. They try to produce Cérons every year to satisfy their clients, who demand a regular supply of the wine. The gravelly soil is planted with 80 per cent Sémillon, 15 per cent Sauvignon and 5 per cent Muscadelle. No wood is used and the style of the wine is closer to *moelleux* than *liquoreux*. The balance is usually a trifling 12.5° of alcohol and about 3° of residual sugar. Production rarely exceeds 15,000 bottles, though they could double the output were there sufficient demand. Pierre Tourré told me he likes the style of his 1992, hardly a great vintage for sweet wines, so it is not surprising that these wines are rather feeble. The estate works closely with Bordeaux *négociants*, who seem to dictate the style of the wine. Prices are low, but the quality, even in good years such as 1989, is mediocre.

Mlle Anne Expert, Château des Moulins à Vent, Cérons, 33720 Podensac, telephone: 56 271423, fax: 56 270124

CLOS BOURGELAT

Lafosse is one of the most engaging characters in Cérons, garrulous, ebullient, hospitable. He has 13 ha. which can be used to produce Cérons and almost all of them are planted with Sémillon. The must is fermented in stainless-steel tanks and about one-third is aged in *barriques* for at least twelve months before being blended with the rest of the wine. Most of the barrels are two or three years old. No 1991 was bottled and there will only be about 6,000 bottles in 1992. The maximum production of Cérons here is 20,000 bottles. Prices are moderate.

The 1988 was an attractive but rather simple wine and the oak gave it a dry finish rather than any pronounced vanilla flavours. The 1990 is richer, more botrytized and tastes of ripe melons, as Sémillon often does, but overall the wine is rather light for the vintage.

Dominique Lafosse, Clos Bourgelat, Cérons, 33270 Podensac, telephone: 56 270173

GRAND ENCLOS AU CHÂTEAU DE CÉRONS

This fine vineyard was once part of the domaine of the Marquis de Calvimont, who lived at the Château de Cérons. It became separated from the château after the *route nationale* was built, prompting the Marquis to sell his estate in three lots. In 1875, the Lataste family acquired the property, which since 1985 has been run by the tall, dapper Olivier Lataste. There are 26 ha. planted here and only the oldest vines are used to make Cérons; 1.5 ha. survive from 1921. The enclosed vineyard behind the house is planted half with Sémillon and half with Sauvignon, but throughout the estate the proportions are different, with 80 per cent Sémillon. The Sauvignon is usually reserved for his excellent dry wine, as Lataste also produces a fine Graves, Château Lamouroux.

Lataste uses a hydraulic press for his Cérons and keeps the must chilled until the *trie* is completed. He then blends the lots and fermentation begins. Since 1988, the Cérons has been barrel-fermented without added yeasts. In 1989, he had exceptionally rich musts and the first *trie* had 26° of potential alcohol from yields of

26 hl./ha. The 1989 vintage yielded 10,000 bottles. In 1990, there was a single *trie* since the botrytis was uniform in the vineyard; in this vintage he used 50 per cent new oak and produced 15,000 bottles. In 1991, the frost limited production severely and only 2,400 bottles were released. There was no Cérons in 1992 or 1993. Prices are moderately high; in 1994, the 1990 was priced at 60 francs, the 1991 at 70 francs.

The 1988 had a melony nose, and was creamy and elegant, though a touch light on the palate; it was well balanced, but lacked extract and complexity. The 1989, which I have tasted only once, showed poorly; it was loose in structure and hard-edged on the palate, yet with good length. The very rich 1990 is a splendid wine, with tropical fruits on the nose and masses of botrytis, and stylish and concentrated on the palate, with superb length. The 1991 is outstanding for the vintage: a ripe, spicy wine with real concentration and exemplary balance.

Olivier Lataste, Grand Enclos au Château de Cérons, Cérons, 33720 Podensac, telephone: 56 270153

18

Sauternes Vintages

Sauternes is not like other wines and in many respects it defies conventional wisdom. Vintages are certainly important in Sauternes, yet on many occasions I have been astonished to encounter a little-known wine from a little-known vintage, only to discover that it is, at worst, worth making its acquaintance and, at best, a wonderful glass of wine. Sauternes is rich in the components that help wine to age and improve in bottle: alcohol, acidity and sugar. The finer the balance between these elements, the greater the chance that the wine will age gracefully. A simple wine will never become complex because it has been aged; but a simple wine can none the less evolve, and sometimes in interesting ways. I would never recommend cellaring a wine that in its youth is insipid and feeble; a modest Sauternes that is cracking up after ten years in bottle is not an enjoyable experience. Yet the wine lover is more likely to encounter pleasant surprises among old Sauternes than among old Médocs. Moreover, old bottles do turn up quite frequently at auction and often sell for surprisingly modest prices, so there is less risk in bidding for an old Sauternes than for a red wine of comparable age, and a greater chance of finding something rewarding once the cork has been pulled.

Nineteenth-century vintages are unlikely to pass your lips, or mine, very often. The most celebrated vintage of the early nineteenth century was the 1811 'Comet' vintage; 1822 and 1825 were also exceptional. The 1847 and 1848 Yquems are of legendary reputation. Other vintages noted as exceptional include the 1858, 1859, 1865, 1869 (especially for Yquem) and 1874. In the very famous vintage of 1893, picking began, at Yquem at any rate, on 28 August. Subsequent vintages of outstanding quality were 1896, 1899, 1900, 1904, 1906 and 1909. Exceedingly hot weather in

1921 provoked another early vintage, with picking commencing on 14 September. The wines were notably lush.

The good 1926 vintage was overshadowed by the celebrated pair of 1928 and 1929. Of the two, the 1928 tended to be better balanced and has aged more successfully. There were two fine vintages in the 1930s, 1934 and the outstanding 1937, which if properly cellared should still be holding up well.

The 1940s provided a series of superb wines, beginning with the rich 1942, picked from early October onwards. The 1943 is the most celebrated wartime vintage and picking began in mid-September; many wines from this vintage are still in excellent condition. The 1945 was another early vintage and resulted in many great wines; as a vintage it equals, and sometimes surpasses, the celebrated 1947, another truly glorious year. In October 1949, hardly a drop of rain fell and another superb and healthy vintage was brought in. The wines have darkened quite rapidly.

There were good vintages in the 1950s too: 1950; 1953, elegant but comparatively rapid in its evolution; the abundant yet rich 1955; and the small but outstanding 1959, an exceptionally hot year that gave intensely flavoured wines.

It is tempting to assume that because 1961 was a fabulous year for claret it was equally successful for Sauternes. In fact, the conditions were not that suitable for botrytized wines, and 1961 Sauternes tend to be quite baked and raisiny. None the less, there are good wines to be had from this vintage.

In fact, 1962 is the better-balanced vintage, with elegant fruity wines brought to full ripeness by a very warm summer. There was a disastrous harvest in 1963. The 1964 might have been excellent had not torrential rain wrecked the harvest; a few estates picked early and produced serviceable wine. The weather in 1965 was equally wet and the vintage even worse in quality. The 1966s are lean and light and unlikely to improve, since they lack basic fruitiness.

1967 A vintage with a formidable reputation, thanks to the outstanding Yquem. The climatic pattern was classic: a hot, dry summer, a wet September, then a sunny October during which picking began. Botrytis, however, was slow to develop and only those estates which picked late made first-rate wine, although the overall standard is high.

1968 Ghastly. Unripe and, if any still exists in bottle, probably undrinkable.

1969 A cool year, though a warm autumn proved helpful. None the less, acidity was very high and the wines are not particularly enjoyable.

1970 The warm, dry autumn helped the grapes to ripen perfectly, but did not encourage the development of noble rot. The upshot was a sweet, succulent vintage that lacked the complexity that botrytis alone can bring. Many of the wines are powerful, plump and fruity, and are ageing well.

1971 There is some dispute as to whether this vintage is superior to the 1970. There was certainly more botrytis, although the raw material may have been less rich than in 1970. The 1971s have the virtue of being very well balanced and should enjoy a healthy future.

1972 An unsatisfactory growing season ended with a very late harvest. The wines have proved slightly better than the reputation of the vintage, and some Barsac estates, notably Climens and Nairac, made perfectly acceptable wines that now need to be drunk up.

1973 Rain in September resulted in a modest vintage: distinctly light wines, lacking in botrytis, but fresh and agreeable in their youth. Most will have been drunk up by now, but Nairac is still very pleasant and there may well be other surprises lurking in the cellar.

1974 Poor, since the autumn was exceptionally wet. The wines are thin and only slightly sweet. Those wines that were bottled should have been drunk up.

1975 The first of a fine pair of vintages, and bottles from both can fuel many a blind tasting as Sauternes fanciers debate which is superior. Despite some spring frost in Barsac, climatic conditions were excellent, with warm weather throughout the spring and summer until some rain marred the end of August; in September, dry weather resumed and the humid period had not harmed the grapes. Botrytis was widespread, but did not take hold until well into October, so it is not always reflected in the wines. After a succession of poor vintages, some growers were in a hurry to harvest. All the wines, whether botrytized or not, are characterized by freshness and good acidity. The best wines are still youthful and will age beautifully.

1976 This is the more opulent vintage of the two. The summer was very hot, but there was also ample rain in August and mid-September. Picking began on 21 September and botrytis continued to spread in October, rewarding those growers who waited before harvesting. Many of the wines have a dark colour from the outset, possibly from a slight oxidation that affected wines made from grapes that had been storm-damaged. In general, the 1976s are rich and lush and honeyed, but some of them lack structure and have become prematurely blowsy. The best wines are superb, but quite a few are now falling apart and should be drunk up. Generalizations are tricky, but 1976 is the richer, more opulent of the two vintages, whereas 1975 has more elegance and restraint and staying power.

1977 An awful year, wet and dull. The few acceptable wines were made after very late picking, but not even they had much richness or character. Surviving bottles should probably be drunk soon.

1978 A curious year, notable for its lack of botrytis. The summer was wretched, but the autumn was fine and dry, which brought the grapes to maturity without conferring much botrytized character on them. Some estates produced attractive, correct wines from desiccated grapes with little personality. Best drunk soon.

1979 The summer was cool and botrytis came to the vineyards late in the year and irregularly. The wines tend to be floral, lightly honeyed, medium-bodied, attractive if slightly bland and low in sustaining acidity. The vintage has been overlooked and I have no doubt there are some pleasant surprises to be encountered. Some of the best wines, such as Raymond-Lafon, are holding up very well and there is no rush to drink them.

1980 An underrated year. The spring was poor and flowering uneven. The summer began badly with a cool, wet July; August was very warm, but September cool and humid. It was not until late October that the dry weather returned and botrytis gradually enveloped the vineyards. So 1980 was a late harvest, with much of the best fruit being picked well into November. Some have written off the vintage as mediocre, but anyone who has tasted Yquem, Fargues or Nairac can vouch for its delicious fruit – from those estates that took the risk of waiting for botrytis.

1981 A wet early summer has also blighted the reputation of this vintage. As in 1980, August was hot, but late September and early October were uncomfortably wet. Dry weather returned and with it botrytis; the grapes retained good acidity. In the early years of its evolution, the 1981s were awkward and lacked generosity. But with age the best of them are beginning to show well. It seems clear that overall 1981 is superior to 1979, but whether it is, as many claim, better than 1980 is more debatable.

1982 As in 1961, the fabulous success of the red Bordeaux vintage in this year has led some to suppose that the Sauternes is of comparable quality. In Sauternes the summer was promisingly warm, and grew hotter as autumn approached. The fine weather broke in early October; thereafter it rained and rained. However, many estates, notably Suduiraut, had harvested much of the crop in September and ended up with ripe if not exceptional wines, while the more courageous estates that waited for fine late-autumn weather were disappointed. There are plenty of enjoyable wines, but they have developed quite rapidly and will probably be at their best by 1995, though a few will keep well.

1983 A humid August caused some anxiety, as grey rot gripped some bunches, especially in Bommes, and these had to be removed. Thereafter the weather improved and a superb October allowed many estates to make some outstanding wines, despite the slow onset of botrytis. A year such as this was what the growers had been waiting for. There had been good years in 1979–81, but not great ones, and the promise of 1982 had not been fulfilled. It looked like being a splendid year in 1983, much like 1975. The temptation was to pick too soon, before botrytis was thoroughly installed in the vineyards, but those who exercised patience harvested some superlative grapes and made great wines. Many of the best *tries* were picked in November. Horizontal tastings of the 1983s in recent years have revealed a less even vintage than had been originally supposed: at some estates the winemaking was still slapdash; at others, the wines lacked richness and complexity. None the less, it proved the best vintage since 1976 and far more consistent, despite individual shortcomings.

1984 A cold, wet May spelt trouble at the flowering stage in June, when there was much *coulure*. After a pleasant summer, September was cold and wet, culminating in Cyclone Hortense on 5 October. Fine weather returned later in October, but by then there was only a small crop remaining on the vines. Some estates declassified the entire harvest. The best 1984s, such as Lafaurie-Peyraguey, have been enjoyable from the start; charming, flowery wines with no great depth or structure. They should be drunk up.

1985 Apart from a very wet and blustery May, 1985 was a normal year. Localized hail in Barsac diminished the crop at some estates. For tourists, the weather must have been delightful; for vine growers less so, as the dry conditions inhibited botrytis. Most estates picked in November, but a handful, notably Yquem, picked well into December in the search for botrytized grapes. Not surprisingly, there were some frozen bunches at this time of the year and one or two estates, such as Filhot, produced a special *cuvée* in the style of ice wine. The 1985 is not a classic Sauternes vintage: botrytis is simply not sufficiently abundant, but the grapes were wonderfully ripe and the best properties declassified a large proportion of their crop in order to bottle only the richest and most concentrated wine. Many estates, such as Climens and Raymond-Lafon, are thoroughly satisfied with their wines in 1985, but the vintage was to be eclipsed by the more classic 1986.

1986 The spring was cold and wet, but in May the weather cleared up and remained fine throughout the summer. Flowering proceeded normally. September was wetter than usual, especially between the 15th and 25th, but dry weather returned in October. Botrytis spread rapidly in the vineyard and light rain at various times in October sustained it. Grey rot also made an appearance, so harvesters had to be vigilant. None the less, the fruit was of exceptional quality, rich in botrytis if slightly low in acidity. Picking continued in excellent conditions until mid-November. Those who did not rush to pick everything in early October tended to make the best wines, though low acidity in some of the final *tries* led them to be declassified.

At the time, 1986 provoked great excitement in the region because some estates had not encountered so much botrytis in many years. Unfortunately the other factors required to make a truly great Sauternes were not necessarily present. Some of the fruit was not as ripe as in 1976 or 1983, and low acidity has given the wines a certain amiable softness rather than vigour and excitement. Recent tastings of many 1986s have been disappointing, but the inherent richness of the wines is such that they will no doubt bounce back, though they are unlikely to be as long-lived as the other top vintages of the 1980s.

1987   This year did not begin well. There was localized frost in January and snow remained on the ground for two weeks. April was mild, but a wet June did not aid even flowering. The summer was irregular, but August and September were hot and dry. Unfortunately, heavy rain began to fall just as the grapes were ready to be harvested. This was the vintage when cryo-extraction was used on a wide scale for the first time, with satisfactory results. There was a rapid spread of botrytis in late October, but from now on it was necessary to pick fast, as rain returned in early November and effectively put an end to the harvest. The crop was small, the quality modest, much wine was declassified, but everyone was agreed that 1987 was superior to 1984. Quite a few estates, such as Doisy-Védrines, bottled no 1987; other estates argued that it was preferable to release a small quantity of good wine than to skip a vintage, thus denting further the reputation of the year. The best wines do have some botrytis, but they are rather soft and shallow; they should not be kept too long, but should be enjoyed while they retain their youthful fruit.

1988   The winter was mild and followed by a wet spring. Dry weather in June allowed flowering in perfect conditions. The summer was fine, and September hot and dry, threatening a blocking of the ripening process by drought, but most of the grapes were fully mature by the end of the month. Some rain and misty conditions characterized early October and botrytis followed, helped by morning dew, and sunny conditions returned later in the month. In short, a near perfect year, with a long growing season culminating in ripe, botrytized fruit. The best grapes were probably harvested during the last week in October and the first week in November, and many estates required up to eight *tries*. Château de Fargues did not complete the harvest until 23 November.

Despite the lateness of the harvest, the grapes were in excellent condition and had not become raisined or excessively *rôti*. This resulted in wines of exquisite balance, with ample fruit, generous botrytis and heart-stopping elegance. Of the great trio of vintages in the late 1980s, the 1988 is the most classic, the most refined. The 1989 and 1990 are richer, more powerful and initially more impressive, but it would not surprise me if in twenty years' time the top 1988s give as much pleasure.

1989   April was cool and damp, but flowering was as early as late May; the summer that followed was the sunniest and driest in thirty years. In early July, hail splattered down on Bommes and Sauternes and did considerable damage, but this had the effect of reducing quantity rather than quality. A little rain in late September and early October provoked the spread of botrytis on perfectly ripe grapes, even though mornings fogs were absent. Many small growers began harvesting in mid-September, picking wonderfully ripe grapes without botrytis. They should have waited. Estates that began to pick in late September and continued through most of October completed the harvest fairly swiftly and brought in perfect grapes with sugar levels higher than 1988.

The richness of the musts was a godsend, but it all posed problems for inexperienced or poorly equipped winemakers, who ended up with rather heavy wines, fat but lacking in finesse. The best wines combine power, lush fruit, concentration and elegance, but will need many years, possibly decades, to reach their peak of perfection. Unfortunately prices rose steeply, which, although justified by the superb quality of the vintage, was tactically unwise, since it coincided with the world recession. Although the vintage is a great one throughout the region, Barsac did especially well, with stunning wines produced at Doisy-Daëne, Doisy-Védrines and many other estates.

1990 There had never been three outstanding vintages in a row in Sauternes, so growers were pleasantly surprised to find that, after a mild winter and warm May, flowering was even more advanced than it had been in 1989. July was exceedingly hot, with the thermometer passing 40°C on some days, but fortunately there was some light rain in the summer so that the drought conditions that threatened the 1989 crop were not present. Storms on 13 and 22–23 August provoked botrytis and fortunately the grapes were ripe enough to benefit from it. September and October remained warmer than usual. The harvest began officially on 11 September and was all over by 10 October. Botrytis spread so rapidly in Sauternes that many estates, including Yquem, needed to make only a single *trie*. Guiraud picked its entire crop between 11 and 21 September. In Barsac, botrytis was more patchy and two or three *tries* were required.

As soon as harvesting began, the growers realized they had an unusual problem on their hands. The musts were *too* rich. In most vintages, estates are more than happy with must weights of 21 or 22°; in 1990, must weights of 28 or 29° were routine. This could cause two problems: difficult fermentations and unbalanced wines. Indeed, some small estates without the means to lower the temperatures of fermentation did encounter problems and there are also a number of wines that are too alcoholic for their own good. Once it became obvious that the musts were going to be exceedingly sweet, the harvesters were instructed to pick less botrytized and less ripe bunches too, to bring the average must weight down to more manageable levels. To the delight of growers, the harvest was not only of sensational quality, but it was also abundant; even at top estates, yields were unusually high.

Curiously, the vintage was greeted cautiously. One British wine writer remarked that many 1990s lacked acidity and backbone, and were too alcoholic. Peter Sichel, in his annual report on the Bordeaux vintage, wrote: 'The sweet white wines have terrific concentration and richness but sometimes lack botrytis character ... It will have been difficult to make wines with the same exceptional elegance as 1988 and 1986.' There are, of course, some unsatisfactory 1990s, but overall I find it a most magnificent vintage. They are big, powerful wines, often with 15° of alcohol or more, but balanced by unusually high residual sugar. Pierre Meslier of Château Raymond-Lafon pointed out that in 1990 only part of the high sugar content of the grapes had been caused by botrytis; desiccation was also present, so the treacle-like, caramel character of over-botrytized wines should have been avoided. The 1990s also have good acidity and I see no reason why they should not develop into very great wines.

There is no consensus on which of this trio of great vintages will turn out best in the long run. My own hunch is that the 1990s will be the best and the 1989s might provide some disappointments as they age. I expect the 1988s to be overlooked with the passage of time, but those fortunate enough to have bottles in their cellars will be able to enjoy beautiful wines with great finesse, while some of the flamboyance of the 1989s may prove to be more short-lived. I could be entirely wrong, of course, and what is clear is that any of these vintages, had it occurred on its own, would have been hailed as stupendous. Instead, the Sauternes lover is spoilt for choice.

1991   This was the year of the frost. On 21 April, the freezing conditions that swept through France afflicted the Sauternais and most of the crop was ruined, especially in Sauternes itself. Some parts of Barsac were relatively unscathed, but that was very much the exception. After the frost, the spring was cool and flowering did not take place until late June. The summer was fine and rain in late August helped botrytis to establish itself. After the frost, a second growth of shoots developed, but the cool spring meant that it was out of sync with what had survived of the original growth. Conse-quently, botrytis attacked the ripe grapes from the original crop, as well as the mostly unripe grapes from the second crop. So selection in the vineyard was as necessary as ever. The harvest began officially on 25 September, although Climens won special dispen-sation to pick earlier and as a result made some extremely good wine. The harvest was rapid, with up to four *tries*. Most estates had finished picking what there was to pick by mid-October. Yields were very low, an average of 9 hl./ha., and La Tour-Blanche was not alone in reporting yields of 3 hl./ha. Moreover, those figures did not reflect subsequent declassification of certain lots.

The quality is better than had been expected and the best wines seem superior to the 1987s. Quite a few estates decided not to release any 1991, but those that are on the market, especially from estates such as Climens, Sigalas-Rabaud and Lafaurie-Peyraguey, are attractive, have botrytis character, and are by no means wines for rapid consumption.

1992 The year began promisingly. The winter was dry and mild, as was the spring; flowering began early, in late May, though cold weather delayed its completion. But the summer was twice as wet as usual. Botrytis began to install itself by mid-September, when the harvest began. Rain fell on 26 September and continued more or less continuously until 7 October. There was a week of fine weather in mid-October, but then the rain resumed and, despite another brief spell of decent weather in early November, more rain on 11 November brought the harvest to an end. As in 1982, those who began to pick early managed to bring in a few *tries* of good grapes, although they were not especially concentrated. Perhaps because of the uneven flowering, there was considerable variation in ripeness levels when harvesting began. Later *tries* had lower sugar levels. The wet weather meant that there was a great deal of grey rot as well as botrytis, so careful selection was crucial. Because of an outbreak of grey rot early in September, many estates treated their vines so heavily against the disease that they also inhibited any development of noble rot.

Some estates, by careful selection, produced a small quantity of decent if unexciting wine for early consumption. Lafaurie-Peyraguey reported a good crop of normal quality and cask samples of the wine were undoubtedly promising. But this was very much the exception; most of the fruit was insufficiently ripe and many properties decided not to release any 1992.

1993 Hail in April did substantial damage in Bommes, especially at those properties close to the Ciron, but in other respects the year was fine. By September, the grapes were in outstanding condition, comparable to their ripeness and health in 1990. As there was little or no botrytis, conscientious growers waited for the onset of noble rot. What they got instead was a steady downpour of rain. Less scrupulous growers had begun picking early and thus had a small quantity of sweet if unbotrytized wine in their cellars. When the harvest began, the grapes were *pourri plein* but not yet properly concentrated. Grey rot set in rapidly as the rain continued and growers rushed to salvage what they could. It was too late; many bunches had interior mould, which tainted the wine. The 300 millimetres of rain washed away glycerol and other compounds, further stripping the must. Barsac suffered more than Sauternes. Some estates availed themselves of cryo-extraction, but not everyone reported good results. However, 1993 was a much better year on the other bank of the Garonne, and some decent wines were produced in Loupiac and Sainte-Croix-du-Mont. In Sauternes, and especially Barsac, this is probably a vintage to forget.

1994   In mid-April frost damaged vines in Barsac, and Châteaux de Myrat, Caillou and Cantegril lost most of their crop. Flowering proceeded normally, but there was imbalance in the process which favoured Sauvignon over Sémillon. As in 1993, the grapes ripened well over the summer, but rain began on 15 September and continued for about two weeks. However, it was only half as wet as it had been in 1993 and the health of the grapes before the rain helped many of them to survive intact. On the other hand, with such humid conditions grey rot and *pourriture aigre* were widespread and most estates reported losses of at least half their crop. Fine weather returned in early October, botrytis was abundant, must weights were a satisfactory 20° and most estates picked quite speedily. Quality is undoubtedly superior to 1992 and 1993, although once again the crop will be small. Cordier puzzlingly announced that Lafaurie-Peyraguey had produced its best wine since 1986.

APPENDIX I

Storing and Serving Sauternes

There are no secrets to storing Sauternes. Like any other wine, it should be kept on its side in a cool cellar and disturbed as little as possible. With age the wine may throw a light deposit of tartrate crystals, which will neither affect the flavour of the wine nor harm your health. Fluctuating temperatures can cause a light leakage from the cork which resembles a drop of treacle beneath the capsule. This should be wiped off; in my experience, a little seepage does not affect the quality of the wine. Storage conditions can also affect the level of the wine. Ideally the wine should still be at neck level, but with wines of thirty years or more the level can drop to the shoulder. Often such wines show no deterioration or premature oxidation, but occasionally they do, though with less frequency than red wines.

Sauternes should never be served on ice. Very light Sauternes intended to be drunk as an aperitif should indeed be well chilled, but any wine from a great estate or a great year should be served at cellar temperature or just below. If the wine is served at the end of the meal, it will warm up swiftly in the glass, so I tend to keep the bottle in the refrigerator until forty minutes before serving. The wine will still be too cool to offer optimal pleasure, but after ten minutes in a glass the bouquet and flavours should emerge strongly. A small, tulip-shaped white wine glass is ideal, as it will capture the bouquet without allowing it to dissipate.

You can decant Sauternes, especially an ageing wine with good colour, but with very old wines it is unwise to pull the cork until shortly before you propose to pour it. Very old wine is fragile and can react dramatically when, after many decades, it suddenly comes into contact with air. Most Sauternes will improve with aeration, but that process can be accelerated by swirling the wine lightly in the glass.

There is no reason not to keep an opened bottle in the refrigerator, preferably under a layer of nitrogen gas, provided by canisters for sale in most wine shops. Even without such isolating protection, the wine should keep well for two days if chilled. It will keep even better if the left-over wine is poured into a clean half-bottle before being refrigerated; this diminishes the quantity of air in the bottle with which the wine is obliged to come into contact.

There is an increasingly fanatical view abroad that all wine, including powerful sweet wines such as Sauternes, must be matched with food. I am not in sympathy with this view and usually prefer to drink Sauternes on its own, at the end of a meal, as a supplementary dessert. With a bowl of nuts, a wedge of dried fruit, or entirely on its own, a glass of Sauternes makes the perfect end to a fine meal, when it can be relished at leisure, sniffed and sipped, and enjoyed without the distraction of other competing flavours and aromas.

On the other hand, I am fully prepared to concede that Sauternes matches certain foods extremely well. The French drink Sauternes with *foie gras* and a delicious combination it is. The question that needs to be posed is whether the palate is prematurely fatigued by such a rich, if satisfying, combination right at the beginning of a meal. Roquefort with Sauternes is another fine match and more satisfactory because it occurs towards the end of a meal, after the red wines have been finished or removed.

The notion that Sauternes is a 'dessert wine' and thus should be served as an accompaniment to dessert is a dangerous one. Many desserts – notably ices, sorbets, or those containing chocolate – will ruin the wine, deadening its flavours. But Sauternes can be a good match with an almond tart or with dried fruits. I have also enjoyed it with strawberries and *fromage frais*, and there is no reason not to eat a peach or nectarine or ripe pear alongside a glass of Sauternes.

It also has its place in the heart of a meal, especially with fish dishes such as turbot in a cream sauce. I have never tried it with *quenelles de brochet*, but am prepared to believe that this works well. I have enjoyed Sauternes with *cèpe* soup and I expect it would work satisfactorily with chestnuts too. Michel Boyer of Château du Cros in Loupiac persuaded me to try his wine with sardines, and very enjoyable it was, although I think I would have preferred a glass of bone-dry *vinho verde*. Sweet wines such as Sauternes can work well with Chinese food, though a single chilli pepper could wreck your palate and the wine with it. Given the price of Sauternes, such combinations strike me as a costly experiment. Moreover, one does not necessarily want to position a sweet wine in the middle of a meal, where it is likely to be followed by a red wine.

Richard Olney's sumptuous book *Yquem* devotes an entire chapter to Sauternes and food, and lists the menus of extraordinary banquets that featured nothing but Sauternes. They must have been remarkable occasions, but only the super-rich could hope to reproduce them. Olney also discusses and sometimes recommends combinations such as Sauternes with oysters and sea urchins, and its role in cooking certain dishes, such as pork and apricots, veal sweetbreads and *sabayon*. I find this makes for fascinating reading, which I warmly recommend, but I am too keen on Sauternes in the glass to want to fling too many measures of a fine old wine into the sauce or marinade.

APPENDIX 2

Growers' Associations

The SYNDICAT VITICOLE of Sauternes, in which almost all growers participate, deals with choices that affect the economic and technical aspects of vine-growing and winemaking. Founded in 1908, the Syndicat offers advice on pruning, herbicides, personnel and many other matters. In conjunction with INAO (the Institut National des Appellations d'Origine) the Syndicat organizes the Label, the compulsory blind tasting set up to control the quality of wines bottled under the appellation label. If a wine fails, the producer is given a second chance, and if the reason for the wine's failure is a technical fault, the Syndicat will advise him on how to correct that fault or which lots to eliminate. If the wine fails for a second time, it is dispatched for distillation.

Place de la Mairie, 33210 Sauternes, telephone: 56 766037, fax: 56 766967

The SYNDICAT VITICOLE of Barsac was founded in 1907 and maintains an existence independent of the Sauternes Syndicat because its growers have the right, if they wish, to market their wines as Barsac instead of Sauternes.

Grande Rue, 33720 Barsac, telephone: 56 270873

The AMBASSADE DE SAUTERNES is a public-relations organization representing 240 producers, working in conjunction with the Conseil Interprofessionel des Vins de Bordeaux, the umbrella organization that deals with the wines of the entire Bordeaux region and allocates promotional budgets to local organizations such as the Ambassade. The Syndicat Viticole participates in the Ambassade, which publishes maps of the region and assists journalists and other visitors.

Maison du Sauternes, Place de la Mairie, 33210 Sauternes, telephone: 56 766037, fax: 56 766967

The SYNDICAT DES CRUS CLASSÉS DE SAUTERNES ET BARSAC is the organization set up to promote the interests and resolve the problems of the *Crus Classés*. The current president is Comte Xavier de Pontac.

The MAISON DU SAUTERNES, founded in 1982, is a tasting and sales room and also provides information to tourists and other visitors. It is also the sole outlet for a *cuvée* of Sauternes sold as Duc de Sauternes.

Place de la Mairie, 33210 Sauternes, telephone: 56 766037, fax: 56 766967

The MAISON DE BARSAC is an offshoot of the Syndicat Viticole and offers tourists information and wines for sale.

Place de l'Église, 33720 Barsac, telephone: 56 271544

The MAISON DU VIGNERON, on the main road through Preignac, is another sales outlet for the wines of the region.

6 rue de la République, 33210 Preignac, telephone: 56 633743

The COMMANDERIE DE BONTEMPS DE SAUTERNES ET BARSAC is a *confrérie*, founded in 1959 by the Comte de Bournazel and modelled on similar organizations in other wine regions. With their stately robes, processions and ceremonial dinners, they confer honorary membership on the local wine trade and on lovers of Sauternes from all walks of life, thus promoting knowledge of and pride in the wines.

Each of the other appellations also has its own Syndicat Viticole:

SYNDICAT VITICOLE DE CÉRONS (president: Jean Perromat), Mairie

de Cérons, Cérons, 33720 Podensac, telephone: 56 270117 or
270113

SYNDICAT VITICOLE DE LOUPIAC (president: Patrick Dejean), BP
10, 33410 Cadillac, telephone: 56 271232

SYNDICAT VITICOLE DE SAINTE-CROIX-DU-MONT (president:
Arnaud de Sèze), BP 10, 33410 Cadillac, telephone: 56 620139 or
620154 or 633138

SYNDICAT VITICOLE DES PREMIÈRES CÔTES DE BORDEAUX ET
CADILLAC, BP 10, 33410 Cadillac, telephone: 56 626718, fax: 56
621982

The minor appellations also have their own Syndicats:

SYNDICAT VITICOLE DES GRAVES ET GRAVES SUPÉRIEURES, Maison
des Graves, 33720 Podensac, telephone: 56 270925

SYNDICAT VITICOLE DES CÔTES DE BORDEAUX SAINT-MACAIRE,
33490 Sainte-Foy-La-Longue, telephone: 56 637142

SYNDICAT VITICOLE DE SAINTE-FOY-BORDEAUX, 33220 Saint-
André-et-Appelles, telephone: 56 460074

The umbrella organization covering the producers of all sweet
wines of Bordeaux is the UNION DES SYNDICATS DES GRANDS VINS
LIQUOREUX DE BORDEAUX, Maison du Vin, 33410 Cadillac, telephone: 56 626718

Selective Bibliography

Benson, Jeffrey, and Mackenzie, Alastair, *Sauternes*, revised edition, Sotheby's, London, 1990

Brook, Stephen, *Liquid Gold*, Constable, London, and Morrow, New York, 1987

Brook, Stephen, *Sauvignon Blanc and Sémillon*, Viking, London and New York, 1992

Coates, Clive, *Grands Vins*, Weindenfeld & Nicolson, London, 1995. Based on articles originally printed in *The Vine* (see below) and other periodicals.

Coates, Clive, *The Vine*. This excellent monthly journal contains many detailed articles on Sauternes estates.

Cocks, Charles, *Bordeaux; Its Wines and the Claret Country*, Longman, London, 1846

Cocks & Féret, *Bordeaux et ses Vins*, eleventh edition, Féret, Bordeaux, 1949

Cocks & Féret, *Bordeaux et ses Vins*, fourteenth edition, Féret, Bordeaux, 1991

Crestin-Billet, Frédérique, *Les Châteaux des Crus Classés des Sauternes et Graves*, Glénat, 1988

Enjalbert, H. and B., *History of Wine and the Vine*, trans. Richard Maxwell and Harriet Coleman, Bardi, Paris, 1987

Féret, Edouard, *Statistique Générale . . . du Département de la Gironde*, G. Masson, Paris, 1874

Flagg, William J., *Three Seasons in European Vineyards*, Harper, New York, 1869

Gayon, U., and Laborde, J., *Vins*, Béranger, Paris, 1912

Healy, Maurice, *Claret*, Constable, London, 1934

Johnson, Hugh, *The Story of Wine*, Mitchell Beazley, London, 1989

Jullien, André, *Topographie de Tous les Vignobles Connus*, fifth edition, Bouchard-Huzard, Paris, 1866

Mouillefert, P., *Les Vignobles et les Vins de France*, Librairie Agricole de la Maison Rustique, Paris, 1891

Olney, Richard, *Yquem*, Dorling Kindersley, London, 1986

Paguierre, M., *Classification et Description des Vins de Bordeaux*, Audot, Paris, 1829

Parker, Robert, *The Wine Buyer's Guide*, third edition, Dorling Kindersley, London, 1994

Penning-Rowsell, Edmund, *The Wines of Bordeaux*, Penguin Books, London, 1989

Peppercorn, David, *Bordeaux*, second edition, Faber and Faber, London, 1991

Redding, Cyrus, *History and Description of Modern Wines*, third edition, Bohn, London, 1851

Ribereau-Gayon, Pascal, *The Wines and Vineyards of France*, Viking, London, 1990

Robinson, Jancis, *Vines, Grapes and Wines*, Mitchell Beazley, London, 1986

Thudichum, J. L. W., *A Treatise on Wines*, Bell, London, 1894

Index

INDEX

Haut-Goutey, Ch., 203, 229
Haut-Mayne, Ch., 106
Hermitage, Ch. L', 168–9
Huradin, Ch., 242
Jean-Fonthenille, Ch., 225
Justices, Ch. Les, 8, 11, 14, 42, 170, 172–3
Labatut-Bruchard, Ch., 232
Lafaurie-Peyraguey, Ch. (previously Ch. Peyraguey), xv, 3, 5, 7, 13, 28, 36, 47, 69, 71–5, 78, 79, 82, 84, 85, 98, 130, 188, 251, 255, 256, 257
Lafite-Rothschild, Ch., 94
Lafon, Ch., 3, 185–6, 188
Lafon-Laroze, Ch., 190
Lagrange, Ch., 71
Lamaringue, Ch., 186
Lamontagne, Ch. (later Ch. Bastor-Lamontagne), 3
Lamothe, Ch., 4, 5, 10, 136–7, 138
Lamothe-Bergey, Ch., 136, 137–8
Lamothe-Despujols, Ch., 136
Lamothe-Guignard, Ch., 6, 7, 8, 136, 137–40, 156
Lamourette, Ch., 186–7
Lamoureux, Ch., 244
Landiras, Ch., xxiii
Lardiley, Ch., 230
Laribotte, Ch., 173–4
Larrouquey, Ch., 242
Lasalle, Ch., 3
Levant, Ch. du, 151
Lionne, Graves, Ch., 220
Liot, Ch., 151–2
Loubens, Ch., 197, 198, 205–7, 212
Loupiac-Gaudiet, Ch., 218–19
Loustalot, Ch., 225
Lousteau-Vieil, Ch., 207–8, 237
Lynch-Bages, Ch., 97
Madère, Ch. de, 242–3
Mailles, Ch. des, 208–9
Malagar, Verdelais, Ch., 227
Malle, Ch. de, xxn, 3, 4, 6, 7, 8, 132, 140–43
Marcottes, Ch. Les, 209, 237
Mareillac, Ch., 3
Martillac, Ch., 219
Martindroit, Ch., 270
Mayne, Ch. du, 152
Mayne des Carmes, Ch., 95
Mémoires, Ch., 219–20, 229, 232
Ménota, Ch., xv, 114, 152–3, 237

Meyney, Ch., 72
Mirat, Ch., 4
Montalier, Ch., 7, 174
Mont Célestin, Verdelais, Ch. de, 231
Moulins à Vent, Ch. des, 243–4
Moyne, Ch. Le, 220
Myrat (Mirat), Ch. de, xvii–xix, xxi, 3, 5, 6, 23, 102, 116–18, 257
Myrat-Broustet, Ch., 102, 116
Nairac, Ch. (previously Nérac), xv, 3, 4, 6, 8, 12, 32, 40, 102, 118–26, 182, 197, 248, 250
Navarro, Ch., 127, 128
Ormes (property), Ch. des, 164
Ormes (second wine), Ch. des, 165
Ormes (later Ch. d'Armajan-Ormes), Ch. Les, 3
Pajot, Ch., 54
Partarrieu, Ch., 168
Pascaud-Villefranche, Ch., 49, 153
Payre, Ch. du, 233
Pechotte, Ch., 3
Pernaud, Ch., 3
Petit Mayne, Ch., 106
Pexoto, Ch., 4, 75, 93
Peyraguey (later Ch. Lafaurie-Peyraguey and Clos Haut-Peyraguey), Ch., 3, 4, 5
Peyrere, Ch. La, 210
Peyruchet, Ch., 230
Peyxotto, Ch., 5
Piada, Ch., 48, 64, 118, 132, 154–5, 242
Pichard, Ch., 71
Pichon-Longueville-Baron, Ch., 97
Pin-France, Ch. de, 205
Pineau de Rey, Ch., 133
Piot, Ch., 155
Piot-David, Ch., 155, 232
Poncet, Ch., 232–3
Pontac, Ch., 218, 219
Portail Rouge, Ch., 222
Prioulette, Ch. La, 230
Prost, Ch., 12, 155–6, 238
Rabaud, Ch., 15, 75, 77, 81, 93
Rabaud-Promis, Ch., xix, xxn, 3, 5, 7, 42, 47, 72, 75–8, 221
Rahoul, Ch., 222
Rame, Ch. La, 21, 44, 196, 197, 210–12, 229–30
Raymond-Lafon, Ch., xix, xxi–xxii,

Pebayle, 151
Pédesclaux, M., 126
Peppercorn, David, xxii, xxiii, 56
Pepys, Samuel, xi
Perpezat, Jean-Charles, 118–19
Perromat, Jean, 130, 131, 155, 156,
    214, 236, 238–9, 263
Perromat, Michel, 164, 238
Perromat, Pierre, 130, 138, 238
Perromat, Suzanne, 238
Perromat, Xavier, 238
Perromat-Machy, Mme, 165
Perrot family, 116
Pessac, Graves, 17–18
pesticides, movement away from, 21
Petit Verdot, 15
Pétrie, Mme Carol, 168
Peynaud, Emile, 15–16
Peyrondet, François, 224
phylloxera, xviii, 17
Pichard, Jean de, 63
Pichard family, 63, 69, 132
picking: number of *tries*, 40; and *pourri
    plein* grapes, 26–7; selective, 27,
    28–9; separate vinification, 40, 41;
    timing of, 24, 28
Pierre, Marie-José, 105
Pignéguy, François de, 153
Pinsan-Lataste family, 154
Pivonet, Alain, 142, 143
planting, density of, 196
Planty, Xavier, 25, 89–93
pneumatic press, 32, 42
Podensac, 235
Poitevin, Pierre-Alexandre, 132
Pontac, Albert de, 78
Pontac, Vicomte Gabriel de, 78
Pontac, Jacques de, 116
Pontac, Comte Maximilien de, xviii,
    116
Pontac, Comte Xavier de, xxi, xxiv,
    116, 117–18, 262
Pontac, de, family, 116
Pontallier, Louis, 188
Pouchappadesse, Mme (née Garros),
    127
pourri plein grapes, 26–7, 28, 256
pourriture aigre, 26, 257
pourriture grise see grey rot
Preignac, 9, 11–12, 140, 141, 164
Preignac: character, 13; classification,
    3–8; compared with Sauternes,
    11; *Deuxièmes Crus*, 140–43;

dominant varieties in, 15; and
    Muscadelle, 90; other wines of,
    163–76; *Premiers Crus*, 97–101
Premier Grand Cru, 4, 5, 47, 64
Premières Côtes de Bordeaux, xix, 155,
    200, 225, 232, 233
Premières Côtes de Bordeaux (wine),
    xiii, 202, 203, 211, 227, 228,
    229, 233
Premiers Crus, 3–6, 13, 17, 42, 47; of
    Barsac, 58–68; of Bommes,
    69–87; of Fargues, 93–7; of
    Preignac, 97–101; of Sauternes,
    88–93
presshouse, 28, 29, 31
pressing, 29, 31–2, 33
prix de sortie, 86, 91
Promis, M. Adrien, 75, 81
Prost, Elizabeth, 118
Prueras, 15
Prunilla, 15
pruning, 261; *guyot double*, 196, 213;
    guyot simple, 18, 196, 213, 235;
    leaf, 22; severe, 19, 27; spur-, 18;
    taille à cot, 18, 196, 213, 235;
    taille courte, 18
Pujols, Graves, 67

Queyrens, Bernard, 217, 230
Queyrens, Jean, 199, 205

'R', 96
racking wine, 37, 38
rain: and botrytis, 26; and harvest, 41;
    and maturation process, 24
Rayne, Baron de, 78
Rayne, Catherine Marie de, 78
Reay-Jones, Dr Nigel, 10, 180, 181
refractometer, 20, 27
Remparts de Bastor, Les, 166, 167
replanting, 18
residual sugar, xii, xiii
Rhône valley, 15
Ribereau-Gayon, Professor Pascal, xii
Ribet, Alfred, 59
Ricard, Claude, 225
Ricard, Louis, 174, 175, 176
Ricaud, Yves, 242
Riesling, xxiv, 14–15
Rions, 227
Rival, Paul, 88–93
Robinson, Jancis, 15n